Moving from IBM® SPSS® to R and RStudio®

To Jennifer

Sara Miller McCune founded SAGE Publishing in 1965 to support the dissemination of usable knowledge and educate a global community. SAGE publishes more than 1000 journals and over 600 new books each year, spanning a wide range of subject areas. Our growing selection of library products includes archives, data, case studies and video. SAGE remains majority owned by our founder and after her lifetime will become owned by a charitable trust that secures the company's continued independence.

Los Angeles | London | New Delhi | Singapore | Washington DC | Melbourne

Moving from IBM® SPSS® to R and RStudio®

A Statistics Companion

Howard T. Tokunaga

Department of Psychology

San Jose State University

Los Angeles | London | New Delhi
Singapore | Washington DC | Melbourne

FOR INFORMATION:

SAGE Publications, Inc.
2455 Teller Road
Thousand Oaks, California 91320
E-mail: order@sagepub.com

SAGE Publications Ltd.
1 Oliver's Yard
55 City Road
London EC1Y 1SP
United Kingdom

SAGE Publications India Pvt. Ltd.
B 1/I 1 Mohan Cooperative Industrial Area
Mathura Road, New Delhi 110 044
India

SAGE Publications Asia-Pacific Pte. Ltd.
18 Cross Street #10-10/11/12
China Square Central
Singapore 048423

Printed in Canada

Library of Congress Cataloging-in-Publication Data

Names: Tokunaga, Howard, author.

Title: Moving from IBM SPSS to R and RStudio : a statistics companion/Howard T. Tokunaga, Department of Psychology, San Jose State University.

Description: Los Angeles : SAGE, [2022] |

Identifiers: LCCN 2020040155 | ISBN 9781071817001 (paperback) | ISBN 9781071817018 (epub) | ISBN 9781071817025 (epub) | ISBN 9781071817049 (pdf)

Subjects: LCSH: Social sciences—Statistical methods—Data processing. | R (Computer program language) | SPSS (Computer file)

Classification: LCC HA32 .T65 2022 | DDC 005.5/5—dc23 LC record available at https://lccn.loc.gov/2020040155

This book is printed on acid-free paper.

Acquisitions Editor: Leah Fargotstein
Editorial Assistant: Kelsey Barkis
Production Editor: Gagan Mahindra
Copy Editor: Integra
Typesetter: C&M Digitals (P) Ltd.
Proofreader: Eleni Maria Georgiou
Cover Designer: Ginkhan Siam
Marketing Manager: Victoria Velasquez

MIX
Paper from responsible sources
FSC® C103567
www.fsc.org

21 22 23 24 25 10 9 8 7 6 5 4 3 2 1

BRIEF CONTENTS

About the Author   xiii

Acknowledgments   xv

Introduction   1

Chapter 1 • Introduction to R   5

Chapter 2 • Preparing to Use R and RStudio   15

Chapter 3 • R Terms, Concepts, and Command Structure   25

Chapter 4 • Introduction to RStudio   33

Chapter 5 • Conducting Rstudio Sessions:
                 A Detailed Example   43

Chapter 6 • Conducting Rstudio Sessions: A Brief Example   75

Chapter 7 • Conducting Statistical Analyses Using
                 This Book: A Detailed Example   91

Chapter 8 • Conducting Statistical Analyses Using
                 This Book: A Brief Example   109

Chapter 9 • Working With Data Frames and Variables in R   123

Chapter 10 • Conducting Statistical Analyses Using
                  SPSS Syntax   127

Appendix A: Data Transformations   141

Appendix B: Statistical Procedures   165

Further Resources   293

DETAILED CONTENTS

About the Author   xiii

Acknowledgments   xv

Introduction   1

Chapter 1 • Introduction to R   5

1.1 What Is R?   5

1.2 Why are Some Features of R?   5

1.3 Installing R and Getting Help Learning R   6
    Downloading and Installing the Latest Version of R   6
    Using R To Conduct Statistical Analyses: Getting Help   7
    Identifying and Locating Packages   7

1.4 Conducting Statistical Analyses in Spss Versus R:
    A First Example   8
    Conducting Statistical Analyses Using SPSS   8
    Conducting Statistical Analyses Using R   9
    A First Example of SPSS Versus R: Conducting a *t*-Test   10
    Relevant Types of Files: SPSS and R   12

1.5 Comparing Spss and R   13

Chapter 2 • Preparing to Use R and Rstudio   15

2.1 Tasks to Perform Before Your First R Session   15
    Install R   15
    Install RStudio   15
    Install the "Basic" Version of MIKTeX   16
    Create the Working Directory   16

2.2 Tasks to Perform Before Any R Session   18
    Prepare Files in SPSS or Excel for Importing into R   18
      Issue: Missing Data   18
      Issue: Retaining Variables in Data Files   19
    Save Prepared Data Files as CSV (Comma-Separated Value) Files   20
      Saving SPSS Data Files as CSV Files   20
      Saving Excel Worksheet Files as CSV Files 22
    Place CSV Files in the Working Directory   22

2.3 Tasks To Perform During Any R Session   23
    Use RStudio to Conduct and Document Statistical Analyses 23

Chapter 3 • R Terms, Concepts, and Command Structure　　　25

3.1 Data-Related Terms　　　25
　　Vectors, Elements, and Data Frames　　　25
　　Factors　　　26
3.2 Command-Related Terms　　　26
　　Commands, Functions, and Arguments　　　26
　　Writing Commands: Some Rules and Guidelines　　　27
　　Scripts　　　29
　　Comments　　　29
3.3 Object-Related Terms　　　30
　　Objects and Workspace　　　30
　　Naming Objects: Some Rules and Guidelines　　　31
3.4 File-Related Terms　　　32
　　Script Files and Markdown Files　　　32
　　Markdown Documents　　　32

Chapter 4 • Introduction to Rstudio　　　33

4.1 What Is RStudio?　　　33
4.2 Installing RStudio　　　33
4.3 Components of RStudio　　　34
4.4 Writing and Executing R Commands in RStudio　　　35
　　Writing and Executing R Commands in the Console　　　35
　　Writing and Executing R Commands in a Script File　　　37
　　Writing and Executing R Commands in a Markdown File　　　41
　　The Console, Script Files, and Markdown Files—
　　　Which One Should You Use?　　　41

Chapter 5 • Conducting Rstudio Sessions: A Detailed Example　　　43

5.1 1. Start RStudio　　　46
5.2 2. Create a New Script File (Optional)　　　46
5.3 3. Define the Working Directory　　　47
　　Creating a Default Working Directory　　　48
5.4 4. Import CSV File to Create a Data Frame　　　49
5.5 5. Change Any Missing Data in Data Frame to NA　　　50
　　Converting Missing Values into NAs: Some Examples　　　53
5.6 6. Save Data Frame With NAs As CSV File in the
　　Working Directory　　　54
5.7 7. Read the Modified CSV File to Create a Data Frame　　　56
　　Reading Files Created by the Write.csv Function:
　　　The Mysterious "X" Variable　　　57
5.8 8. Download and Install Packages (If Not Already Done)　　　58

5.9 9. Load Installed Packages (As Needed) 60
5.10 10. Conduct Desired Statistical Analyses 61
5.11 11. Open a New Markdown File 62
    Document Information 64
    Code 65
    Comments 66
5.12 12. Copy Commands and Comments into the Markdown File 67
5.13 13. Knit the Markdown File to Create a Markdown Document 69
    R Markdown Files Versus Spss Output Files 71
5.14 Exiting Rstudio (Save the Workspace Image?) 71
5.15 Getting Help With R 72

Chapter 6 • Conducting Rstudio Sessions:
A Brief Example **75**

6.1 1. Start RStudio 78
6.2 2. Create a New Script File (Optional) 78
6.3 3. Define the Working Directory 78
6.4 4. Import CSV File to Create a Data Frame 78
6.5 5. Change Any Missing Data in Data Frame to NA 79
6.6 6. Save Data Frame with NAs as CSV File in the
    Working Directory 79
6.7 7. Read the Modified CSV File to Create a Data Frame 80
6.8 8. Download and Install Packages (If Not Already Done) 81
6.9 9. Load Installed Packages (As Needed) 82
6.10 10. Conduct Desired Statistical Analyses 82
6.11 11. Open a New Markdown File 84
6.12 12. Copy Commands and Comments into the Markdown File 85
6.13 13. Knit the Markdown File to Create a Markdown Document 86
6.14 Exiting RStudio 88

Chapter 7 • Conducting Statistical Analyses Using
This Book: A Detailed Example **91**

7.1 1. Start RStudio 94
7.2 2. Copy and Paste an Example Script into a Script File 94
7.3 3. Modify the Example Script as Needed for the Desired
    Statistical Analysis 97
7.4 4. Execute the Script to Confirm It Works Properly 100
7.5 5. Copy and Paste the Script into a Markdown File 102
7.6 6. Knit the Markdown File to Create a Markdown Document 105

Chapter 8 • Conducting Statistical Analyses Using This Book: A Brief Example   **109**

8.1 1. Start RStudio   111

8.2 2. Copy and Paste an Example Script into a Script File   111

8.3 3. Modify the Example Script as Needed for the Desired Statistical Analysis   113

8.4 4. Execute the Script to Confirm it Works Properly   115

8.5 5. Copy and Paste the Script into a Markdown File   116

8.6 6. Knit the Markdown File to Create a Markdown Document   119

Chapter 9 • Working With Data Frames and Variables in R   **123**

9.1 Working with Data Frames   123

Display the Contents of a Data Frame   123

List the Number of Participants (Rows) in a Data Frame   124

List the Number of Variables (Columns) in a Data Frame   124

List the Names of the Variables in a Data Frame   124

Refer to a Specific Variable in a Data Frame   124

Remove a Variable from a Data Frame   124

Sort the Rows in a Data Frame by a Variable   125

Create a New Data Frame With No Missing Data   125

Create a New Data Frame With Only Selected Variables From a Data Frame   125

Create a New Data Frame With Only Selected Cases From a Data Frame   125

Save a Data Frame as a Csv File   126

9.2 Working With Variables   126

Convert Numeric Values of a Variable to String (Alphanumeric) Values   126

Convert a Numeric Variable into a String Variable (Factor)   126

Chapter 10 • Conducting Statistical Analyses Using SPSS Syntax   **127**

10.1 Conducting Analyses in SPSS Using Menu Choices   128

10.2 Conducting Analyses in Spss Using Syntax Commands   130

Writing SPSS Syntax Commands: Some Rules and Guidelines   132

Getting Information About SPSS Syntax Commands: The Syntax Reference Guide   133

Executing SPSS Syntax Commands   135

10.3 Editing SPSS Output Files   136

Selecting Aspects of Output Files to be Printed   136

Setting the Number of Decimal Places in Output Files   137

Appendix A: Data Transformations   141

Reverse Score a Variable (Recode)   146

Reduce the Number of Groups in a Categorical Variable (Recode)   147

Create a Categorical Variable from a Continuous Variable (Recode)   149

Create a Variable From Other Variables (Compute)   151

Create a Variable from Other Variables (Minimum Number of Valid Values) (Compute)   153

Create a Variable from Occurrences of Values of Other Variables (Count)   155

Perform Data Transformations When Conditions are Met (IF)   156

Perform Data Transformations Under Specified Conditions (DO IF/END IF)   158

Perform Data Transformations Under Different Specified Conditions (DO IF/ELSE IF/END IF)   160

Use Numeric Functions in Data Transformations (ABS, RND, TRUNC, SQRT)   162

Appendix B: Statistical Procedures   165

Descriptive Statistics (All Variables)   168

Descriptive Statistics (Selected Variables)   169

Descriptive Statistics (Selected Variables) by Group   170

Frequency Distribution Table   171

Histogram   172

t-Test for One Mean   174

Confidence Interval for the Mean   176

T-Test for Independent Means   177

T-Test for Dependent Means (Repeated-Measures T-Test)   179

One-Way Anova and Tukey Post-Hoc Comparisons   181

One-Way Anova and Trend Analysis   183

Single-Factor Within-Subjects (Repeated Measures) Anova   187

Two-Factor Between-Subjects Anova   190

Two-Factor Between-Subjects Anova (Simple Effects)   194

Two-Factor Between-Subjects Anova (Simple Comparisons)   197

Two-Factor Between-Subjects Anova (Main Comparisons)   200

Two-Factor Mixed Factorial Anova   202

Two-Factor Within-Subjects Anova   206

Three-Factor Between-Subjects Anova   211

Pearson Correlation (One Correlation)   215

Pearson Correlation (Correlation Matrix) 217

Scatterplot 220

Internal Consistency (Cronbach's Alpha) 221

Principal Components Analysis (Varimax Rotation) 224

Principal Components Analysis (Oblique Rotation) 228

Factor Analysis (Principal Axis Factoring) 232

Linear Regression 237

Multiple Regression (Standard) 239

Multiple Regression (Hierarchical With Two Steps) 241

Multiple Regression (Hierarchical With Three Steps) 244

Multiple Regression (Testing Moderator Variables Using
    Hierarchical Regression) 249

Multiple Regression (Portraying A Significant Moderating Effect) 252

Multiple Regression (Stepwise) 260

Multiple Regression (Backward) 264

Multiple Regression (Forward) 268

Canonical Correlation Analysis 272

Discriminant Analysis (Two Groups) 278

Discriminant Analysis (Three Groups) 284

Cross-Tabulation and the Chi-Square Test of Independence 289

Further Resources 293

ABOUT THE AUTHOR

Howard T. Tokunaga is a Professor of Psychology at San Jose State University, where he serves as Coordinator of the MS Program in Industrial/Organizational (I/O) Psychology and teaches undergraduate and graduate courses in statistics, research methods, and I/O psychology. He received his bachelor's degree in psychology at UC Santa Cruz and his PhD in psychology at UC Berkeley. In addition to his teaching, he has consulted with a number of public-sector and private-sector organizations on a wide variety of management and human resource issues. He is author of *Fundamental Statistics for the Social and Behavioral Sciences* and coauthor (with G. Keppel) of *Introduction to Design and Analysis: A Student's Handbook*.

ACKNOWLEDGMENTS

I start by expressing my indebtedness to Leah Fargotstein, my editor at SAGE. Leah listened carefully and responded thoughtfully to all my conviction and doubts about this book, and I feel truly blessed to have twice been given the opportunity to work with someone of her wisdom, humor, and kindness. I also am grateful for my graduate students at San Jose State, without whom this book would have never been a possibility, let alone a reality. Working with such motivated and gifted students is something I will always cherish. I'd also like to convey much appreciation to Valerie Carr, whose skill and devotion to teaching data science was a guiding light for this book, and to Megumi Hosoda, Arlene Asuncion, Cheryl Chancellor-Freeland, and Mildred Alvarez for being such wonderful friends and colleagues. I thank my kids, Meagan and Will, for their love and support over these last two years that were, to say the least, challenging, and Joe and Stephen Butler for their data analytic acumen and simply for being great people.

I would like to thank the following people at SAGE: Leah Fargotstein, Gagan Mahindra, Ivey Mellem, Rashmi Motiwale, Eleni M. Georgiou, Victoria Velasquez. SAGE and the author would also like to thank the following reviewers for their valuable contributions to the development of this manuscript:

Behrouz Bakhtiari, McMaster University

Evan Curtis, Booth University College

Daniel DePaulo, Borough of Manhattan Community College

Lindsay Greenlee, Texas Tech University

Abdy Javadzadeh, St. Thomas University

Tae Kuen Kim, Adelphi University School of Social Work

Charles P. Kost II, Colorado Technical University

Cleborne Maddux, University of Nevada, Reno

Joshua Maxwell, University of New Mexico

Sylvia Reyes, Bakersfield College

Aditi Sachdev, Hofstra University

Beverley Searle, University of Dundee

Laura Solitare, Texas Southern University

Alisia (Giac-Thao) Tran, Arizona State University

INTRODUCTION

As someone raised in academia, I learned to analyze data using SPSS. I hesitate to admit it, because it reveals more about my age than I'd like, but I knew SPSS not only before it was IBM SPSS Statistics, but before it was PASW, SPSS Statistics, and SPSS-X, which means I knew SPSS when you didn't have to get a new version of it seemingly every year. In fact, I knew SPSS when the letters S, P, S, and S actually represented something! But I digress. I learned SPSS because that was how many college students learned to conduct statistical analyses if your major was something other than math or computer science, especially in the era(s) before personal computers and the Internet.

After graduating from college, I continued to use SPSS in my research, in my courses as a graduate teaching assistant at Cal, and as a faculty member at San Jose State. One of my reasons for using SPSS was my familiarity with the software, but an equally important reason was its relatively quick learning curve for the students I was teaching. Because students knew much about clicking on menu choices and buttons, it was easy for them to learn to analyze data using SPSS, thus allowing them to focus their time and energy on the results rather than the process of data analysis. However, as time passed and I stayed in touch with my former undergraduate and graduate students, I came to the realization that although there is much value in learning SPSS, it has one critical limitation: students are often unable to continue to use it after graduation because of its cost and licensing requirements. Consequently, my former students sought alternatives to SPSS, which often led them to R. Feeling both the duty and the desire to help my students ultimately resulted in the writing of this book.

The main goal of this book is to help those familiar with the SPSS statistical software package learn how to use the R software environment to analyze data and conduct statistical analyses. R is an increasingly popular alternative to traditional data analytic software such as SPSS. Consequently, it's helpful for students and researchers to learn how to use R to analyze data and conduct statistical analyses. However, for a variety of reasons, the learning curve for R is much steeper than software such as SPSS. First, because R is a programming language, it takes longer to learn to write and execute commands than software such as SPSS that provides a menu-driven, point-and-click graphic user interface (GUI). Second, rather than being a packaged software program, the statistical capabilities of R are dependent on users who contribute to an ever-growing library of additions to R. Consequently, identifying, evaluating, and using this library can be a laborious process. Third, there are relatively few books designed for researchers that focus on how commonly used data transformations and statistical procedures can be conducted using R. Hopefully, this book will help address this third issue.

This book is structured around three main purposes. The first purpose is to introduce R and RStudio, a software tool designed for users of R. Toward this purpose, the first two chapters of this book discuss how to install and get help with R, illustrate critical differences between SPSS and R, and cover tasks that must be completed before conducting statistical analyses using R. The second purpose is to illustrate how statistical analyses may be conducted using R. Chapters 3–9 provide a brief overview of R terms and concepts, introduce RStudio, which is software designed to facilitate the use of R, and provide several examples of how statistical analyses can be conducted using RStudio. The third purpose, addressed in Appendices A and B of this book, is to demonstrate how a variety of common data transformation tasks and statistical procedures may be conducted using R. As it's assumed readers of this book are familiar with SPSS, the use of R will be illustrated by comparing it side-be-side with SPSS. For each data transformation task and statistical procedure, how the analysis may be conducted using SPSS will first be presented, immediately followed by a presentation of how the same or similar results can be produced using R.

It's critical to understand that this book is **not** designed to teach statistics or provide an extended introduction to SPSS. In order to focus on how to conduct statistical analyses using R, it will be assumed that readers will rely upon their previous training in statistics and SPSS to extract and interpret the relevant information from the results of statistical analyses. Also, although R has very powerful graphics capabilities, this book will focus instead on analyzing data rather than visualizing data.

As with any book, it is assumed this one can be corrected and improved upon in an infinite number of ways. Any such, any and all feedback is most welcome and may be sent to howard.tokunaga@sjsu.edu.

* * * * *

NOTE: This book was last updated in January 2020 using version 4.0.0 (Arbor Day) of R (Windows 64-bit), version 1.3.959 of RStudio, version 2.9.7442 of MiKTex, and version 25 of SPSS (Windows).

NOTE: In this book, different font styles will be used to designate four aspects of R and SPSS: R terms and concepts, R commands that are common to all users, R commands that are optional to each user (e.g., files and variables named by the user), and SPSS commands. How these four aspects will be represented in this book are illustrated in the table below:

Aspect	Font	Example
R term or concept	Bold italic	*packages*
R command	Courier New	`df1 <- read.csv("MISC.csv")`
User-option R command	Courier New (colored)	`DATATRANS.csv`
SPSS command	Arial	COMPUTE SCORE = 1

1

INTRODUCTION TO R

1.1 WHAT IS R?

According to the R Project (https://www.r-project.org/), "R is a free software environment for statistical computing and graphics . . . R is an integrated suite of software facilities for data manipulation, calculation and graphical display." R was started by Robert Gentleman and Ross Ihaka and was influenced by the S language, originally developed at Bell Laboratories.

The base R distribution consists of *code* that can be written to create *commands* that are executed to perform a desired task; interrelated sets of commands are known as *functions*. For example, the command cc(set1, set2) utilizes the cc function to conduct a canonical correlation analysis between the two sets of variables set1 and set2. Commands and functions may be executed to produce an *object* such as a data set or the results of a statistical analysis. For example, the command df1 <- read.csv("MISC.csv") creates an object, a data frame (i.e., data set) named df1, by reading the file MISC.csv. Commands, functions, and objects are introduced in Chapter 3 (R terms, concepts, and command structure) and discussed throughout this book.

1.2 WHY ARE SOME FEATURES OF R?

R has a number of defining features. Focusing on the features relevant to this book, R is an open-source programming language, which the World Wide Web Consortium (https://www.w3.org/) defines as "software whose source code is freely distributed and modifiable by anyone." Being open-source implies that

R is freely available and requires no license to use. Also, R is supported and maintained by a very large and active community of users that do such things as maintain blogs and websites, write manuals, hold boot camps, and conduct workshops, seminars, and training sessions.

Because R is open-source, it is continuously evolving. This is because users of R may extend the capabilities of the base R distribution by creating sets of functions known as **packages**, also referred to as *libraries*. For example, the psych package can be downloaded and installed within R to calculate descriptive statistics and Pearson correlations, whereas the CCA package can be used to conduct the canonical correlation analysis mentioned above. Packages, which have been created for a wide variety of academic disciplines as well as businesses, are made freely available to users by being contributed to the repository at the Comprehensive R Archive Network (CRAN) (https://CRAN.R-project.org/). *CRAN* is a worldwide collection of websites that provide access to the R language, packages, and documentation. As of September 2020, over 16,000 packages are available at CRAN. Packages that can be used to conduct the statistical analyses covered in this book are identified in Chapter 5 (Conducting RStudio sessions: A detailed example).

In addition to the support and contributions of its community, R has risen in prominence for a number of technical reasons, many of which are beyond the scope of this book. One of the most popular features of R is its large collection of sophisticated static and interactive graphics and data visualization packages. R also has the ability to present the results of statistical analyses and graphics in web pages, Word documents, and PowerPoint presentations. More broadly, R is a comprehensive programming language, which means it can facilitate both statistical computing as well as software development such as the creation of web-based applications. R also supports cross-platform compatibility such that it can be used on many different operating systems, such as Windows, MacOS, and Linux. As a powerful programming language, R is designed to work with many different types of data, databases, and other programming languages.

1.3 INSTALLING R AND GETTING HELP LEARNING R

Downloading and Installing the Latest Version of R

The "base" distribution of R may be found at the CRAN website (https://cran.r-project.org/). Links to Linux, Windows, and Mac versions of R are located within the "Download and Install R" selection.

Using R to Conduct Statistical Analyses: Getting Help

There are a seemingly infinite number of books, online tutorials, and cheat sheets designed to help people learn R. Here are a few resources specifically geared toward the statistical analysis of data (thanks to my colleague Valerie Carr for her recommendations):

Interactive tutorials

- Swirl: http://swirlstats.com

- edX: https://www.edx.org/course/data-science-r-basics

Written tutorials

- Personality project: http://personality-project.org/r/r.guide.html

Website for calculating statistics using R (*extremely* helpful website!)

- Quick-R: http://www.statmethods.net

Website for creating figures (bar charts, line graphs, scatterplots, etc.)

- ggplot2: https://ggplot2.tidyverse.org/

Identifying and Locating Packages

As mentioned earlier, R users have extended the capabilities of the base R distribution by creating sets of functions known as packages. Packages needed to conduct some of the statistical analyses in this book are indicated in Chapter 5 (Conducting RStudio sessions: A detailed example); however, you may need to locate other packages for your specific situation.

One strategy to identify and locate packages is to use an Internet search engine such as Google. For example, in conducting multiple regression (MRC) analyses for this book, it was concluded that executing the lm function in the base R package does not provide standardized regression coefficients (betas) for the predictor variables. To find a package that provides these coefficients, "standardized coefficients MRC CRAN package" was searched for within Google, which identified the lm.beta package. Note that "CRAN" was included in the search rather than "R" because including just the letter "R" returns many irrelevant results. Searching, downloading, and installing packages are illustrated in Chapter 5 (Conducting RStudio sessions: A detailed example).

1.4 CONDUCTING STATISTICAL ANALYSES IN SPSS VERSUS R: A FIRST EXAMPLE

As you may have deduced, R is similar to statistical software such as SPSS in terms of its primary purposes: data manipulation, data analysis, and graphical display. In other words, both SPSS and R provide the ability to define and modify data, conduct statistical analyses, and represent data visually using graphs and figures. However, there are many fundamental differences between SPSS and R in how data are handled and how statistical analyses may be conducted.

As this book is primarily designed to help SPSS users learn how to use R, this section introduces these differences by providing an example of how an analysis may be conducted using SPSS and then how the same analysis may be conducted using R. The steps and concepts introduced in this example are the basis for many of the later chapters in this book.

Conducting Statistical Analyses Using SPSS

Students and researchers who have learned to use SPSS may be in the situation of needing to analyze data in an SPSS data file. If so, the following four steps may be followed to conduct statistical analyses using SPSS:

1. Start SPSS

2. Open an SPSS data file

3. Open a syntax file to enter and execute commands (optional)

4. **Conduct desired statistical analyses to create output file**

There are several things to note regarding the above steps. First, these steps did not include creating a new data file by defining variables (variable names, formats, labels, missing values, etc.) and entering raw data into the file. Because this book is written for researchers who already possess a working knowledge of SPSS, it's assumed readers of this book know how to create data files using SPSS or Excel. Second, the step "Open a syntax file to enter and execute commands (optional)" implies desired statistical analysis may be conducted by writing commands into a syntax file rather than by selecting menu choices. In presenting the SPSS output for each analysis, this book will provide the syntax used to generate the output. Chapter 10

(Conducting statistical analyses using SPSS syntax) provides a brief summary of how statistical analyses may be conducted in SPSS using syntax commands.

Conducting Statistical Analyses Using R

Listed below is one way statistical analyses may be conducted using R. The terms and concepts introduced in these steps will be discussed in later chapters of this book, particularly in Chapter 3 (R terms, concepts, and command structure) and Chapter 5 (Conducting RStudio sessions: A detailed example):

1. Start RStudio

2. Create a new script file (optional)

3. Define the working directory

4. Import CSV file to create a data frame

5. Change any missing data in data frame to NA

6. Save data frame with NAs as CSV file in the working directory

7. Read the modified CSV file to create a data frame

8. Download and install packages (if not already done)

9. Load installed packages (as needed)

10. **Conduct desired statistical analyses**

11. Open a new markdown file

12. Copy commands and comments into the markdown file

13. Knit the markdown file to create a markdown document

Besides the sheer number of steps, a critical difference between SPSS and R occurs in the first step, "Start RStudio." **This book will access R by starting another program, RStudio.** In essence, RStudio is a software program, known as an integrated development environment (IDE), that is designed to help people use R more efficiently. Chapter 4 (Introduction to RStudio) introduces the purpose and components of RStudio; Chapters 5–8 illustrate how RStudio may be used to conduct statistical analyses.

In addition to how the steps begin, another difference between SPSS and R is that using R requires additional steps both before and after step 10, "Conduct desired statistical analyses." In terms of steps required by R **before** conducting statistical analyses, these steps involve actions such as "download," "install," and "load." These words represent a critical distinction between SPSS and R: although SPSS is a stand-alone software program in which statistical procedures are preinstalled, **R is an ever-changing programming environment in which users must locate and evaluate different methods for conducting a statistical analysis, and then bring the desired method into R in an interactive manner**. These steps are discussed in Chapter 5 (Conducting RStudio sessions: A detailed example).

Another difference between SPSS and R that takes place before conducting statistical analyses involves accessing data files. In SPSS, users typically open a data file that has been created within the SPSS software. **In using R, however, this book will show how data files in R may be created by importing and modifying files first created in Excel or SPSS**. Creating data files for use in R is discussed in Chapter 2 (Preparing to use R and RStudio).

In terms of differences between SPSS and R that take place **after** statistical analyses are conducted, conducting statistical analyses in SPSS automatically creates an output file that includes the results of the analyses. However, **after determining how to conduct a desired statistical analysis, users of R must then create a file, known as a markdown document, that is the equivalent of an SPSS output file**. Markdown documents are introduced in Chapter 5 (Conducting RStudio sessions: A detailed example).

A First Example of SPSS Versus R: Conducting a *t*-test

To provide an initial illustration of similarities and differences between SPSS and R, imagine you're a researcher who has a set of data in an SPSS data file. Using this data file, you want to test the difference between the means of two groups (gender: Male, Female) on a dependent variable named defp using the *t*-test for independent means.

Using SPSS, conducting this *t*-test can involve the following steps:

1. Start SPSS

2. Open an SPSS data file

3. Open a syntax file to enter and execute commands to conduct a *t*-test

4. Conduct the *t*-test to create output file

Below is what the output of this analysis could resemble using the T-TEST command in SPSS (note that the syntax commands that conduct this analysis are provided at the top of the output):

```
T-TEST GROUPS=gender(1 2)
   /MISSING=ANALYSIS
   /VARIABLES=defp
   /CRITERIA=CI(.95).
```

T-Test

Group Statistics

	gender	N	Mean	Std. Deviation	Std. Error Mean
defp	1 Male	56	2.9095	.65589	.08765
	2 Female	57	3.0988	.55947	.07410

Independent Samples Test

		Levene's Test for Equality of Variances		t-test for Equality of Means						
		F	Sig.	t	df	Sig. (2-tailed)	Mean Difference	Std. Error Difference	95% Confidence Interval of the Difference Lower	Upper
defp	Equal variances assumed	2.296	.133	-1.651	111	.101	-.18928	.11461	-.41640	.03783
	Equal variances not assumed			-1.649	107.690	.102	-.18928	.11478	-.41679	.03823

To conduct this same analysis using R, we could follow the steps below (we realize these steps are introduced without explanation—they will be discussed in later chapters of this book):

1. Start RStudio

2. Create a new script file and enter commands that accomplish steps 3–9 above:

   (a) Define the working directory

   (b) Import a CSV file to create a data frame

   (c) Change any missing data in the data frame to NA

   (d) Save the data frame with NAs in a new CSV file in the working directory

   (e) Read the modified CSV file to create a data frame

   (f) Load a package that conducts a t-test for independent means

   (g) Write commands to conduct the t-test

3. Conduct the t-test

Below is what the output of this analysis could look like in R (the commands used to conduct this analysis are provided at the top of the output to the right of the > symbols and will be discussed in later chapters):

```
> setwd("e:/R output")
> df1 <- read.csv("MISC.csv")
> df1[, 2:2] [df1[, 2:2] == 0] <- NA
> df1[, 3:3] [df1[, 3:3] == 9.99] <- NA
> write.csv(df1, "MISC_NA.csv", row.names=FALSE)
> df1 <- read.csv("MISC_NA.csv")
> library(psych)
> describeBy (df1$defp, df1$gender)

 Descriptive statistics by group
group: 1
    vars  n mean   sd median trimmed  mad  min  max range skew kurtosis   se
X1     1 56 2.91 0.66   2.88    2.89 0.64 1.22 4.72   3.5 0.34     0.59 0.09
----------------------------------------------------------------
group: 2
    vars  n mean   sd median trimmed  mad  min  max range skew kurtosis   se
X1     1 57  3.1 0.56   3.12    3.09 0.48 1.89 4.67  2.78 0.28     0.71 0.07
> t.test(df1$defp ~ df1$gender, var.equal=TRUE, paired=FALSE)

        Two Sample t-test

data:  df1$defp by df1$gender
t = -1.6515, df = 111, p-value = 0.1015
alternative hypothesis: true difference in means is not equal to 0
95 percent confidence interval:
 -0.41639771  0.03783276
sample estimates:
mean in group 1 mean in group 2
       2.909489        3.098771

>
```

Comparing these two outputs, they calculate the same descriptive statistics for the two groups (Male ($M = 2.91$, sd = .66), Female ($M = 3.10$, sd = .56)) and the same value for the t-test ($t(111) = -1.65$, $p = .10$). However, the commands needed to conduct this analysis using R are greater in number and complexity.

It is also important to note that the above R output is **not** automatically placed into a file similar to an SPSS output file. In other words, at this point we have only reached step 10 of the 13 steps listed earlier; additional steps are needed to generate a file that includes the R commands and the results of executing the commands. These last three steps are introduced in Chapter 5 (Conducting RStudio sessions: A detailed example).

Relevant Types of Files: SPSS and R

Using software to conduct statistical analyses primarily involves working with three types of computer files: (1) files that contain data, (2) files that contain code or commands that carry out data manipulation and data analysis activities, and (3) files that provide the results of executing commands or code. Listed below are the names given to these three types of files in SPSS versus R:

Contents of file	SPSS	R
Data	Data file (.sav)	CSV file (.csv) → Data frame
Commands/ Comments	Syntax file (.sps)	Script file (.r) or markdown file (. Rmd)
Results of executing commands	Output file (.sav)	Markdown document (.md)

The types of files used within R and similarities and differences with their SPSS counterparts will be discussed throughout the remainder of this book.

1.5 COMPARING SPSS AND R

Now that we've illustrated how statistical analyses can be conducted in SPSS and R and the types of files they utilize, it's appropriate to compare them along a number of aspects that may be of concern to those wishing to analyze their data. This comparison, provided in the next table, suggests that the relative advantages of SPSS are that it is relatively easier and faster to learn to use due to its reliance on a menu-driven ("point and click") graphic use interface (GUI) that facilitates the display and manipulation of data. The relative strengths of R are that it's freely available, has more sophisticated graphing capabilities, and provides greater support to its users from its large and active community of users.

Aspect	SPSS	R
Cost	Commercial product	Free
Ease of use	Easier	More difficult
Learning curve	Shorter	Longer
User interface	Primarily menu-driven GUI	Primarily command (syntax) driven
Display and manipulation of raw data	Data displayed and manipulated in spreadsheet-like fashion	Data displayed and manipulated by executing commands
Graphing	A few functional graphs with minor changes	Many customizable and interactive graphs
Support	Official support provided by publisher	Informal/Professional support provided by users/companies
Documentation	Fewer available sources, some of which are free	Many available sources, many of which are free
Community	Smaller, less active community of users	Large, very active community of users
Capabilities/ Functionality	Changes occasionally with published updates	Constantly changing and growing due to user-created packages

* * * * *

Having provided an overview of the steps and files involved in using R to conduct statistical analyses, the next chapter lists specific tasks users of R must complete both before and during their use of R.

2

PREPARING TO USE
R AND RSTUDIO

Chapter 1 introduced steps that can be taken to conduct statistical analyses using R. However, there are several critical tasks that must first be performed before any statistical analyses can be conducted. This chapter is a bridge between the previous chapter, which provided a listing of the steps taken to conduct statistical analyses using R, and the following chapters, which discuss and illustrate each of these steps in greater detail.

2.1 TASKS TO PERFORM BEFORE YOUR FIRST R SESSION

Install R

The first step is to install the base R distribution. To do this, go to https://cran.r-project.org/, click on the appropriate operating system (**Linux**, **Mac**, **Windows**) in the "Download and Install R" box, and download the "base" distribution.

Note: This book is based on Windows 64-bit version 4.0.0 (Arbor Day).

Install RStudio

In addition to installing R, we recommend that you install RStudio, which is a software program developed to help use R more efficiently and effectively. To install RStudio, go to https://www.rstudio.com/products/rstudio/, click on

RStudio Desktop, and under "Open Source Edition," click on **DOWNLOAD RSTUDIO DESKTOP** and download the free Windows or Mac version under "Installers for Supported Platforms."

Note: This book is based on Windows 7+ version 1.3.959 (64-bit).

Install the "Basic" Version of MiKTeX

MiKTeX (pronounced "mick-tech") creates pdf files within RStudio that are the equivalent of SPSS output files. MiKTeX is introduced in Chapter 5 (Conducting RStudio sessions: Introduction). To install MiKTeX, go to https://miktex.org/download, click on the **Windows** or **Mac** tab located below the words "Getting MiKTeX" and download and install the "basic" version—if asked, install any requested files and say "Yes" to "Install missing packages on-the-fly." Mac users should note the message on the MiKTeX website that states, "To set up a TeX/LaTeX system on macOS, download and open this disk image. Then drag the MiKTeX icon onto the Applications folder." Mac users are strongly advised to read the tutorial "Install MiKTeX on macOS" to insure the installation is complete and that the MiKTeX Console is installed to access LaTeX and TeX.

Note: This book is based on Windows 7+ version 2.9.7442 (64-bit).

Create the Working Directory

Within SPSS, files containing data (i.e., data files) can be located anywhere on one's computer (Desktop, hard drive, flash drive, etc.). However, before using R, a computer folder must be created that will hold the data files to be analyzed—this folder will be referred to as the ***working directory***. Furthermore, all data files to be analyzed must be placed in the working directory **before** conducting any statistical analyses.

The working directory can be anywhere of your choosing, such as the computer's Desktop, hard drive, or an external flash drive. For the examples in this book, the working directory is a folder named "R output" on a flash drive (the "e:" drive of a Windows computer) thus referred to as "**e:/R output**." If the "R output" folder had instead been created within the RStudio program on the hard drive of a Windows-based computer, the working directory would have been stated as "C:/Program Files/RStudio/R output."

To find the location (i.e., path) of the folder designated as the working directory, right click the folder and select "Properties" (Windows) or "Get info" (Mac). It's **very** important to remember the path of the working directory as it may be provided every time you use R. A Windows example of identifying the location of the working directory for this book (e:/R Output) is provided below:

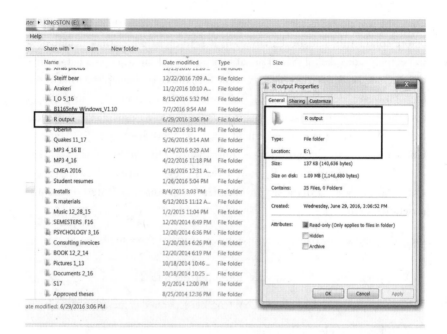

One bit of confusion for Windows users is that even though the location of the R Output folder is stated using a backslash (E:\), the location must be written within R using a forward slash (E:/). In other words, the working directory will be referred to as "e:/R Output" rather than "e:\R Output."

For Mac users, we've found the path information provided by "Get info" to be somewhat confusing. Consequently, the working directory for Mac users may be best placed on the Desktop, which results in the path, "/users/*username*/Desktop/*foldername*." For example, if the author of this book had created the "R Output" folder on the desktop of a Mac, the path to the working directory would be "/users/howard/Desktop/R Output."

Note that multiple working directories can be created for different projects or purposes. For example, you might want to create one working directory for your thesis and a second working directory for your job. In this book, this could consist of creating two additional folders inside the "e:/R Output" folder: one folder named "thesis" and another named "job." The location of these two working directories would be "e:/R Output/thesis/" and "e:/R Output/job/," respectively.

2.2 TASKS TO PERFORM BEFORE ANY R SESSION

Once the working directory has been created, the next step that must be taken before conducting statistical analyses in R is to prepare files that include data to be analyzed. Like SPSS, statistical analyses in R may be conducted on files that include variables (the columns of the file) and participants (the rows of the file). However, defining variables and entering data within R is surprisingly complicated and cumbersome; this is because R doesn't provide the ability to create a file that is the equivalent of an Excel worksheet or SPSS data file. Consequently, this chapter discusses how to create files in SPSS or Excel that may then be imported into R; how R reads these imported files to conduct statistical analyses is discussed in Chapter 5 (Conducting RStudio sessions: A detailed example).

Preparing and saving data files for use in R consists of three steps:

1. Prepare files in SPSS or Excel for importing into R

2. Save prepared data files as CSV (comma separated value) files

3. Place CSV files in the working directory

Each of these three steps is discussed and illustrated below.

Prepare Files in SPSS or Excel for Importing into R

IMPORTANT: After creating a data file in SPSS or Excel, it's a good idea to save a backup copy of the file before performing the R-related modifications or preparations discussed in this chapter.

In preparing SPSS or Excel files for importing into R, there are two critical issues: missing data and which variables to retain in the data file. Each of these issues is discussed below.

Issue: Missing Data

It is often the case that, in collecting data, valid data is not obtained on all variables for all participants. Consequently, the issue of missing data must be addressed in a clear and explicit manner. As it turns out, R handles missing data **much** differently than SPSS. There are two things to keep in mind:

First, the main value R recognized as missing data is *NA*. More specifically, R uses NA to represent missing data for <u>all</u> types of variables (numeric, string, etc.). As a result, any and all missing data in an SPSS or Excel file (often designated using blank spaces, periods, 0, 9, 99, X, etc.) must be converted into NAs. Note: this conversion is not done within SPSS or Excel, but rather after the file has been imported into R. How to convert missing data to NAs is illustrated in Chapter 5 (Conducting RStudio sessions: A detailed example). <u>Suggestion: One way to expedite the conversion of missing values to NAs is to use blank spaces or periods (rather than numbers such as 9 or 99 or letters such as X) for all missing data in the SPSS or Excel file.</u>

Second, some (but not all) statistical procedures within R will only execute if the data file contains <u>no</u> missing data. That is, even if missing data have been converted into NAs, some procedures do not allow for any missing data (i.e., these procedures do not perform "listwise" or "pairwise" deletion). Consequently, for some statistical procedures, any participants with any missing data must be deleted from the data file before conducting the statistical procedure. Again, this deletion is not done while creating the data file in SPSS or Excel, but rather after the file is imported into R. This book will indicate which procedures require no missing data and commands that may be used to remove participants with any missing data. <u>Suggestion: One resolution to this issue is to replace any missing data in the SPSS or Excel file with valid values so that there are no missing data—this ensures that all analyses conducted on a data file are based on the same sample size.</u>

It should be noted that R actually utilizes another missing value: ***NaN*** ("not a number"). The missing value NaN is used by R to represent an impossible value for a variable. For example, if you attempted to divide a value of a variable by zero (e.g., 5/0) or take the square root of a negative number (e.g., $\sqrt{-4.25}$), the result of these calculations would be assigned an NaN. An NaN is generally treated the same way as an NA.

Issue: Retaining Variables in Data Files

In addition to missing data, a second data file issue pertains to the variables in the data set. **Some R packages require that the data file contains <u>only</u>**

the variables to be used in the desired analysis. As an example, imagine you want to use the `alpha` command in the `psych` package to calculate Cronbach's alpha on variables X1 to X5, but your data file also contains variables Y1 to Y7. If so, Cronbach's alpha will be calculated using all 12 variables. However, this does not mean you need to create SPSS or Excel files that only contain certain variables (e.g., you don't need to create one file that contains X1–X5 and a second file that contains Y1–Y7). Instead, within R, temporary data sets can be created that contain subsets of variables from existing data files; this will be illustrated for the statistical procedures that have this requirement. Suggestion: Because creating temporary data sets requires knowing the exact location of the variables in the data file, it's helpful to have a record of what variables are in the SPSS or Excel file and the location (i.e., column number) of each variable.

Save Prepared Data Files as CSV (Comma Separated Value) Files

Once a data file has been prepared for use in R, the next step is to save the file in the correct format. Files created by software have what are known as "extensions." For example, a Word document has the extension .docx, such that the full name for the Word document XXX is XXX.docx. An SPSS data file has an .sav extension and an Excel worksheet has an .xlsx extension.

In order to be used in R, an SPSS or Excel data file must be saved as a comma separated value (CSV) file with a .csv extension. To save an SPSS data file or Excel worksheet as a CSV file, open the file within its particular software, select the "Save as" menu choice, and select the CSV option. How this may be accomplished in SPSS and Excel is demonstrated below.

Saving SPSS Data Files as CSV Files

1. Open the SPSS data file (.sav)

2. Click on the **File** menu, select **Save As**, click **Comma delimited (*.csv)** within the "Save as type:" menu, and click the **Save** button. IMPORTANT: Be sure the **Write variable names to file** box is checked so that the names are included in the top row of the CSV file.

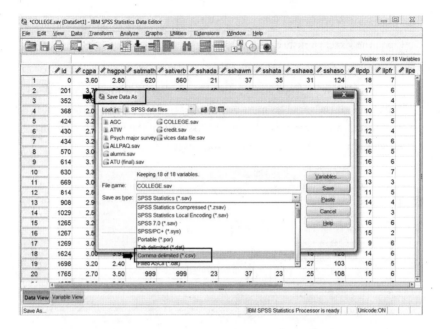

3. OPTIONAL: To save only a subset of the variables in the CSV file, before clicking on the **Save** button, click on **Variables** and **Keep** the desired variables.

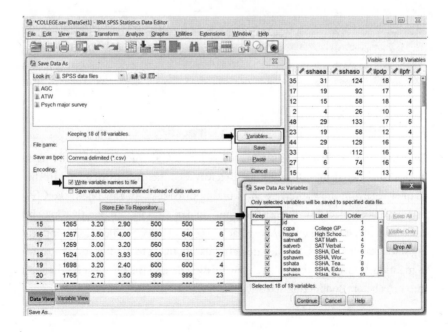

Saving Excel Worksheet Files as CSV Files

1. Open the Excel worksheet (.xlsx)

2. Click on the **File** menu, select **Save As**, click **CSV (Comma delimited)** within the "Save as type:" menu, and click the **Save** button. IMPORTANT: The names of the variables must be provided in the first row of the worksheet (in the screenshot below, the first row of the Excel file contains variable names such as "id," "cgpa," and "hsgpa").

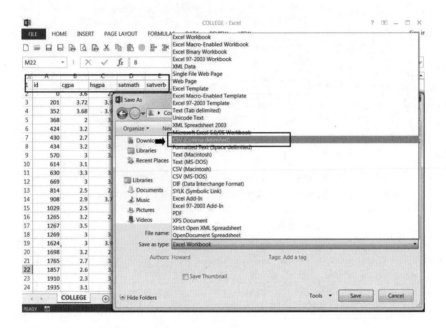

Place CSV Files in the Working Directory

Once the SPSS or Excel file has been saved as a CSV file, the CSV file must be placed or saved into the working directory (see the earlier discussion in this chapter regarding how to create the working directory). In this book, the CSV files have been placed in the "e:/R output" folder. As with any file that may be later modified, it's advisable to save a backup copy of the CSV file before conducting statistical analyses. CSV files are particularly subject to modification because, as mentioned earlier in this chapter, any missing data in the file must be changed into NAs before conducting statistical analyses.

2.3 TASKS TO PERFORM DURING ANY R SESSION

Use RStudio to Conduct and Document Statistical Analyses

Once the above preliminary steps have been completed, you're ready to conduct statistical analyses! Although statistical analyses may be conducted directly in R, this book will utilize RStudio, a software program known as an integrated development environment (IDE) that helps people use R more efficiently. Conducting statistical analyses using RStudio requires its own set of steps, which are discussed and illustrated in Chapter 5 (Conducting RStudio sessions: A detailed example).

* * * * *

Now that the above preliminary steps have been accomplished, we are ready to return to a discussion of R and RStudio. The next chapter defines terms, concepts, and commands that will be mentioned in later chapters that discuss the conducting of statistical analyses within R.

3

R TERMS, CONCEPTS, AND COMMAND STRUCTURE

Up to this point, we've discussed tasks that need to be accomplished before using R: installing necessary software, creating a folder known as the working directory, preparing data files for use in R, and saving these files as CSV files in the working directory. Before we move on to the next chapters, it's useful to become acquainted with terms and concepts you'll encounter when using R.

3.1 DATA-RELATED TERMS

Vectors, Elements, and Data Frames

Regarding how data may be described, a *vector* is a vertical column consisting of *elements*. In essence, a vector is what SPSS users refer to as a "variable" and elements are "data for a variable." A *matrix* is a two-dimensional array (rows and columns) of numbers. A *data frame* is a matrix in which names have been assigned to the columns in the matrix—a data frame is what SPSS users would call a "data file" or "data set." In this book, data frames will be created by importing CSV data files created within SPSS and Excel into R that include the names of the variables in the first row of the file.

One critical difference between R data frames and SPSS data files is that R data frames are temporary files that are not saved once an R session is ended. Consequently, the user must write and execute commands to save data frames as files in the working directory. This is the opposite of SPSS data files, which already exist as files and it's assumed the user wants to save them unless they are deliberately deleted. In this book, data frames created within R will be saved as CSV files in the working directory "e:/R output."

Factors

Another data-related term pertains to the type of variable being analyzed. Similar to SPSS, variables in R are typically analyzed as numeric variables, even when the actual variable is alphanumeric (string). For example, the values of the variable Group would typically not be entered into a data file as "Experimental" and "Control" but rather as 1 and 2, where the number 1 is assigned to the Experimental condition and the number 2 is assigned to the Control condition. However, some statistical procedures in R, particularly ANOVA-related procedures that involve the comparison of group means, require variables consisting of groups to be qualitative/categorical variables known as factors.

Factors may be defined as categorical variables whose values are alphanumeric in nature. An example of a factor could be "grade," with the values "Freshman," "Sophomore," "Junior," and "Senior." Given that researchers do not typically enter the values of categorical variables but instead code them numerically (e.g., 1 = Freshman, 2 = Sophomore, 3 = Junior, 4 = Senior), the requirement that a variable be a factor may be problematic. However, it is possible in R to convert numeric variables into factors; the R command that performs this conversion is presented at the end of this chapter and will be included as needed throughout this book.

3.2 COMMAND-RELATED TERMS

Commands, Functions, and Arguments

Running R involves writing and executing *commands*; writing commands is what people sometimes refer to as "writing code" or "coding." Commands in R serve the same purpose as syntax commands in SPSS (such as COMPUTE, MANOVA, and REGRESSION), which is to carry out desired tasks. Starting in the next chapter, we will illustrate how commands in R are executed.

Commands in R are written in the generic form *function*(**arguments**). Functions are lines of code that have been written by R programmers to perform tasks, and arguments are options that customize what is performed by the function. One example of a command is `describe(df1,type=2)`, in which `describe` is a function that calculates descriptive statistics, `df1` is an argument that identifies the data frame (i.e., set of data) on which the statistics will be calculated, and `type=2` is an argument that determines the types of descriptive statistics to be calculated. A second example of a command is `principal(df2, nfactors = 5, rotate = "none")`; `principal` is a function that conducts a principal components analysis, and the arguments `df2`, `nfactors = 5`, and `rotate = "none"` customize how the principal components analysis is conducted.

Below are a few other examples of commands, functions, and arguments that will be presented and discussed in later chapters of this book:

Command	Function	Argument	Purpose of command
`setwd("e:/R output")`	`setwd`	`"e:/R output"`	Set the working directory to the `R output` folder on the `e:` drive
`library(car)`	`library`	`car`	Load the `car` package into R
`abs(df1$VARX)`	`abs`	`df1$VARX`	Calculate the absolute value of the variable `VARX`
`corr.test(df11)`	`corr.test`	`df11`	Calculate Pearson correlations for the variables in the `df11` data frame

As we move through this book, commands and function that are introduced will be accompanied by an explanation of its purpose and format.

Writing Commands: Some Rules and Guidelines

Starting in Chapter 5 (Conducting RStudio sessions: A detailed example), a variety of commands will be introduced, defined, and written to serve a variety of purposes. As such, it's useful to precede these chapters by providing some rules and guidelines that will be followed in writing these commands:

Commands are written in the form *function* (*arguments*), where *function* is the name given to a function by its creator and *arguments* are options that customize the operations performed by the function. Note that there are no blank spaces between the name of the function and the left parentheses symbol (e.g., the generic format is `function(arguments)` rather than *function (arguments)*.

Many commands end in parentheses, even when the parentheses do not contain any arguments (e.g., `summary(linreg)`, `theme_bw()`)

Multiple arguments within parentheses are separated by commas. For example, the command `rnd(df1$VAR1, digits = 0)` contains two arguments: `df1$VAR1`, which identifies the variable `VAR1` in the data frame `df1`, and `digits = 0`, which is the number of digits the values of `VAR1` are to be rounded by the `rnd` function.

Commands may contain brackets and braces. *Brackets* [] encompass data frames, vectors, and matrices. For example, the brackets in the command `df1[, 12:18]` select the variables in columns `12–18` in the data frame `df1`. *Braces* {} group together connected sets of commands and are used in conditional "for" and "if" loops (e.g., `for (i in 1:k) {...}`). Because brackets appear more often in commands used to conduct statistical analyses than are braces, brackets will appear much more often in this book.

Commands may contain comparison operators. R commands may include these commonly used comparison operators:

| == Equal to | < Less than | > Greater than |
| != Not equal to | <= Less than or equal to | >= Greater than or equal to |

In typing comparison operators, note that no spaces should be typed between the two symbols (e.g., == rather than = =) as including spaces will result in an error. For example, including a blank space (= = rather than ==) in the command `df1 [df1 = = 0] <- NA` may result in the error message, *Error: unexpected '=' in "df1 [df1 = =".*

Below are examples of commands in this book that include comparison operators:

Command	Operator	Interpretation of operator
`[df1 == "."]`	==	"If the value of a variable in the data frame `df1` is equal to a period (.)"
`subset(df1, gender == 1)`	==	"Identify those in the data frame `df1` whose `gender` is equal to 1"
`[which(df11$satverb <= 550),]`	<=	"Identify those in the data frame `df1` whose `satverb` is less than or equal to 550"

It should be noted that R commands may include either the double equals sign (==) or the single equals sign (=). However, these two symbols serve very different purposes. The double equals sign (==) is used to make comparisons, whereas a single equals sign (=) is used to assign a value to a vector. For example, gender == 1 compares someone's gender with the number 1; this can be represented by the question, "Is someone's gender equal to 1?" On the other hand, gender = 1 assigns a value of 1 to the variable gender; this can be represented by the statement, "Someone's gender is now equal to 1."

Most commands are typically written in lower-case and are case sensitive (e.g., library(psych) rather than *LIBRARY(PSYCH)* or *Library(Psych)*).

Quotation marks within commands (" ") cannot be Word smart quotes (" ").

Commands must be written as a single run-on sentence (i.e., long commands can't be broken across multiple lines using the <Enter> key).

Scripts

A *script* is a set of commands executed in a particular order to produce a desired outcome. The *t*-test example discussed in Chapter 1 of this book involved the script below (later chapters of this book explain the purpose of each command in the script):

```
setwd("e:/R output")
df1 <- read.csv("MISC.csv")
df1[, 2:2] [df1[, 2:2] == 0] <- NA
df1[, 3:3] [df1[, 3:3] == 9.99] <- NA
write.csv(df1, "MISC_NA.csv", row.names=FALSE)
df1 <- read.csv("MISC_NA.csv")
library(psych)
describeBy (df1$defp, df1$gender)
t.test(df1$defp ~ df1$gender, var.equal=TRUE, paired=FALSE)
```

Chapter 5 (Conducting RStudio sessions: A detailed example) illustrates how scripts may be written and executed within R. Appendices A and B of this book (Data Transformation and Statistical Procedures) include examples of a number of scripts designed to conduct common data transformation tasks and statistical procedures.

Comments

Comments are helpful to include when writing R commands and scripts as they provide reminders of the purpose of the command or script. The # symbol is used to signify a comment, such that anything written after the # symbol is treated as text and not executed as a command. Here is an example of a comment:

```
# Perform linear regression predicting cgpa from satmath
  (data frame = df1)
linregoutput <- lm(cgpa ~ satmath, data = df1)
```

In the above example, # Perform linear regression predicting cgpa from satmath (data frame = df1) is a comment used to indicate the purpose of the command below it, which is to conduct a linear regression analysis predicting cgpa from satmath using a data frame named df1.

Comments can also be placed on the same line as a command. Below, comments have been added to the script that conducted the *t*-test to explain the purpose of each command:

```
setwd("e:/R output")  # Set working directory
df1 <- read.csv("MISC.csv")  # Create data frame df1 from
  MISC.CSV
df1[, 2:2] [df1[, 2:2] == 0] <- NA # Convert 0's to missing,
  col 2 variable
df1[, 3:3] [df1[, 3:3] == 9.99] <- NA # Convert 9.99's to
  missing, col 3 variable
write.csv(df1, "MISC_NA.csv", row.names=FALSE) # Save df1 data
  frame in a CSV file
df1 <- read.csv("MISC_NA.csv")  # Create data frame df1 from
  MISC_NA.CSV file
library(psych)  # Load psych package into R
describeBy (df1$defp, df1$gender)  # Calculate descriptive
  stats of defp by gender
t.test(df1$defp ~ df1$gender, var.equal=TRUE, paired=FALSE)
  # t-test(defp by gender)
```

Although comments add a bit of clutter, they are extremely useful in documenting the steps and logic of a script or statistical analysis.

3.3 OBJECT-RELATED TERMS

Objects and Workspace

Within R, an **object** is what is produced by executing a command or script. An object is anything created in an R session—examples of objects are a variable, a data frame, or the output of a statistical analysis. The collection of objects created within a session of R is known as a ***workspace***.

The symbol <- (the "less than" symbol followed by a minus sign) is included in an R command that creates an object, with the name of the object located to the left of the <-. For example, looking at the above script that conducted a *t*-test, the command df1 <- read.csv("MISC.csv") creates the object df1, which is a data frame created by reading the CSV file MISC.csv. As another example, in the command linregoutput <- lm(cgpa ~ satmath, data = df1), the object linregoutput is the output created by running a linear regression analysis predicting cgpa from satmath using the df1 data frame. Given the many commands that are typed when using R, it may be helpful to know that a shortcut way to type <- is to press the Alt and minus (-) keys (i.e., Alt-minus).

Below are a few other examples of commands and objects:

Command	Object	Purpose of command
df1 <- read. csv("MISC.csv")	df1	Create the data frame df1 by reading the MISC csv file
df1 [df1 == 0] <- NA	df1 [df1 == 0]	Change zeroes (0) in the df1 data frame to NA
df1$GPA <- NULL	df1$GPA	Remove the variable GPA from the df1 data frame
df1$NX4<- recode(df1$X4,"1=2; 2=1")	df1$NX4	Create the variable NX4 by recoding the values of X4

Naming Objects: Some Rules and Guidelines

There are some rules that should be followed in giving names to objects:

Object names should only consist of letters (a-z), numbers, and underscores (_) (e.g., myvar, myvar1, and my_var are acceptable, but *myvar!* is not)

Object names cannot start with a number (e.g., df2 is acceptable, but *2df* is not)

Object names cannot contain spaces or commas (e.g., happy1 is acceptable, but *happy 1* or *happy,1* are not)

Object names are case-sensitive (e.g., a created object named `newvar` cannot later be typed as *NEWVAR* or *Newvar*)

Object names should not be the same as the names of R functions (e.g., `describe`, `mean`)

If you use the same object name as one used earlier in the R session, the new object replaces the old object (e.g., if two commands in the same script or R session start with `df1 <-`, the second `df1` replaces the first `df1`).

3.4 FILE-RELATED TERMS

Script Files and Markdown Files

Commands, scripts, and comments may be written and saved into a file—two ways to do this in R are to create either a ***script file*** or a ***markdown file***, both of which are essentially the equivalent of an SPSS syntax file. Creating script and markdown files provide a way of documenting and recording commands and scripts for later reference and use. Script files and markdown files will be introduced and illustrated in the next chapter of this book, Chapter 4 (Introduction to RStudio).

Markdown Documents

In addition to saving your commands in a markdown file, you may want to create a file that includes the output produced by executing the markdown file; within R, this file is a ***markdown document***. A markdown document is the equivalent of an SPSS output file and is created by executing ("***knitting***") a markdown file. Markdown documents are introduced in Chapter 5 (Conducting RStudio sessions: A detailed example).

* * * * *

The next chapter of this book describes one way in which R commands and scripts may be written and executed, which is to use the useful tool RStudio.

4

INTRODUCTION
TO RSTUDIO

Much of using R consists of writing and executing individual commands and sets of commands which are known as scripts. Although this can be done directly within R, tools have been developed to do this more easily and efficiently. The purpose of this chapter is to introduce one of these tools, known as RStudio. This chapter will illustrate the main components of RStudio and how commands and scripts may be executed within RStudio. The chapters following this chapter will demonstrate how RStudio can be used to conduct statistical analyses.

4.1 WHAT IS RSTUDIO?

Using R can involve writing and executing commands, examining the results of these executions, creating data frames and figures, and documenting all of these things. To facilitate and organize all of these tasks, RStudio has been created. *RStudio* is a free, open-source integrated development environment (IDE). In essence, R is a programming language; RStudio is a tool that helps you use R more efficiently.

4.2 INSTALLING RSTUDIO

To install RStudio, go to https://www.rstudio.com/products/rstudio/, click **RStudio Desktop**, and under "Open Source Edition," click **DOWNLOAD RSTUDIO DESKTOP** and download the free Windows or Mac version under "Installers for Supported Platforms."

4.3 COMPONENTS OF RSTUDIO

Starting RStudio starts both R and RStudio (you do not need to separately start both of them). After starting RStudio, you will see the ***RStudio interface***, which typically consists of four windows; these windows are described below and illustrated on the next page.

- In the upper left, the ***Script editor*** is used to write and edit sets of commands referred to as scripts, as well as save scripts in files known as script files. Once a script has been written, all or some of the commands in the script may be executed.

- In the lower left is the ***Console***. The R console is the equivalent of a command line, which is where individual commands may be written and executed. In the Console, you'll see the > symbol, which is known as the ***R prompt***. Commands are typed to the right of the R prompt and executed by pressing the <Enter> key. If a command executes successfully, the > R prompt will appear on the next line; if a command contains errors, error messages will be displayed above the next R prompt. Also, the Console is where the results of executed commands and scripts are displayed, such as the results of statistical analyses.

- In the upper right is the ***Environment/History*** window. The **Environment** tab shows the ***workspace***, which is the accumulation of the objects created in the current R session. The **History** tab provides a list of all of the commands executed in the current session. The combined objects in the Environment and History windows make up the ***workspace environment***.

- In the lower right is the ***Files/Plots/Packages/Help*** window. The **Files** tab lets you create new folders (directories) on your computer, as well as move, delete, and rename files. The **Plots** tab contains figures, such as scatterplots or histograms, created in the R session. The **Packages** tab is used to locate and install packages. The **Help** tab provides a way to search for help on R-related tasks.

Within this book, the Console and Script editor windows will be most heavily relied upon as they are used to write and execute commands to conduct statistical analyses.

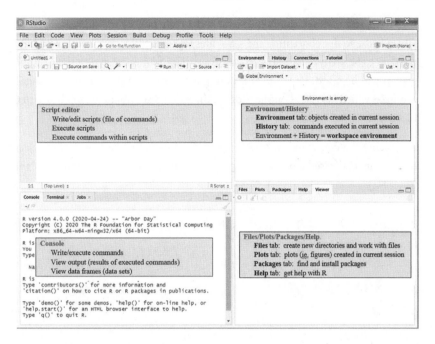

4.4 WRITING AND EXECUTING R COMMANDS IN RSTUDIO

The heart of R consists of writing and executing commands that perform desired tasks such as conducting statistical analyses, creating or modifying data frames and variables, and creating figures. R commands may be written three different ways within RStudio: in the Console, in the Script editor, and in markdown files. Each of these ways is introduced below and discussed in greater detail in Chapter 5 (Conducting RStudio sessions: A detailed example) and Chapter 7 (Conducting RStudio sessions using this book: Introduction).

Writing and Executing R Commands in the Console

Individual commands may be written and executed in the Console, which is the lower left window. More specifically, a command may be written or pasted after the > R prompt and executed by pressing the <Enter> key; the results of executing the command appear immediately in the Console.

To demonstrate how commands may be written and executed in the Console, let's use the command that will begin many of the scripts in this book. This command, the `setwd` command, tells R the location of the working directory, which is the folder containing the CSV files saved in SPSS or Excel that contain the data to be analyzed and is also where any data frames created in the RStudio session will be saved. Because the working directory used in this book is named R output which is located on the e: drive, the `setwd` command would be written as `setwd("e:/R output")`.

To execute the command `setwd("e:/R output")` in the Console, we place the cursor to the right of the > symbol, type in the command, and press the Enter Key:

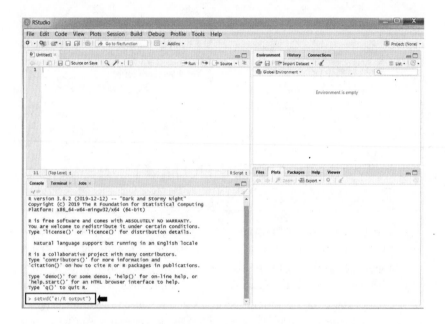

If a command executes without errors, the > R prompt appears below the executed command. However, executing a command that contains errors will result in the displaying of an error message. For example, imagine we incorrectly type the name of the working directory as R _input_ rather than the correct R _output_. Below is what executing the incorrect _setwd("e:/R input")_ command produces.

As is often the case when using software, error messages in R are not particularly informative. The error message in this situation does indicate the command

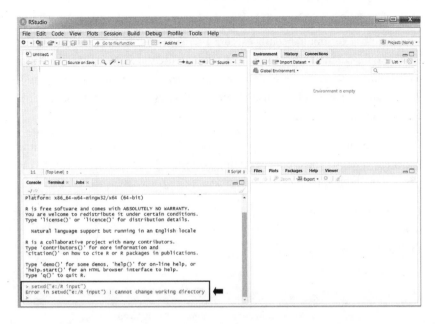

containing the error (*setwd("e:/R input"*)); however, it may not be clear what is meant by "*cannot change working directory*." Searching for the error message in a search engine such as Google may help diagnose and correct any errors.

Once the source of any errors has been identified, the command may be rewritten and re-executed until it runs successfully. One way to think of the Console is as a scratch pad in which commands may be tested, fixed, and modified in a trial-and-error manner until they run correctly and as desired.

It may be helpful to learn that commands previously typed in the Console may be returned to by pressing the up arrow (↑) key). In the above example, if we were to press the ↑ key, the command `setwd("e:/R input")`would reappear, which we could then modify as needed and re-execute.

Writing and Executing R Commands in a Script File

Although commands may be written and executed in the Console, these commands disappear once RStudio is exited, which does not allow them to be saved for your records or later use. Also, rather than executing individual commands, you may want to simultaneously execute a series (aka script) of commands. For these reasons, an alternative to the Console is to use the Script editor (the upper left window) to write and save commands in a ***script file***. A script file is the equivalent of an SPSS syntax file. Creating script files saves commands and scripts in a file for possible reuse in later sessions.

A script file may be created by clicking in the first line of the Script editor (the upper left window) and typing or pasting a command on each line, moving to the next command by pressing the <Enter> key.

In Chapters 1 and 3 of this book, a script was provided that conducts a *t*-test of independent means. Here is what this script would look like if it were entered into the Script editor as a script file:

A script may be saved as a script file by selecting the **File | Save** menu choices or by clicking on the **diskette icon** located directly above the script. It should be noted that script files (which have a .r extension) are not automatically saved in the working directory—in this example, the *TTEST.r* script file will be saved on the Desktop unless we specify a different location.

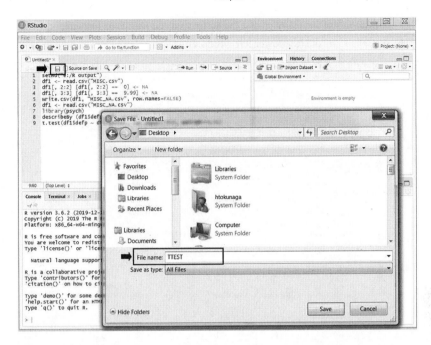

To execute a script file, we move the cursor to the start of the first command, hold down the mouse, drag it over the other commands, release the mouse, and click on the **Run** button:

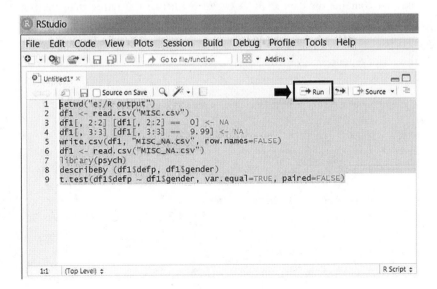

If a script does not have any errors, the script and the results of the script are displayed in the Console (the lower-left window):

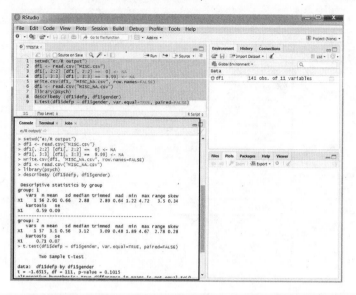

However, if a command in the script contains errors, running the script results in the displaying of error messages in the Console. For example, imagine we include a command (*df1 <- read.csv("MISCC_NA.csv")*) that incorrectly names the CSV file that contains the data as *MISCC_NA* (with two Cs) rather than the correct MISC_NA (with one C) that was part of the previous write.csv(df1, "MISC_NA.csv",row.names=FALSE) command. Here is what executing this script produces:

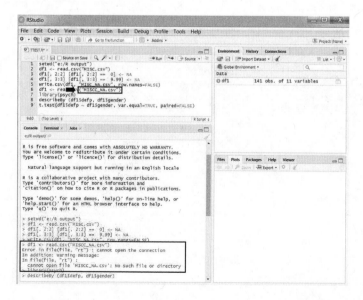

Looking at the Console, the first five commands ran successfully, with the error message being displayed after the command that contains the error. Although this error message is somewhat cryptic, it does indicate the part of the command that is causing the error (*"file 'MISCC_NA.CSV': No such file or directory"*); the phrase "No such file or directory" implies that R could not locate a file named *MISCC_NA.CSV* in the working directory.

Writing and Executing R Commands in a Markdown File

Similar to script files, R commands and comments may be written and executed in what is known as a ***markdown file***. A markdown file is essentially the same as a script file. However, one critical advantage of markdown files over script files is that executing (***knitting***) a markdown file creates what is known as a ***markdown document***, which is a document that may be saved, printed, and distributed. A markdown document is the equivalent of an SPSS output file. The next chapter (Chapter 5 (Conducting RStudio sessions: A detailed example)) discusses how to create and execute markdown files.

The Console, Script Files, and Markdown Files—Which One Should You Use?

In this chapter, we indicated that R commands may be written and executed in one of three ways: in the Console, in a script file, and in a markdown file. Which of these methods do we recommend? As a general strategy, we suggest you initially write and execute individual commands using the Console; once the commands are free from errors and produce the desired results, they can be copied and pasted into a script file or markdown file in order to save the commands for later reference. In this book, we will use markdown files rather than script files in order to produce markdown documents, which are the equivalent of SPSS output files.

In the next chapter, we will first use the Console in order to introduce, define, and discuss individual commands; later in that chapter, these commands will be pasted into a markdown file in order to create a markdown document.

* * * * *

The purpose of this chapter was to introduce the different components of RStudio as well as how R comments and commands may be written. The next chapter, in a step-by-step manner, discusses how an RStudio session may be conducted in order to import a data file and conduct statistical analyses.

5

CONDUCTING RSTUDIO SESSIONS: A DETAILED EXAMPLE

Now that the previous chapter has introduced RStudio, the purpose of this chapter is to describe and illustrate tasks and commands that may be executed when using RStudio to conduct statistical analyses. As a reminder, before conducting your first RStudio session, the following tasks should have been completed following the guidelines discussed in Chapter 2:

- Install R (https://cran.r-project.org/)

- Install the Desktop version of RStudio (https://www.rstudio.com/products/rstudio/)

- Install the basic version of MiKTeX (https://miktex.org/download)

- Create the working directory and note its path (location)

- Save SPSS/Excel data files as CSV files and place them into the working directory.

The example in this chapter will be based on the following research situation: Imagine you've collected data from 11 people on 9 variables: ID, ITEM1 to ITEM4, GROUP, INCOME, SMOKE, and DRINK.

Missing data for all of these variables (except ID) have been assigned one or both of two values: periods (.) and the number 9. Below is a summary of the variables:

Variable	Valid values	Missing value(s)
ID	1–11	None
ITEM1 to ITEM4	1–5	period(.) and 9
GROUP	1–5	period(.) and 9
INCOME	0–999999	period(.)
SMOKE	1–2	period(.) and 9
DRINK	1–2	period(.) and 9

You've created a CSV file (DATATRANS.csv) with the nine variables located in nine columns and have saved the file in the working directory (e:/R output). The CSV file is presented below, with shading provided to highlight the missing data (note that the names of the variables must be provided in the first row of the file):

	A	B	C	D	E	F	G	H	I
1	ID	ITEM1	ITEM2	ITEM3	ITEM4	GROUP	INCOME	SMOKE	DRINK
2	1	2	3	5	1	1	45000	1	1
3	2	3	4	.	1	1	27500	1	2
4	3	1	5	4	2	1	100000	2	1
5	4	5	4	1	2	1	33000	2	2
6	5	3	5	.	3	1	56000	1	2
7	6	2	4	3	3	2	18000	2	.
8	7	4	1	4	4	2	60000	9	1
9	8	.	5	.	4	3	.	.	1
10	9	3	4	3	5	4	48000	9	9
11	10	3	5	1	9	5	35500	1	1
12	11	4	.	.	.		50000	.	.

For the purpose of this example, imagine you want to calculate descriptive statistics (mean, median, standard deviation, etc.) for all nine variables in this set of data. Below is what this output may have looked like had we used the DESCRIPTIVES command in SPSS rather than R:

```
DESCRIPTIVES VARIABLES=ID ITEM1 ITEM2 ITEM3 ITEM4 GROUP INCOME SMOKE DRINK
    /STATISTICS=MEAN STDDEV MIN MAX.
```

Descriptives

Descriptive Statistics

	N	Minimum	Maximum	Mean	Std. Deviation
ID	11	1	11	6.00	3.317
ITEM1	10	1	5	3.00	1.155
ITEM2	10	1	5	4.00	1.247
ITEM3	7	1	5	3.00	1.528
ITEM4	9	1	5	2.78	1.394
GROUP	10	1	5	2.10	1.449
INCOME	10	18000	100000	47300.00	22660.784
SMOKE	7	1	2	1.43	.535
DRINK	8	1	2	1.38	.518
Valid N (listwise)	3				

In showing how RStudio may be used to conduct statistical analyses, the following steps will be covered:

1. Start RStudio

2. Create a new script file (optional)

3. Define the working directory

4. Import CSV file to create a data frame

5. Change any missing data in data frame to NA

6. Save data frame with NAs as CSV file in the working directory

7. Read the modified CSV file to create a data frame

8. Download and install packages (if not already done)

9. Load installed packages (as needed)

10. Conduct desired statistical analyses

11. Open a new markdown file

12. Copy commands and comments into the markdown file

13. Knit the markdown file to create a markdown document

The example in this chapter will introduce, describe, and conduct each of these 13 steps; a summary of the steps for this example is provided at the end of this chapter. However, it's important to understand that some of these steps are not always needed. The main reason we're performing all 13 steps is because it's the first time we're accessing the DATATRANS.csv file. Three of these steps (5 (Change any missing data in data frame to NA), 6 (Save data frame with NAs as CSV file in the working directory), and 7 (Read the modified CSV file to create a data frame)) are only needed the first time a CSV file is imported into R. In this example, these three steps modify the data frame based on DATATRANS.csv file to create a new CSV file we'll save as DATATRANS_NA.csv. Assuming any subsequent analyses will access the modified file (DATATRANS_NA.csv) rather than the original file (DATATRANS.csv), these three steps will not be needed the next time we access this data. As we work through the example in this chapter, steps that may not always be needed will be noted.

It's also important to understand that conducting a particular statistical analysis may require executing commands in addition to those discussed in this chapter (e.g., the commands needed to calculate descriptive statistics are different from those for an ANOVA or a factor analysis). These additional commands are provided for different statistical procedures at the end of this book.

5.1 1. START RSTUDIO

As mentioned earlier, starting RStudio starts both R and RStudio (the two programs are not started separately or sequentially).

5.2 2. CREATE A NEW SCRIPT FILE (OPTIONAL)

Note: This step is performed if the user wants to create a script file rather than only writing and executing individual commands in the Console.

After starting RStudio, many of the tasks to be performed involve writing and executing commands. As discussed in the previous chapter, individual commands may be written and executed in the Console (the lower left window in RStudio) or sets of commands may be written in a script file using the Script editor (the upper left window). In this chapter, we will not create a script file but will instead write and execute individual commands in the Console in order to discuss each command separately. Later in this chapter, these commands will be copied into a markdown file (rather than a script file) to produce a markdown document, which is the equivalent of an SPSS output file.

5.3 3. DEFINE THE WORKING DIRECTORY

Note: This step is performed if a default working directory has not been set within RStudio (see the "Creating a default working directory" section below for more information).

A command is needed to tell R the location of the working directory, which is a folder containing the CSV data files saved in SPSS or Excel. The working directory is also where any data frames, markdown files, and markdown documents created in the RStudio session will be saved. **The working directory used in this book is "R output," located on the "e:" drive** (e:/R output). A command that includes the setwd function may be used to indicate the working directory; this command may be written as follows:

```
Define the working directory

    Command:    setwd("path and folder name")

    Example:    setwd("e:/R output")
```

The above example command, relevant to the situation in this chapter, defines the working directory as a folder named R output located on the e: drive.

As we illustrated in the previous chapter, writing and executing commands in the Console consists of typing the command to the right of the > R prompt and pressing <Enter>. If the command has been correctly written, either the > prompt will appear on the next line or the result of executing the command will appear in the Console. However, if the command is written incorrectly, an error message will appear in the Console. Also, if you want to edit or rerun a previous command, press the up arrow (↑) key—see Chapter 3 (Writing commands: Some rules and guidelines) for help in writing commands.

In using the `setwd` function, the path for the working directory should include a forward slash (/) rather than a backwards slash (\). For example, incorrectly defining the working directory as "e:\R Output" rather than the correct `"e:/R Output"` may result in an error message such as, '\R' *is an unrecognized escape in character string starting ""e:\R"*. Also, incorrectly typing the name of the working directory (e.g., R Input rather than R Output) or trying to access a working directory that R cannot locate (e.g., f:\R Output rather than e:\R Output) may result in an error message that says, "*cannot change working directory.*"

As discussed in Chapter 4, the "**path and folder name**" for the working directory is written differently for a Mac than a Windows computer. For example, if the author of this book had created the "R Output" folder on the desktop of a Mac, the setwd command may have be written as, `setwd("/users/howard/Desktop/R Output")`.

Creating a Default Working Directory

If you use the same working directory every time you use RStudio, you can avoid having to execute the `setwd` function (i.e., you can eliminate step 3 (Define the working directory)) by setting a default working directory within RStudio. To do this, start by clicking on the **Tools** menu and select **Global Options**:

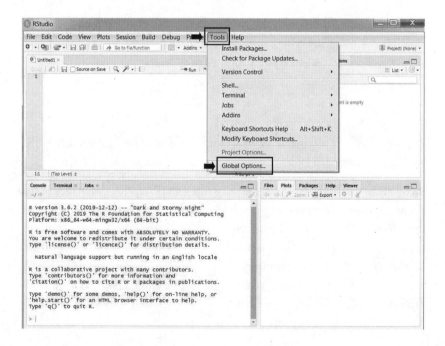

Within the "General" selection within "Options," the working directory's path and name can be typed in the "Default working directory" box or located by clicking the **Browse** button:

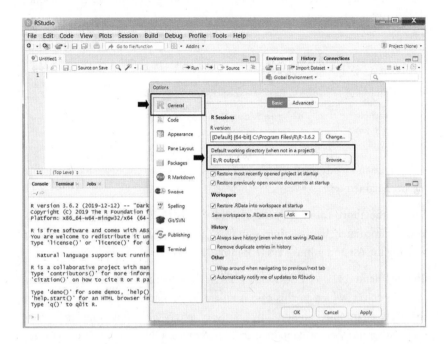

Setting a default working directory implies you do not need to use the `setwd` function to define the working directory. However, you would need to write a command if you wanted to access a different working directory in an R session. For example, if you needed to access a working directory named `thesis` that's located within the `R Output` working directory, you would need to execute the command, `setwd("e:/R output/thesis/")`. Furthermore, if you wanted to return to the `R Output` working directory later in the same R session, you'd need to execute the command, `setwd("e:/R output")`.

5.4 4. IMPORT CSV FILE TO CREATE A DATA FRAME

The next step is to import the file containing the data to be analyzed; importing a file implies reading the file to create what R calls a data frame. As mentioned earlier, the files used to create data frames in this book are comma-separated

(CSV) files created in SPSS or Excel. *Important*: Before importing the file into R, you should confirm that the file is a CSV file located in the working directory.

Data frames are created from CSV files by executing a command that includes the `read.csv` function:

Import a CSV file into a data frame

    Command: *dataframe* **<- read.csv(**"*file name*"**)**

    Example: df1 **<- read.csv(**"DATATRANS.csv"**)**

This command reads the CSV file DATATRANS.csv to create a data frame that has been named df1.

Within the above command, the symbol <- is the less than symbol (<) followed immediately by the minus sign (–). The <- symbol can also be typed by pressing the Alt and minus keys (Alt-minus).

The command df1 <- read.csv("DATATRANS.csv") creates what R refers to as an object, which in this case is a data frame named df1. As a reminder, the name of an object should only consist of letters (a–z) and numbers, cannot start with a number, or contain spaces or commas. Object names are also case-sensitive, such that the data frame df1 cannot be later referred to as *DF1* or *Df1* as doing so results in an "*object not found*" error message—see Chapter 3 (Naming objects: Some rules and guidelines) for help in naming objects.

5.5 5. CHANGE ANY MISSING DATA IN DATA FRAME TO NA

Note: This step is performed if a data frame contains missing data. Also, this step is only performed once for a data frame, assuming the modified data frame is saved as a CSV file in the working directory for later access.

As discussed in Chapter 2, one of the critical differences between R and SPSS is the handling of missing data. Rather than allow for user-defined missing values such as 9, period (.), or a blank, R represents <u>all</u> missing data with the symbol *NA*. Consequently, <u>all</u> user-defined missing values in the data frame must be replaced with NAs.

In the example in this chapter, missing data for the variables in the DATATRANS.csv file have been assigned two values: periods (.) and the number 9. First, to convert periods (.) for all of the variables in the data frame into NAs, the command below may be written and executed in the Console:

Change periods (.) to NA

    Command: `dataframe [dataframe == "."] <- NA`

    Example: `df1 [df1 == "."] <- NA`

This command assigns the missing value NA to periods (.) for all of the variables in the data frame df1.

In writing the above command, note that there should be no blank spaces between the two equals (=) signs. For example, including a blank space (= = rather than ==) in this command (e.g., *df1 [df1 = = "."] <- NA*) may result in the error message, *Error: unexpected '=' in "df1 [df1 = =".*

In terms of the other missing value (9), imagine that 9 is a missing value for the variables ITEM1 to ITEM4, GROUP, SMOKE, and DRINK, but not for ID or INCOME (i.e., 9 is a valid value for ID and INCOME). Consequently, we only want to convert a 9 into NA for the variables ITEM1 to ITEM4, GROUP, SMOKE, and DRINK. In order to do this type of selective conversion to NAs, you must determine the location of the targeted variables—that is, the columns of the data frame that contain these variables. You must do this because R identifies variables by their column numbers rather than by their variable names.

Looking at the below image of the CSV file, we find ITEM1 to ITEM4 and GROUP are located in columns 2–6 (columns B–E) and SMOKE to DRINK are located in columns 8–9 (columns H–I):

	A	B	C	D	E	F	G	H	I
	ID	ITEM1	ITEM2	ITEM3	ITEM4	GROUP	INCOME	SMOKE	DRINK
1	ID	ITEM1	ITEM2	ITEM3	ITEM4	GROUP	INCOME	SMOKE	DRINK
2	1	2	3	5	1	1	45000	1	1
3	2	3	4	.		1	27500	1	2
4	3	1	5	4	2	1	100000	2	1
5	4	5	4	1	2	1	33000	2	2
6	5	3	5	.	3	1	56000	1	2
7	6	2	4	3	3	2	18000	2	.
8	7	4	1	4	4	2	60000	9	1
9	8	.	5	.	4	3	.	.	1
10	9	3	4	3	5	4	48000	9	9
11	10	3	5	1	9	5	35500	1	1
12	11	4	.	.	.		50000	.	.

Once the column locations of the targeted variables have been determined, the missing value (9) for these variables may be converted into NAs by writing and executing the two commands below:

Selectively change missing values to NA by including column location of variables

```
Command:    dataframe[,startcol#:endcol#][dataframe
            [,startcol#:endcol#]

            == missing value] <- NA

Example:    df1[, 2:6] [df1[, 2:6] == 9] <- NA

Example:    df1[, 8:9] [df1[, 8:9] == 9] <- NA
```

The first command in the above example converts a 9 into NA for the variables located in columns 2–6 (2:6) in the data frame df1 (ITEM1 to ITEM4 and GROUP). The second command converts a 9 into NA for the variables located in columns 8–9 (8:9) in the data frame df1 (SMOKE and DRINK).

Successfully executing these two commands simply results in the displaying of two > symbols in the Console. If we want to confirm that the conversion of the missing values into NAs has been attained, we can view the current contents of the data frame by typing the name of the data frame in the Console and press <Enter>:

View contents of data frame

```
Command:    dataframe

Example:    df1
```

Presented below are the contents of the df1 data frame. If you compare this data frame with the DATATRANS.csv file presented at the start of this chapter, you see that all of the periods (.) and missing values of 9 have been converted into NAs (note that the ID of 9 has not been changed to NA).

```
> df1
   ID ITEM1 ITEM2 ITEM3 ITEM4 GROUP INCOME SMOKE DRINK
1   1     2     3     5     1     1  45000     1     1
2   2     3     4  <NA>     1     1  27500     1     2
3   3     1     5     4     2     1 100000     2     1
4   4     5     4     1     2     1  33000     2     2
5   5     3     5  <NA>     3     1  56000     1     2
6   6     2     4     3     3     2  18000     2  <NA>
7   7     4     1     4     4     2  60000  <NA>     1
8   8  <NA>     5  <NA>     4     3   <NA>  <NA>     1
9   9     3     4     3     5     4  48000  <NA>  <NA>
10 10     3     5     1  <NA>     5  35500     1     1
11 11     4  <NA>  <NA>  <NA>  <NA>  50000  <NA>  <NA>
```

Given the small size of the Console window, viewing a data frame is not particularly useful when the data frame consists of a large number of variables and/or a large number of observations.

Converting Missing Values into NAs: Some Examples

The purpose of this section is to provide, in one place, how three common types of missing values (numbers, periods, and blanks) may be converted into NAs for use in R:

Change numeric missing value (e.g., 0) to NA

   Command: `dataframe [dataframe == numeric missing value] <- NA`

   Example: `df1 [df1 == 0] <- NA`

Change periods (.) to NA

   Command: `dataframe [dataframe == "."] <- NA`

   Example: `df1 [df1 == "."] <- NA`

Change blank cells to NA

   Command: `dataframe [dataframe == ""] <- NA`

   Example: `df1 [df1 == ""] <- NA`

The first command ("Change numeric missing value…") changes any values of 0 in the data frame df1 to NAs. The second command ("Change periods(.) . . .")

changes any periods (.) in the data frame df1 to NAs, and the third command ("Change blank cells . . .") changes any blank (i.e., empty) cells in the data frame df1 to NAs.

It's common to assign different missing values for different variables. For example, imagine you used a missing value of 9 for variables X1 to X7 (which you determine are located in columns 12–18 of a data frame), but a missing value of 99 for GRADE (located in column 19). Below is how missing data for these variables could be converted to NAs:

Selectively change missing values to NA by including column location of variables

Command: `dataframe[,startcol#:endcol#][dataframe[,startcol#:endcol#]`

            `== missing value] <- NA`

Example: `df1[, 12:18][df1[, 12:18] == 9] <- NA`

Example: `df1[, 19:19][df1[, 19:19] == 99] <- NA`

The first command converts a 9 into NA for the variables located in columns 12–18 (12:18) in the data frame df1 (which we stated were X1 to X7). The second command converts a 99 into NA for the variable located in column 19 (19:19) in the data frame df1 (which we stated was GRADE).

5.6 6. SAVE DATA FRAME WITH NAs AS CSV FILE IN THE WORKING DIRECTORY

Note: This step is performed if a data frame contains missing data that has been converted into NAs (i.e., step 5 was performed).

Once missing values have been changed to NAs, it's a good idea to save the modified data frame in a new CSV file so that future importing of the CSV file doesn't require changing the missing values into NAs. Creating CSV files may be done using the write.csv function:

Save a data frame into a CSV file

Command: **write.csv(*dataframe*, "*file name*.csv",
row.names=FALSE)**

Example: write.csv(df1, "DATATRANS_NA.csv",
row.names=FALSE)

This command saves the modified df1 data frame as a CSV file named DATATRANS _ NA.csv in the working directory.

The name of the new CSV file (DATATRANS _ NA.csv) differs from the original CSV file (*DATATRANS.csv*) in order to prevent the new file from overwriting the original file. Below is a picture of the DATATRANS_NA.csv file:

	A	B	C	D	E	F	G	H	I
1	ID	ITEM1	ITEM2	ITEM3	ITEM4	GROUP	INCOME	SMOKE	DRINK
2	1	2	3	5	1	1	45000	1	1
3	2	3	4	NA	1	1	27500	1	2
4	3	1	5	4	2	1	100000	2	1
5	4	5	4	1	2	1	33000	2	2
6	5	3	5	NA	3	1	56000	1	2
7	6	2	4	3	3	2	18000	2	NA
8	7	4	1	4	4	2	60000	NA	1
9	8	NA	5	NA	4	3	NA	NA	1
10	9	3	4	3	5	4	48000	NA	NA
11	10	3	5	1	NA	5	35500	1	1
12	11	4	NA	NA	NA	NA	50000	NA	NA

As you can see, the periods (.) and missing values of 9 have been converted into NAs.

The command using the write.csv function ends with the argument row.names=FALSE; this is included to prevent R from adding a new variable to the CSV file. More specifically, in using the write.csv function, R adds a new first column to the CSV file that numbers the rows of the data frame. In our example, if we had not included row.names=FALSE and had instead written the command as *write.csv(df1, "DATATRANS_NA.csv")*, below is what the new CSV file would look like:

	A	B	C	D	E	F	G	H	I	J
1		ID	ITEM1	ITEM2	ITEM3	ITEM4	GROUP	INCOME	SMOKE	DRINK
2	1	1	2	3	5	1	1	45000	1	1
3	2	2	3	4	NA	1	1	27500	1	2
4	3	3	1	5	4	2	1	100000	2	1
5	4	4	5	4	1	2	1	33000	2	2
6	5	5	3	5	NA	3	1	56000	1	2
7	6	6	2	4	3	3	2	18000	2	NA
8	7	7	4	1	4	4	2	60000	NA	1
9	8	8	NA	5	NA	4	3	NA	NA	1
10	9	9	3	4	3	5	4	48000	NA	NA
11	10	10	3	5	1	NA	5	35500	1	1
12	11	11	4	NA	NA	NA	NA	50000	NA	NA
13										

As you can see, the first column (column A) of this CSV file does not have a name in the top cell and consists of the row numbers of the file (in this case, 1–11). We suggest you include the row.names=FALSE argument so that the column numbers of the variables do not change from the first CSV file to the modified CSV file (i.e., ID is in column 1 of both files). As you saw in step 5 (Change any missing data in data frame to NA), there are times in which you may need to indicate the column numbers of your variables—not including the row. names=FALSE argument may result in indicating incorrect columns.

5.7 7. READ THE MODIFIED CSV FILE TO CREATE A DATA FRAME

Note: This step is performed if a data frame contains missing data that has been converted into NAs and the data frame has been saved as a new CSV file (i.e., steps 5 and 6 were performed).

Once the modified data frame has been saved into a new CSV file, the next step is to create a data frame from this new file to use for subsequent statistical analyses. We do this by writing and executing another read.csv command:

Import a modified CSV file into a data frame

Command: *dataframe* <- **read.csv(**"*file name*"**)**

Example: df1 <- read.csv("DATATRANS_NA.csv")

This command imports the DATATRANS _ NA.csv file into a data frame named df1.

You may have noticed that df1 is the same name as the data frame created in step 4 (Import CSV file to create a data frame) which imported the original CSV file—this new version of df1 replaces the earlier version. As was mentioned in Chapter 3, if you use the same name for an object as one used earlier in the R session, the new object replaces the old one. We've chosen to replace the earlier version of df1 to avoid accessing the wrong data frame.

Reading Files Created by the write.csv Function: The Mysterious "X" Variable

What would have happened in this step if the write.csv function in step 6 did not end with the row.names=FALSE argument? As it turns out, after writing the CSV file and then reading the modified CSV file into a data frame, the new first column created by the write.csv function would be given the name "X." Because this column has not been assigned a name (i.e., the cell at the top of the column was blank), R calls it "X" by default. Below is what this data frame would look like:

```
> df1 <- read.csv("DATATRANS_NA.csv")
> df1
     X ID ITEM1 ITEM2 ITEM3 ITEM4 GROUP INCOME SMOKE DRINK
1    1  1     2     3     5     1     1  45000     1     1
2    2  2     3     4    NA     1     1  27500     1     2
3    3  3     1     5     4     2     1 100000     2     1
4    4  4     5     4     1     2     1  33000     2     2
5    5  5     3     5    NA     3     1  56000     1     2
6    6  6     2     4     3     3     2  18000     2    NA
7    7  7     4     1     4     4     2  60000    NA     1
8    8  8    NA     5    NA     4     3     NA    NA     1
9    9  9     3     4     3     5     4  48000    NA    NA
10  10 10     3     5     1    NA     5  35500     1     1
11  11 11     4    NA    NA    NA    NA  50000    NA    NA
>
```

As has been boxed, the first column of the data frame contains the label "X" and consists of the row numbers of the data frame (in this case, 1–11). As mentioned in the previous step, we suggest you include the row.names=FALSE argument as part of the write.csv function so that the column numbers of the variables do not change from the first CSV file to the modified CSV file.

5.8 8. DOWNLOAD AND INSTALL PACKAGES (IF NOT ALREADY DONE)

Note: Packages only need to be installed once, <u>not</u> every time you conduct an RStudio session. In other words, if you installed a package during a previous R session, you do not need to install it again.

In order to conduct many of the statistical procedures in this book, you'll need to install packages, which are sometimes referred to as *libraries*. Packages are sets of functions written by R users to extend the capabilities of the base R distribution.

Identifying packages appropriate for a desired statistical analysis typically involves using Internet search engines. For example, to identify packages that conduct factor analyses, "factor analysis package CRAN" was searched for within Google; "CRAN" (the Comprehensive R Archive Network that houses many packages) was included rather than "R" because including just "R" returns many irrelevant results:

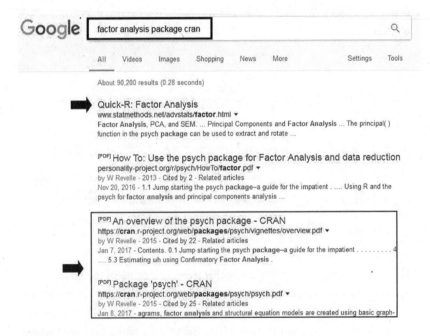

In the above screenshot, several search results have been noted that may be particularly useful in conducting statistical analyses. The first noted search result, "Quick-R: Factor Analysis," leads to an excellent website (Quick-R) for statistics-related issues. The second noted search leads to CRAN; users who develop packages contribute documentation regarding their packages to CRAN.

For the example in this chapter, we've determined that the `psych` package can calculate descriptive statistics. A package can be installed by writing a command in the Console that uses the `install.packages` function:

Install a package (library)

    Command: **install.packages("*package name*")**

    Example: `install.packages("psych")`

This command downloads and installs the `psych` package on the computer's hard drive.

There are four things to note about installing packages. First, you must be connected to the Internet to install packages. Second, a package only needs to be installed once, not every time you conduct an RStudio session—a package installed during a previous R session does not need to be installed again. However, reinstalling a package does not result in an error message. Third, a package may be installed at any point in an RStudio session, not just at the beginning of the session. Fourth, the `install.packages` command can be typed and executed in the Console but should <u>not</u> be included in a script or markdown file—including the `install.packages` command in script or markdown files may result in errors.

The following packages will be used to conduct the statistical analyses in this book—as such, we recommend you install these packages after downloading and installing RStudio:

```
psych      ggplot2  phia      GPArotation  lm.beta
lmSupport  CCA      candisc   gmodels
```

In addition to executing the `install.packages` function in the Console, packages may also be located and installed within RStudio using the **Packages** tab in the **Files-Plots-Packages-Help-Viewer** window (the lower right window):

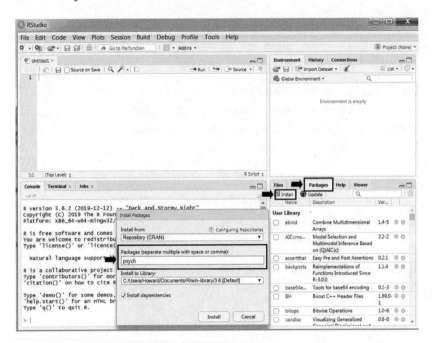

5.9 9. LOAD INSTALLED PACKAGES (AS NEEDED)

The next step is to load an installed package (i.e., bring a package into R) in order to conduct a desired statistical analysis. Packages may be loaded using the library function:

Load a package (library)

> Command: **library(*package name*)**

> Example: library(psych)

This command loads the psych package into the current R session so that its functions may be accessed.

It is important to understand that packages must be loaded each time you start an RStudio session—"loading" a package is different than "installing" a package, which only needs to be done once. This implies that the command with the library function needs to be typed and executed in the Console as well as included in a script or markdown file in every RStudio session. Also, packages may be loaded at any point in an R session, not just at the start of a session.

The scripts included in Appendix B of this book (Statistical Procedures) will indicate whether and what specific packages must be loaded for a particular statistical procedure.

5.10 10. CONDUCT DESIRED STATISTICAL ANALYSES

Once the data frame has been modified and read, and needed packages have been installed and loaded, the next step is to conduct desired statistical analyses (finally!). For the example in this chapter, we want to calculate descriptive statistics for the nine variables in the DATATRANS CSV file; the describe function may be used for this purpose:

Conduct a desired statistical analysis

    Example command: **describe(***dataframe***, type=2)**

    Example: describe(df1, type=2)

This command calculates descriptive statistics for all of the variables in the data frame df1; the argument type=2 has been included to have R calculate skewness and kurtosis the same way as does SPSS. Within Appendix B (Statistical Procedures) at the end of this book, a script for this research situation ("Descriptive statistics (all variables)") is provided.

After executing the describe function, the results of this command are immediately displayed in the Console:

```
> describe(df1, type=2)
        vars  n      mean        sd  median   trimmed        mad    min     max
ID         1 11      6.00      3.32     6.0      6.00       4.45      1      11
ITEM1      2 10      3.00      1.15     3.0      3.00       1.48      1       5
ITEM2      3 10      4.00      1.25     4.0      4.25       1.48      1       5
ITEM3      4  7      3.00      1.53     3.0      3.00       1.48      1       5
ITEM4      5  9      2.78      1.39     3.0      2.78       1.48      1       5
GROUP      6 10      2.10      1.45     1.5      1.88       0.74      1       5
INCOME     7 10  47300.00  22660.78  46500.0  44375.00  18161.85  18000  100000
SMOKE      8  7      1.43      0.53     1.0      1.43       0.00      1       2
DRINK      9  8      1.38      0.52     1.0      1.38       0.00      1       2
        range   skew  kurtosis        se
ID         10   0.00     -1.20      1.00
ITEM1       4   0.00      0.08      0.37
ITEM2       4  -1.72      3.42      0.39
ITEM3       4  -0.39     -1.11      0.58
ITEM4       4   0.15     -1.06      0.46
GROUP       4   1.16      0.20      0.46
INCOME  82000   1.33      2.86   7165.97
SMOKE       1   0.37     -2.80      0.20
DRINK       1   0.64     -2.24      0.18
>
```

At this point, it's important to note a critical difference between SPSS and R. In SPSS, the results of statistical analyses such as the one at the start of this chapter are automatically pasted into an output file, which can be saved and printed. However, this is <u>not</u> the case in R—if we were to now exit RStudio, the results of any analyses displayed in the Console would no longer exist. In order to document the output of an analysis, a file known as a markdown file must be created—this is discussed in the next step.

5.11 11. OPEN A NEW MARKDOWN FILE

At this point, commands have been written that (a) define the working directory, (b) import and modify a CSV file to create a data frame, (c) save and read the modified data frame, (d) install and load packages, and (e) conduct statistical analyses to generate desired output. One limitation of writing and executing commands in the Console or in a script file is that neither creates a permanent record of the results of executing R-related tasks. When such a record is desired, R commands and comments can be written or pasted into a ***markdown file***, which is then executed ("knitted") to create a ***markdown document***. A markdown document is the equivalent of an SPSS output file.

To open a new markdown file, within RStudio, select **File | New File | R Markdown** (Note: The first time you create a markdown document, you may be asked to install packages):

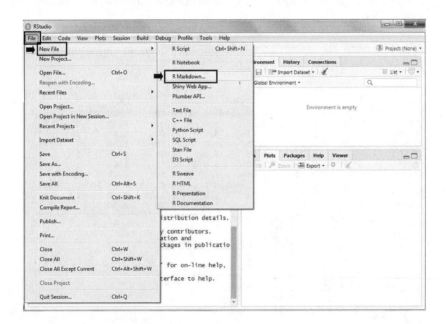

When you start a new markdown file, the following window may appear:

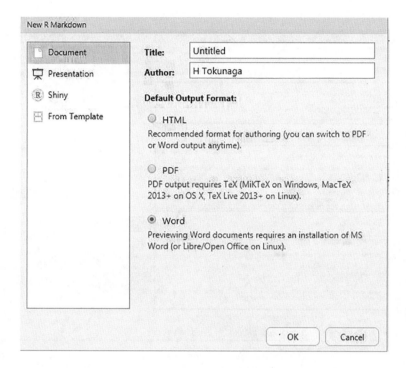

In this window, you can replace the word "Untitled" with a title you want to appear at the top of the markdown document (we will not do so in this example).

In terms of the "Default Output Format" in this window, markdown documents can be saved in different types of files: html, pdf, or Microsoft Word. As there are advantages and disadvantages to the different types in terms of file size and ability to edit the file, we recommend you try the different types and use the one that best meets your needs and preferences. In this book, the markdown files will be Word documents. In order to create pdf markdown documents, you must first install the basic version of MiKTeX (https://miktex.org/download). Mac users should ensure that the MiKTeX Console is installed and started in order to access LaTeX and TeX. However, as we've seen users (particularly Mac users) have problems creating pdf markdown files, you may wish to instead use a Word or html format.

After writing a title and selecting the output format, you'll see a window that looks something like the one below, which is a template file that includes examples of some of the main components of markdown files: document information, code, and comments. Each of these three components is described below.

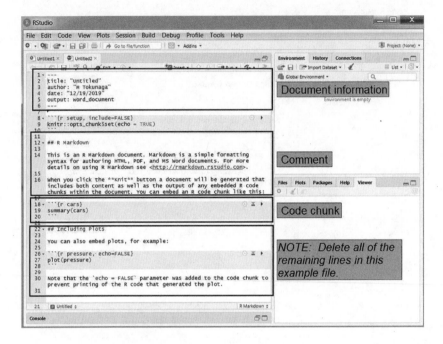

Document Information

At the top of the markdown file, the information listed after "title:," "author:," and "output:" was provided earlier by the user when the new markdown file was opened. As shown below, this information will be printed at the top of the markdown document that is created when the markdown file has been executed (knitted):

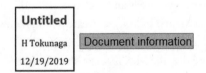

R Markdown

This is an R Markdown document. Markdown is a simple formatting syntax for authoring HTML, PDF, and MS Word documents. For more details on using R Markdown see http://rmarkdown.rstudio.com.

When you click the **Knit** button a document will be generated that includes both content as well

Code

R code is executed in a markdown file by writing or pasting commands into what is known as a ***code chunk***. The markdown file that's opened when a new file is created includes an example code chunk consisting of the command, `summary(cars)`; `cars` a data frame included in the base R distribution:

```
``` {r cars}
summary(cars)
```
```

As you can see, the first line of a code chunk contains three back tick marks (``` ``` ```) and `{r}` (the word `cars` is unique to this particular example), and the last line consists of three back tick marks (``` ``` ```). Also, code chunks are shaded in light gray or blue.

Once a markdown file has been knitted, the output produced by a code chunk is included in the markdown document. Below is the output created by executing the `summary(cars)` code chunk (this code chunk should be deleted or modified before conducting your desired statistical analysis):

```
When you click the Knit button a document will be generated that includes both content as well
as the output of any embedded R code chunks within the document. You can embed an R code
chunk like this:

summary(cars)

##     speed           dist
##  Min.   : 4.0   Min.   :  2.00
##  1st Qu.:12.0   1st Qu.: 26.00        Execution of code chunk
##  Median :15.0   Median : 36.00
##  Mean   :15.4   Mean   : 42.98
##  3rd Qu.:19.0   3rd Qu.: 56.00
##  Max.   :25.0   Max.   :120.00
```

There are many ways to modify what is included in the markdown document as the result of running code chunks. For example, executing commands often generates messages that may or may not be of interest to you. To modify a markdown document, options can be included after `{r}` in the first line of back ticks (``` ``` ```). Here are a few of these options (more than one option can be included within the `{ }` braces):

To hide the displaying of messages: ``` ```{r message = FALSE} ```

To set width of plots (figures) created (in inches): ``` ```{r fig.width = #} ```

To set height of plots (figures) created (in inches): ``` ```{r fig.height = #} ```

Comments

Comments, which are optional, are used to indicate or remind the reader of the purpose of the document or different aspects of the document. Comments can be included in a markdown file by placing the cursor in any blank line and writing or pasting the comment. The comment included in the markdown file that's opened when a new file is created is shown below (this comment should be deleted or modified before conducting your desired statistical analyses):

R Markdown   `Comment`

This is an R Markdown document. Markdown is a simple formatting syntax for authoring HTML, PDF, and MS Word documents. For more details on using R Markdown see http://rmarkdown.rstudio.com.

When you click the **Knit** button a document will be generated that includes both content as well as the output of any embedded R code chunks within the document. You can embed an R code chunk like this:

The example comment illustrates different ways comments may be formatted (e.g., font size and type (plain, bold-face, etc.)). Different formats for comments are illustrated in the box below:

Formatting comments in markdown documents

Headings and subheadings

Syntax	Result
Header 1: **#**	Level 1 heading
Header 2: **##**	Level 2 heading
Header 3: **###**	Level 3 heading

Font style

Syntax	Result
Italicized: *italicized text*	*italicized text*
Bold: **bold text**	**bold text**
Bold italicized: **_bold italicized text_**	***bold italicized text***

Indented comment

Syntax	Result
> indented comment	Indented comment

Including links to web pages

Syntax	Result
<http://www.example.com>	http://www.example.com

5.12 12. COPY COMMANDS AND COMMENTS INTO THE MARKDOWN FILE

Once a new markdown file has been opened, the next step is to place commands and comments into the markdown file as a code chunk. As mentioned above, commands must be placed between the two lines of back tick marks (` ``` `). For the example in this chapter, the commands we've written and executed thus far in the Console will be pasted as a script into the markdown file:

```
``` {r}
setwd("e:/R output")
df1 <- read.csv("DATATRANS.csv")
df1 [df1 == "."] <- NA
df1[, 2:6][ df1[, 2:6] == 9] <- NA
df1[, 8:9][ df1[, 8:9] == 9] <- NA
write.csv(df1, "DATATRANS_NA.csv", row.names=FALSE)
df1 <- read.csv("DATATRANS_NA.csv")
library(psych)
describe (df1, type = 2)
```
```

In copying and pasting commands into the markdown file, one way to retrieve commands written in the Console is to use the up arrow and down arrow (↑ and ↓) keys. However, do <u>not</u> copy and paste an `install.packages` command into a markdown file as doing so results in errors in executing the code.

Below is what the above code chunk looks like within the markdown file:

As a reminder, a code chunk must start and end with the two lines of back tick marks (` `` `). Failing to include the tick marks implies that the commands pasted into the markdown file are <u>not</u> commands to be executed but rather are comments. Code chunks differ from comments in that code chunks are shaded in light blue or gray.

It's worth noting that not all of the commands in this code chunk need to be included in the markdown file. More specifically, it isn't necessary to include the commands that read and modify the DATATRANS.csv file because we've saved these modifications in a new CSV file (DATATRANS_NA.csv). In this example, we could have simply moved from `setwd("e:/R output")` to `df1 <- read.csv ("DATATRANS_NA.csv")` and not included the five intermediate commands. However, we've chosen to include all of the commands in the code chunk in order to have them displayed in the markdown document to provide a record of all of the steps.

Comparing the above image of the markdown file with the example file that's opened when a new markdown file is created (the file with `summary(cars)`), you see that the code chunk for our statistical analysis replaced <u>all</u> of the lines in the example file that followed the document information lines (i.e., everything after the Document information has been deleted). This was done so that the markdown document included only the output of our analysis.

Before moving onto the next step, which is to execute (knit) the markdown file, there are several things you might want to do. First, as was just illustrated, you should delete any unwanted comments or code chunks. Second, it's a good idea to save the markdown file for future reference and use. After clicking on the **diskette** icon, we'll navigate to the working directory (e:/R output) and save the markdown file as a file (with an .Rmd file extension) named "Example markdown file (Chapter 5)":

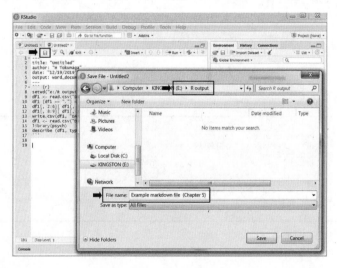

Note: After writing or pasting code into a code chunk, it's possible to run the code before knitting the file to ensure the code chunk runs properly. To run a code chunk, place the cursor anywhere between the two lines of back tick marks (```) and select **Run | Run Current Chunk**:

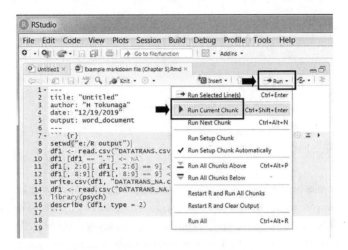

The output produced by running the code chunk will appear in the Console. However, running individual code chunks is <u>not</u> recommended because it may make the final markdown document unnecessarily large because an executed code chunk may appear multiple times in the document. Instead, it's preferable to ensure the code runs properly in the Console or a script file <u>before</u> copying it into the markdown file.

5.13 13. KNIT THE MARKDOWN FILE TO CREATE A MARKDOWN DOCUMENT

Executing the commands and comments in a markdown file consists of "knitting" the file (sometimes referred to as *rendering* the file). Knitting a markdown file executes the code chunks and comments in the markdown file to create a markdown document.

To knit a markdown file, click the ball of yarn **Knit** icon ( ) and select the type of file to be created; in this example, we will **Knit to Word** (the first time you knit a markdown file, you may be asked to install packages). As mentioned earlier, we recommend you try knitting to the different types of files (html, pdf, Word) to determine which type best fits your needs:

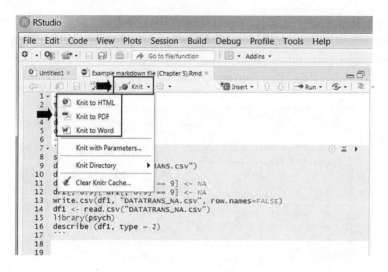

After you select the type of file, you may be asked to provide a name for the file and where you want the file to be saved. In this example, a new Word document will be saved in the same directory as the markdown file (the e:\R output folder) with the same name as the markdown file ("Example markdown file (Chapter 5)"). Below is what the markdown document looks like:

Untitled

H Tokunaga

12/19/2019

```
setwd("e:/R output")
df1 <- read.csv("DATATRANS.csv")
df1 [df1 == "."] <- NA
df1[, 2:6][ df1[, 2:6] == 9] <- NA
df1[, 8:9][ df1[, 8:9] == 9] <- NA
write.csv(df1, "DATATRANS_NA.csv", row.names=FALSE)
df1 <- read.csv("DATATRANS_NA.csv")
library(psych)
describe (df1, type = 2)
```

```
##          vars  n     mean       sd  median  trimmed      mad    min     max
## ID          1 11     6.00     3.32     6.0     6.00     4.45      1      11
## ITEM1       2 10     3.00     1.15     3.0     3.00     1.48      1       5
## ITEM2       3 10     4.00     1.25     4.0     4.25     1.48      1       5
## ITEM3       4  7     3.00     1.53     3.0     3.00     1.48      1       5
## ITEM4       5  9     2.78     1.39     3.0     2.78     1.48      1       5
## GROUP       6 10     2.10     1.45     1.5     1.88     0.74      1       5
## INCOME      7 10 47300.00 22660.78 46500.0 44375.00 18161.85  18000  100000
## SMOKE       8  7     1.43     0.53     1.0     1.43     0.00      1       2
## DRINK       9  8     1.38     0.52     1.0     1.38     0.00      1       2
##          range  skew kurtosis       se
## ID          10  0.00    -1.20     1.00
## ITEM1        4  0.00     0.08     0.37
## ITEM2        4 -1.72     3.42     0.39
## ITEM3        4 -0.39    -1.11     0.58
## ITEM4        4  0.15    -1.06     0.46
## GROUP        4  1.16     0.20     0.46
## INCOME   82000  1.33     2.86  7165.97
## SMOKE        1  0.37    -2.80     0.20
## DRINK        1  0.64    -2.24     0.18
```

R Markdown Files Versus SPSS Output Files

Comparing the output created from R with the SPSS output presented at the beginning of this chapter, we see many similarities. In this example, both the SPSS output and the R markdown file provide the names of the variables, the sample size for each variable (N), and some critical statistics (mean, standard deviation (sd), minimum (min), and maximum (max)). However, there are several fundamental differences between the two.

One difference between R and SPSS is that R may calculate different statistics than SPSS (e.g., "trimmed," "mad"). To understand the nature and logic of these statistics, users of R must rely on their statistical training as well as documentation on the CRAN website (https://cran.r-project.org/) provided by the developer of the package used to calculate the statistics. A second difference is that markdown files cannot be edited. For example, none of the information in the markdown file can be deleted, the width of the columns cannot be changed, and the number of decimal places displayed (e.g., the mean of 2.78 for the variable ITEM4) cannot be increased or decreased, all of which are very different from SPSS output files.

Appendices A and B of this book (Data Transformations and Statistical Procedures) display SPSS and R output side by side for a wide variety of situations. As noted at the start of this book, our goal is not to teach you statistics – as such, we must rely upon you to determine what aspects of the analyses are important to you.

5.14 EXITING RSTUDIO (SAVE THE WORKSPACE IMAGE?)

When you quit RStudio, a message regarding the "workspace image" may appear:

The "workspace image" is a snapshot of the workspace environment, which consists of the objects created (data frames, variables, output, etc.) and commands executed in the current R session. You normally **Don't save** the workspace image and instead save any desired objects in files.

The steps discussed in this chapter are summarized in the table on the next page. As mentioned earlier, three of these steps (5 (Change any missing data in data frame to NA), 6 (Save data frame with NAs as CSV file in the working directory), and 7 (Read the modified CSV file to create a data frame)) are only needed the first time a CSV file is imported into R; subsequent R sessions analyzing this data should read the modified CSV file created in step 6 rather than the original CSV file.

5.15 GETTING HELP WITH R

As you can imagine, there may be many times in which you will need assistance when using R. The help function can be executed to get help with an R function:

To get help with R functions

    Command: **help(***function***)**

    Example: help(aov)

The above help(aov) command asks for help on the aov function, which may be used to conduct different types of analysis of variance (ANOVA) analyses.

To get examples of R functions

    Command: **example(***function***)**

    Example: example(subset)

The above example(subset) command asks for examples of commands that include the subset function, which is used to select variables and observations from a larger set of data, such as selecting only people who are older than 40 from a sample.

> To get help with R packages
>
> Command: **help(package =** *package name***)**
>
> Example: help(package = psych)

The above `help(package = psych)` command requests help with the `psych` package.

* * * * *

This chapter discussed a number of issues and concerns in using RStudio. The purpose of the next chapter is to use a second example to more succinctly illustrate these steps.

Conducting RStudio Sessions: A Detailed Example

Step	Command/Menu	Example
1. Start RStudio		
2. Create a new script file (optional)		
3. Define the working directory	**setwd(**"*path and folder name*"**)**	setwd("e:/R output")
4. Import CSV file to create a data frame	*dataframe* **<- read.csv(**"*file name*"**)**	df1 <- read.csv("DATATRANS.csv")
5. Change any missing data in data frame to NA (*)	*dataframe* [*dataframe* **==** *number*] **<- NA** *dataframe* [*dataframe* **==** "."] **<- NA** *dataframe* [*dataframe* **==** ""] **<- NA**	df1 [df1 == 0] <- NA df1 [df1 == "."] <- NA df1 [df1 == ""] <- NA
6. Save data frame with NAs as CSV file in working directory (*)	**write.csv(***dataframe,* "*file name*.csv", **row.names=FALSE)**	write.csv(df1, "DATATRANS_NA.csv", row.names=FALSE)

(Continued)

(Continued)

Step	Command/Menu	Example
7. Read modified CSV file to create a data frame (*)	*dataframe* **<- read. csv(**"*file name*"**)**	df1 <- read. csv("DATATRANS _ NA.csv")
8. Download and install packages (if not already done)	**install.packages ("***package name***")**	install.packages ("psych")
9. Load installed packages (as needed)	**library(***package name***)**	library(psych)
10. Conduct a desired statistical analysis	describe(dataframe, type=2)	describe(df1, type=2)
11. Open a new markdown file	**File	New File	R Markdown**	
12. Copy commands and comments into the markdown file		
13. Knit the markdown file to create a markdown document	**Knit (⚙)**	

(*) Conducted the first time a CSV file is imported into R

CONDUCTING RSTUDIO SESSIONS: A BRIEF EXAMPLE

C hapter 5 introduced steps that can be performed in RStudio to conduct statistical analyses. Having provided this introduction, the purpose of this chapter is to use a second example to more quickly demonstrate an RStudio session.

* * * * *

This chapter will be based on the following research situation: You've collected data from 115 people on 6 variables: EWB1 to EWB5 and AGE. All of the variables have been assigned a missing value of 0. Below is a summary of the variables:

Variable	Valid values	Missing value(s)
EWB1 to EWB5	1–7	0
AGE	1–99	0

The data are in an Excel worksheet (EWB.xls) with the variable names (EWB1 to EWB5, AGE) in the top row. The worksheet, illustrated below, has been saved as a CSV file (EWB.csv) in the working directory (e:/R output):

⊿	A	B	C	D	E	F	
1	EWB1	EWB2	EWB3	EWB4	EWB5	AGE	
2	6	6	4	6	6	22	
3	3	6	6	5	5	21	
4	6	0	7	6	6	21	
5	6	6	6	7	6	21	
6	6	6	2	6	3	21	
7	7	7	0	7	0	21	
8	2	5	4	5	6	21	
9	5	5	3	7	5	21	
10	6	6	6	5	5	22	
11	5	5	4	7	7	20	
12	5	5	4	5	2	21	

You wish to use R to create a matrix of Pearson correlations between the variables EWB1 to EWB5—note that AGE will <u>not</u> be included in the matrix. Below is what this correlation matrix could look like if it were created using the CORRELATIONS command in SPSS:

```
CORRELATIONS
  /VARIABLES=EWB1 EWB2 EWB3 EWB4 EWB5
  /PRINT=TWOTAIL NOSIG
  /MISSING=PAIRWISE.
```

Correlations

Correlations

		EWB1	EWB2	EWB3	EWB4	EWB5
EWB1	Pearson Correlation	1	.388**	.393**	.187	.153
	Sig. (2-tailed)		.000	.000	.050	.106
	N	115	111	112	110	113
EWB2	Pearson Correlation	.388**	1	.418**	.366**	.217*
	Sig. (2-tailed)	.000		.000	.000	.024
	N	111	111	108	106	109
EWB3	Pearson Correlation	.393**	.418**	1	.115	.230*
	Sig. (2-tailed)	.000	.000		.240	.015
	N	112	108	112	107	111
EWB4	Pearson Correlation	.187	.366**	.115	1	.353**
	Sig. (2-tailed)	.050	.000	.240		.000
	N	110	106	107	110	108
EWB5	Pearson Correlation	.153	.217*	.230*	.353**	1
	Sig. (2-tailed)	.106	.024	.015	.000	
	N	113	109	111	108	113

**. Correlation is significant at the 0.01 level (2-tailed).

*. Correlation is significant at the 0.05 level (2-tailed).

Import a CSV file into a data frame

Command: *dataframe* **<- read.csv(**"*file name*"**)**

Example: df1 <- read.csv("EWB.csv")

In this example, this command reads the EWB.csv file and creates a data frame named df1.

6.5 5. CHANGE ANY MISSING DATA IN DATA FRAME TO NA

Before proceeding, any missing values in the CSV file must be replaced with NAs. In this example, missing data for all of the variables in the EWB.csv file were assigned a value of 0. The command below replaces numeric missing values with NAs:

Change numeric missing value (e.g., 0) to NA

Command: *dataframe* **[***dataframe* **==** *numeric missing value***] <- NA**

Example: df1 [df1 == 0] <- NA

In the above command, all values of 0 in the df1 data frame are replaced with NAs (note there should be no blank spaces between the two equals (=) signs).

6.6 6. SAVE DATA FRAME WITH NAs AS CSV FILE IN THE WORKING DIRECTORY

The next step is to save the modified data frame in a new CSV file using the write.csv function:

Save a data frame into a CSV file

Command: **write.csv(*dataframe*, "*file name*.csv",
           row.names=FALSE)**

Example: write.csv(df1, "EWB_NA.csv",
           row.names=FALSE)

In this command, the data frame df1 is saved as the CSV file EWB _ NA.csv in the working directory. As mentioned in the previous chapter, the argument row. names=FALSE was included to prevent R from adding the unnecessary "X" variable to the first column of the CSV file.

6.7 7. READ THE MODIFIED CSV FILE TO CREATE A DATA FRAME

Before conducting the desired statistical analyses, we again need a command with the read.csv function to create a data frame from the modified CSV file:

Import a CSV file into a data frame

Command: *dataframe* <- **read.csv("*file name*")**

Example: df1 <- read.csv("EWB_NA.csv")

This command creates a data frame named df1 from the file EWB _ NA.csv. The df1 data frame created by this command replaces the df1 data frame created by the read.csv function that imported the original CSV file (EWB.csv). We've purposely done this in order to avoid accessing incorrect data.

If so desired, we can confirm that the missing values have been converted into NAs by using the dataframe command to view the modified CSV file:

View the contents of a data frame

Command: *dataframe*

Example: df1

By typing the name of the data frame (df1) in the Console and pressing <Enter>, the contents of the data frame are immediately displayed in the Console:

```
> df1
    EWB1 EWB2 EWB3 EWB4 EWB5 AGE
1      6    6    4    6    6  22
2      3    6    6    5    5  21
3      6   NA    7    6    6  21
4      6    6    6    7    6  21
5      6    6    2    6    3  21
6      7    7   NA    7   NA  21
7      2    5    4    5    6  21
8      5    5    3    7    5  21
9      6    6    6    5    5  22
10     5    5    4    7    7  20
11     5    5    4    5    2  21
12     6    5    2    6    6  21
13     3    3    1   NA    3  21
14     6    7    7    7    6  22
15     5    6    4    4    3  23
```

Looking at the new data frame allows us to confirm that the previous missing values of zero (0) have been converted into NAs.

6.8 8. DOWNLOAD AND INSTALL PACKAGES (IF NOT ALREADY DONE)

As mentioned in the previous chapter, many of the statistical procedures in this book require the identification, downloading, and installation of packages. To create the matrix of Pearson correlations for this chapter's example, we've determined that the psych package is appropriate. After ensuring we're connected to the Internet, this package may be installed using the install.packages command:

Install a package (library)

Command: **install.packages("*package name*")**

Example: install.packages("psych")

Running this command downloads and installs the psych package on your computer. As you may recall, the psych package was installed in the previous chapter of this book. Because a package only needs to be installed once, it was not necessary to execute the `install.packages("psych")` command in this chapter. However, if we were to issue this command again, the `psych` package would be reinstalled and replace the previous version without incident (i.e., no error or warning messages would be issued).

6.9 9. LOAD INSTALLED PACKAGES (AS NEEDED)

The next step is to load an installed package to conduct the desired statistical analyses using the `library` function:

Load a package (library)

    Command: **`library(`*`package name`*`)`**

    Example: `library(psych)`

This command loads the `psych` package into R. Again, you may recall that this package was loaded in the previous chapter. However, assuming we're conducting this analysis in a new RStudio session (i.e., we exited and reentered RStudio), this package would need to be loaded again. That is, unlike installing a package, packages must be loaded in each new RStudio session.

6.10 10. CONDUCT DESIRED STATISTICAL ANALYSES

We're ready to execute commands to conduct a desired statistical analysis. For the example in this chapter, we want to calculate Pearson correlations between the variables EWB1 to EWB5. However, as it turns out, the `psych` package calculates statistics on all of the variables in the data frame (i.e., it does not allow users to pick and choose variables for a particular analysis).

Because the data frame `df1` includes a variable (AGE) we do not want to include in the correlations, we need to create a new data frame that includes only the variables of interest (EWB1 to EWB5). This new data frame is created using the `subset` function (Chapter 9 (Working with data frames) discusses other ways data frames may be manipulated):

Create a new data frame with only selected variables

Command:
```
newdataframe <- subset(dataframe, ,select 
= c(variable, variable, variable...))
```

Example:
```
df11 <- subset(df1, ,select = c(EWB1, 
EWB2, EWB3, EWB4, EWB5))
```

This command creates the data frame `df11` that consists of the variables EWB1 to EWB5 selected from the data frame `df1`. There are two things to note about the `df11` data frame. First, it was named `df11` rather than `df1` so that the data frame with all of the variables (`df1`) can be accessed as needed for other statistical analyses in this RStudio session. Second, `df11` could be saved as a CSV file by writing another command that includes the `write.csv` function; however, we will not do this as these variables already exist in the larger EWB_NA.csv file.

Now that a data frame has been created that includes the variables of interest, we can execute a command to create a matrix of Pearson correlations. This command uses the `corr.test` function:

Conduct a desired statistical analysis

Example command:
```
corr.test(newdataframe, 
use = 'pairwise')
```

Example:
```
corr.test(df11, use = 'pairwise')
```

The above command calculates a matrix of Pearson correlations for all of the variables in the data frame df11; the argument `use = 'pairwise'` performs pairwise deletion, which implies participants are excluded from a Pearson correlation if they're missing data on one of the two variables. The alternative argument `use = 'complete'` would have performed listwise deletion, in which only participants with valid data on all variables are included in the analysis.

After executing the `corr.test` function, the results of the command are displayed in the Console:

```
> corr.test(df11, use = 'pairwise')
Call:corr.test(x = df11, use = "pairwise")
Correlation matrix
     EWB1 EWB2 EWB3 EWB4 EWB5
EWB1 1.00 0.39 0.39 0.19 0.15
EWB2 0.39 1.00 0.42 0.37 0.22
EWB3 0.39 0.42 1.00 0.11 0.23
EWB4 0.19 0.37 0.11 1.00 0.35
EWB5 0.15 0.22 0.23 0.35 1.00
Sample Size
     EWB1 EWB2 EWB3 EWB4 EWB5
EWB1 115  111  112  110  113
EWB2 111  111  108  106  109
EWB3 112  108  112  107  111
EWB4 110  106  107  110  108
EWB5 113  109  111  108  113
Probability values (Entries above the diagonal are adjusted for multiple tests.)

     EWB1 EWB2 EWB3 EWB4 EWB5
EWB1 0.00 0.00 0.00 0.15 0.21
EWB2 0.00 0.00 0.00 0.00 0.09
EWB3 0.00 0.00 0.00 0.24 0.08
EWB4 0.05 0.00 0.24 0.00 0.00
EWB5 0.11 0.02 0.02 0.00 0.00
```

6.11 11. OPEN A NEW MARKDOWN FILE

Once the above commands have been successfully written and executed in the Console, they may be pasted as a script into a markdown file to create a markdown document. As demonstrated in Chapter 5, to open a new markdown file within RStudio, select **File | New File | R Markdown**. Within the newly opened markdown file, a title may be provided and a "Default Output Format:" can be selected:

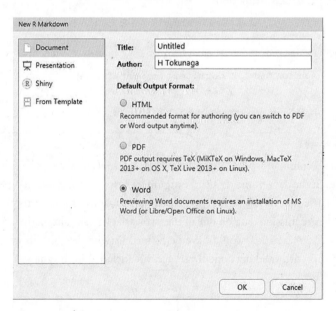

In this example, we'll change the "Untitled" title to "Conducting RStudio sessions: A second example" and we'll choose a Word format for the markdown document.

6.12 12. COPY COMMANDS AND COMMENTS INTO THE MARKDOWN FILE

The next step is to place commands and comments into the markdown file to create a code chunk. For the example in this chapter, here is the code chunk for the commands we've written and executed in the Console (these commands were retrieved from the Console using the up and down arrow (↑↓) keys):

```
``` {r}
setwd("e:/R output")
df1 <- read.csv("EWB.csv")
df1 [df1 == 0] <- NA
write.csv(df1, "EWB_NA.csv", row.names=FALSE)
df1 <- read.csv("EWB_NA.csv")
library(psych)
df11 <- .subset(df1, ,select = c(EWB1, EWB2, EWB3, EWB4, EWB5))
corr.test(df11, use = 'pairwise')
```
```

As a reminder, commands must be placed between the two lines of back tick marks (```). The code chunk, shaded in light gray, is illustrated below (note that the `install.packages` command was not pasted into the code chunk as this would result in errors in executing the code):

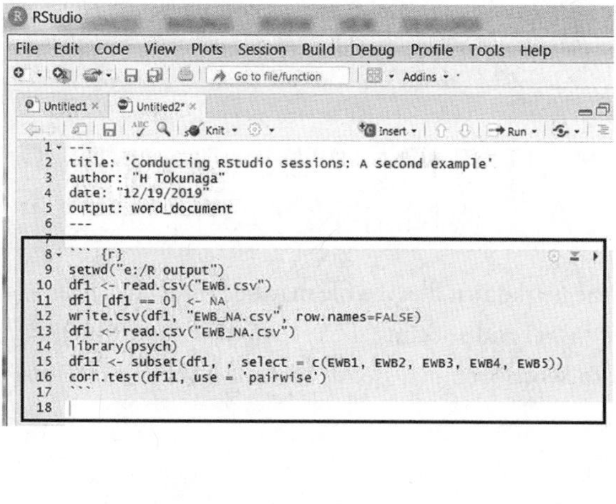

Looking at this markdown file, the code chunk for our statistical analysis has replaced <u>all</u> of the lines in the example file after the Document information lines in order to avoid executing any unwanted code chunks or comments. Also, as in the previous chapter, it wasn't necessary to include the three commands between `setwd("e:/R output")` and `df1 <- read.csv("EWB_NA.csv")` in the code chunk because these commands have already been written and executed in the Console. However, we've included them in order to have them displayed in the markdown document to record all of the steps we've followed.

Before knitting the markdown file, we'll save the markdown file by clicking on the **diskette** icon, navigating to the working directory (e:/R output), and saving the file as "Second example markdown file (Chapter 6)."

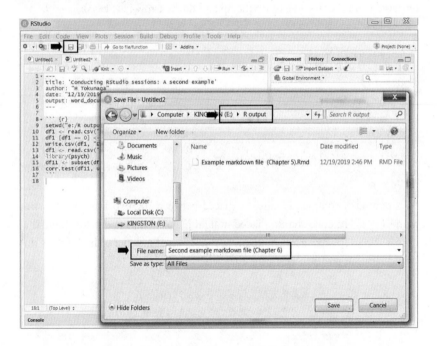

6.13 13. KNIT THE MARKDOWN FILE TO CREATE A MARKDOWN DOCUMENT

After saving the markdown file, the file may be knitted by clicking on the ball of yarn **Knit** icon (🧶) and selecting the type of file to be created. In this example, we will **Knit to Word** (you may decide that the html or pdf format works better for you):

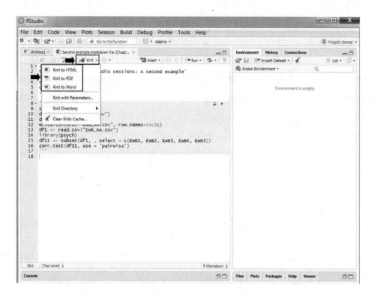

Knitting this markdown file creates and saves a Word document in the same directory as the markdown file (e:\R output folder) with the same name as the markdown file. This markdown document is shown below:

Conducting RStudio sessions: A second example

H Tokunaga

12/19/2019

```
setwd("e:/R output")
df1 <- read.csv("EWB.csv")
df1 [df1 == 0] <- NA
write.csv(df1, "EWB_NA.csv", row.names=FALSE)
df1 <- read.csv("EWB_NA.csv")
library(psych)
df11 <- subset(df1, , select = c(EWB1, EWB2, EWB3, EWB4, EWB5))
corr.test(df11, use = 'pairwise')

## Call:corr.test(x = df11, use = "pairwise")
## Correlation matrix
##       EWB1 EWB2 EWB3 EWB4 EWB5
## EWB1 1.00 0.39 0.39 0.19 0.15
## EWB2 0.39 1.00 0.42 0.37 0.22
## EWB3 0.39 0.42 1.00 0.11 0.23
## EWB4 0.19 0.37 0.11 1.00 0.35
## EWB5 0.15 0.22 0.23 0.35 1.00
## Sample Size
##       EWB1 EWB2 EWB3 EWB4 EWB5
## EWB1  115  111  112  110  113
## EWB2  111  111  108  106  109
## EWB3  112  108  112  107  111
## EWB4  110  106  107  110  108
## EWB5  113  109  111  108  113
## Probability values (Entries above the diagonal are adjusted for multiple
tests.)
##       EWB1 EWB2 EWB3 EWB4 EWB5
## EWB1 0.00 0.00 0.00 0.15 0.21
## EWB2 0.00 0.00 0.00 0.00 0.09
## EWB3 0.00 0.00 0.00 0.24 0.08
## EWB4 0.05 0.00 0.24 0.00 0.00
## EWB5 0.11 0.02 0.02 0.00 0.00
##
##  To see confidence intervals of the correlations, print with the
short=FALSE option
```

As in the example in Chapter 5, comparing the output created by R with the SPSS output presented at the start of this chapter reveals both similarities and differences. Perhaps the most critical difference is the inability to edit the output in the markdown file. For example, the "Probability values" of the Pearson correlations are only displayed to two decimal places, which makes it difficult to report the exact probability of a correlation in the text (e.g., what exactly *is* the probability of a correlation with "p = 0.00"?) as well as in a table (e.g., is a correlation with "p = 0.05" *less* or *greater* than the traditional .05 cutoff?)

6.14 EXITING RSTUDIO

As in the last chapter, a message regarding the "workspace image" may appear when you quit RStudio:

The workspace image is a snapshot of the workspace environment, which consists of all the objects created and commands executed in the R session. Having saved your output in a markdown file, you normally **Don't save** the workspace image.

The steps covered in conducting the analysis in this chapter are summarized in the table on the next page. Similar to the example in Chapter 5, steps 5–7 (Change any missing data in data frame to NA, Save data frame with NAs as CSV file in the working directory, and Read the modified CSV file to create a data frame) are needed the first time a CSV file is imported; step 4 (Import CSV file to create a data frame) of subsequent R sessions should read the modified CSV file rather than the original CSV file.

* * * * *

The goal of Chapters 5 and 6 was to introduce RStudio and steps within RStudio that can be used to conduct statistical analyses. As you may have deduced from these chapters, many of these steps are common to any RStudio session—what changes are the specific commands needed to perform a particular analysis in a particular research situation. Consequently, it is possible to develop sets of commands (scripts) to conduct different statistical procedures that can be placed into markdown files and modified as needed.

Appendix B of this book (Statistical procedures) provides scripts for a variety of common statistical procedures. The next chapter provides an example of how these scripts may be utilized within R to obtain results similar to those obtained in SPSS.

Conducting RStudio Sessions: A Brief Example

Step	Command/Menu	Example
1. Start RStudio		
2. Create a new script file (optional)		
3. Define the working directory	`setwd("path and folder name")`	`setwd("e:/R output")`
4. Import CSV file to create a data frame	`dataframe <- read.csv("file name")`	`df1 <- read.csv("EWB.csv")`
5. Change any missing data in data frame to NA (*)	`dataframe [dataframe == number] <- NA`	`df1 [df1 == 0] <- NA`
6. Save data frame with NAs as CSV file in working directory (*)	`write.csv(dataframe, "file name.csv", row.names=FALSE)`	`write.csv(df1, "EWB_NA.csv", row.names=FALSE)`
7. Read modified CSV file to create a data frame (*)	`dataframe <- read.csv("file name")`	`df1 <- read.csv("EWB_NA.csv")`

(Continued)

(Continued)

8.	Download and install packages (if not already done)	`install.`
		`packages("package`
		`name")`
			`install.`
			`packages("psych")`

9.	Load installed packages (as needed)	`library(package name)`	`library(psych)`

10.	Conduct desired statistical analyses	`newdataframe <-`
		`subset(dataframe,,`
		`select = c`
		`(variable,variable...))`
		`corr.test`
		`(newdataframe,use`
		`='pairwise')`
			`df11 <-`
			`subset(df1,`
			`,select = c(EWB1,`
			`EWB2, EWB3, EWB4,`
			`EWB5))`
			`corr.test(df11,`
			`use = 'pairwise')`

11.	Open a new markdown file	**File | New File | R Markdown**	
12.	Copy commands and comments into the markdown file		
13.	Knit the markdown file to create a markdown document	**Knit (✦)**	

(*) Conducted the first time a CSV file is imported into R

7

CONDUCTING STATISTICAL ANALYSES USING THIS BOOK: A DETAILED EXAMPLE

The previous two chapters described and illustrated different commands that may be executed in an RStudio session to conduct statistical analyses. Although these commands can be executed one by one in the Console, a combined set (aka script) of these commands can instead be written or pasted into a markdown file; the file can then be executed (knitted) to produce a markdown document, which is the equivalent of an SPSS output file. As Appendix B of this book includes scripts for a variety of different statistical procedures, the purpose of this chapter is to demonstrate how these scripts may be used to produce results similar to those produced by SPSS to conduct the same analysis.

Conducting statistical analyses using this chapter is based on three prerequisite assumptions:

(1) **The file containing the data to be analyzed has been prepared for use in R and placed in the working directory**. Following the guidelines presented in Chapter 2, this implies that (a) the SPSS or Excel file has been saved as a CSV file, (b) the CSV file has been imported into R and any missing data in the data file have been changed to NAs, and (c) the data frame with NAs has been saved as a new CSV file in the working directory (e.g., the example in this chapter will import

the modified CSV file COLLEGE_NA.csv rather than the original COLLEGE.csv file). As a reminder, in this book the working directory is the folder "R output" on the "e:" drive (e:/R Output); in using the scripts in this book, please remember that you'll need to indicate your working directory.

(2) **The packages needed to conduct the statistical procedures in this book have been downloaded and installed**. In Chapter 5, these packages were identified as psych, ggplot2, phia, GPArotation, lm.beta, lmSupport, CCA, candisc, and gmodels. It is, of course, quite likely that statistical procedures not discussed in this book will require installation of other packages.

(3) **The user of this book understands how to write and execute commands that define the working directory, import CSV files to create data frames, and load packages into R**. Commands that use the functions setwd, read.csv, and library to perform these tasks were introduced and discussed in Chapters 5 and 6.

This chapter will be based on the following research situation: You've collected data from 116 college seniors on nine variables: *id, cgpa, hsgpa, satmath, satverb, sshada, sshawm, sshata,* and *sshaea*. Below is a summary of these variables:

Variable	Description	Valid values	Missing value
id	ID number	1–116	–
cgpa	College GPA	0.00–4.00	9.99
hsgpa	High school GPA	0.00–4.00	9.99
satmath	SAT Math score	200–800	999
satverb	SAT Verbal score	200–800	999
sshada	SSHA Delay Avoidance	0–50	99
sshawm	SSHA Work Methods	0–50	99
sshata	SSHA Teacher Approval	0–50	99
sshaea	SSHA Education Acceptance	0–50	99

Any missing data have been converted into NAs, and the data frame has been saved in a CSV file (COLLEGE_NA.csv) in the working directory—in this chapter, the working directory will be a folder named "STATS" located on the Desktop. A portion of the COLLEGE_NA CSV file is illustrated below:

	A	B	C	D	E	F	G	H	I
1	id	cgpa	hsgpa	satmath	satverb	sshada	sshawm	sshata	sshaea
2	1	3.6	2.8	620	560	21	37	35	31
3	2	3.72	3.95	660	680	19	37	17	19
4	3	3.68	3.94	630	630	6	25	12	15
5	4	2	3.8	400	550	12	8	2	4
6	5	2.7	3.5 NA	NA		23	37	23	25
7	6	3.2	3.8	650	560	23	33	48	29
8	7	2.7	3.7	460	470	4	12	23	19
9	8	3.2	3.8	470	550	25	31	44	29
10	9	2 NA	NA	NA		40	15	4	19
11	10	3	3.5	600	610	31	40	33	8
12	11	3.01	3.5 NA	NA		6	15	23	17
13	12	3.1	4	740	560	12	29	27	6

As you can see, the names of the variables are provided in the first row of the table and all missing values have been changed to NAs. Note: In this file, only 95 of the 116 participants have valid data for all four variables of interest in this chapter (*cgpa*, *hsgpa*, *satmath*, *satverb*).

Imagine you want to conduct a standard (simultaneous) multiple regression analysis predicting college GPA (*cgpa*) from high school GPA (*hsgpa*), SAT Math scores (*satmath*), and SAT Verbal scores (*satverb*). Below is a portion of the output of this analysis if it were conducted using the **REGRESSION** command in SPSS:

```
REGRESSION
   /MISSING LISTWISE
   /STATISTICS COEFF OUTS R ANOVA
   /CRITERIA=PIN(.05) POUT(.10)
   /NOORIGIN
   /DEPENDENT cgpa
   /METHOD=ENTER hsgpa satmath satverb.
```

Regression

Model Summary

Model	R	R Square	Adjusted R Square	Std. Error of the Estimate
1	.393[a]	.155	.127	.37800

a. Predictors: (Constant), satverb, hsgpa, satmath

ANOVA[a]

Model		Sum of Squares	df	Mean Square	F	Sig.
1	Regression	2.382	3	.794	5.556	.002[b]
	Residual	13.003	91	.143		
	Total	15.384	94			

a. Dependent Variable: cgpa
b. Predictors: (Constant), satverb, hsgpa, satmath

Coefficients[a]

Model		Unstandardized Coefficients		Standardized Coefficients	t	Sig.
		B	Std. Error	Beta		
1	(Constant)	1.576	.462		3.408	.001
	hsgpa	.043	.116	.039	.368	.714
	satmath	.001	.000	.323	3.079	.003
	satverb	.001	.001	.144	1.462	.147

The earlier chapters of this book listed 13 steps that can be taken in an RStudio session to conduct statistical analyses. However, because the scripts provided at the back of this book include commands for many of these steps, a smaller number of steps may be used to conduct the statistical analysis in this chapter:

1. Start RStudio

2. Copy and paste an example script into a script file

3. Modify the example script as needed for the desired statistical analysis

4. Execute the script to confirm it works properly

5. Copy and paste the script into a markdown file

6. Knit the markdown file to create a markdown document

In this chapter, we'll work through each of these six steps to conduct our standard multiple regression analysis and save the output of the analysis in a markdown document.

7.1 1. START RSTUDIO

7.2 2. COPY AND PASTE AN EXAMPLE SCRIPT INTO A SCRIPT FILE

In earlier chapters, we wrote and executed individual commands in the Console and then copied and pasted the commands into a code chunk in a markdown file. However, because in this chapter we'll use a preexisting script to conduct our desired statistical analysis, we'll create a script file to first ensure that the commands work properly before pasting the script into a markdown file.

The goal of this step is to copy and paste an appropriate example script into a script file so that the commands may be modified and tested for correctness. For the example in this chapter, we need a script that conducts a standard multiple regression analysis. Looking in the Statistical Procedures at the back of this book, we find, "Multiple regression (standard)." Within this procedure, you'll find an "Example script" that includes the following set of commands:

Example script

```
setwd("e:/R output")
df1 <- read.csv("COLLEGE_NA.csv")
library(lm.beta)
stanmrc <- lm(cgpa ~ satmath + satverb, data = df1)
stanmrcbetas <- lm.beta(stanmrc)
summary(stanmrcbetas)
```

This example script includes commands that perform several of the 13 steps used in the last 2 chapters:

- **Define the working directory**

  Example: `setwd("e:/R output")`

  This command defines the working directory as the `R output` folder on the `e:` drive.

  Note: The `setwd` command may be deleted from the script if a default working directory has been created (see Chapter 5 ("Setting a default working directory") for more information).

- **Read the modified CSV file to create a data frame**

  Example: `df1 <- read.csv("COLLEGE_NA.csv")`

  This command creates a data frame named `df1` from the CSV file `COLLEGE_NA.csv`.

  Note: Be sure the CSV file is in the working directory before executing the `read.csv` function.

- **Load installed packages (as needed)**

  Example: `library(lm.beta)`

  This command loads the `lm.beta` package into R; this package calculates standardized regression coefficients (betas) for predictor variables.

Note: Libraries must be loaded into R <u>before</u> conducting statistical analyses that utilize the library.

These first three commands in this script (`setwd`, `read.csv`, `library`) were used in the previous chapters; what's new in this chapter are the commands needed to conduct our desired analysis:

- **Conduct desired statistical analyses**

    Example: `stanmrc <- lm(cgpa ~ satmath + satverb,`
    `data = df1)`
    `stanmrcbetas <- lm.beta(stanmrc)`
    `summary(stanmrcbetas)`

For each statistical procedure discussed in Appendix B of this book, a brief explanation of these commands is provided. For example, here is the description of commands that conduct a standard multiple regression analysis in R:

Create output of multiple regression analysis

    Command: `result <-lm(dv ~ iv1 + iv2 + iv3...,data`
                      `= dataframe)`

    Example: `stanmrc <- lm(cgpa ~ satmath + satverb,`
                      `data = df1)`

Modify output of multiple regression analysis to include standardized coefficients (betas)

    Command: `resultb <- lm.beta(result)`

    Example: `stanmrcbetas <- lm.beta(stanmrc)`

Display output of multiple regression analysis with standardized coefficients (betas)

    Command: `summary(resultb)`

    Example: `summary(stanmrcbetas)`

The first command creates an object (`stanmrc`) that is the result of a multiple regression analysis using the `lm` function with `cgpa` as the dependent variable and `satmath` and `satverb` as the independent variables, all of which are in the `df1` data frame. The second command applies the `lm.beta` function to the object (`stanmrc`) to calculate standardized regression coefficients (betas) for the independent variables and creates a new object (`stanmrcbetas`). The third command uses the `summary` function to display the results of the object `stanmrcbetas`, which is the results of the multiple regression analysis with the standardized regression coefficients.

In order to save space, this book will not provide detailed explanations of commands and functions used to conduct statistical analyses. Readers who wish to learn more about the intricacies of these commands and functions are strongly encouraged to perform Internet searches to obtain a more comprehensive understanding of their purpose and format.

Once the appropriate example script has been identified, it can be placed into a script file in the Script editor, which is the upper left window of RStudio. Below is our example script for a standard multiple regression analysis:

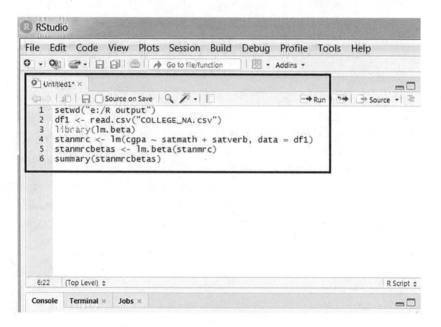

7.3 3. MODIFY THE EXAMPLE SCRIPT AS NEEDED FOR THE DESIRED STATISTICAL ANALYSIS

Once the example script has been copied and pasted into the script file, the next step is to modify the commands in the script as needed for a particular research situation. The colored italicized words in the script are discretionary—in this script, they represent the name and location of the working directory (`e:/R output`), the name of the data frame (`df1`), the name of the CSV file (`COLLEGE_NA.csv`), the desired name of the objects that contains the results of the statistical analysis (`stanmrc` and `stanmrcbetas`), and the names of criterion (`cgpa`) and predictor (`satmath` and `satverb`) variables in the analysis—all of these things can be modified as needed or desired.

In our example, we will modify two of the commands in the script:

First, because the working directory in this example is the "STATS" folder on the Desktop, we must change the first command from `setwd("e:/R output")` to `setwd("C:/Users/howard/Desktop/STATS")`, where `howard` is the name of the author's Windows computer. Note: If you forget to change `"e:/R output"` to your particular working directory, you may get an error message, such as *Error in setwd("e:/R output"): cannot change working directory.*

Second, we need to edit the `stanmrc <- lm(cgpa ~ satmath + satverb, data = df1)` command to `stanmrc <- lm(cgpa ~ hsgpa + satmath + satverb, data = df1)` in order to add the third independent variable `hsgpa`.

Here is the modified script that accesses the STATS working directory on the Desktop, imports the COLLEGE_NA file, loads the `lm.beta` library, and conducts the analysis in this chapter (predicting college gpa (`cgpa`) from high school GPA, SAT Math scores, and SAT Verbal scores (`hsgpa`, `satmath`, and `satverb`)):

```
setwd("C:/Users/howard/Desktop/STATS")
df1 <- read.csv("COLLEGE_NA.csv")
library(lm.beta)
stanmrc <- lm(cgpa ~ hsgpa + satmath + satverb, data = df1)
stanmrcbetas <- lm.beta(stanmrc)
summary(stanmrcbetas)
```

The script file that contains the modified script is illustrated below:

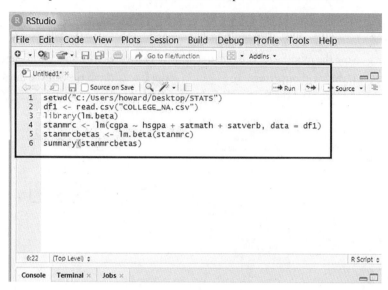

After the example script has been modified, we recommend that the file be saved for future use and reference. In this example, we'll save the script file in the STATS working directory using the name *Ch7_example* (script files have a *.R* file extension).

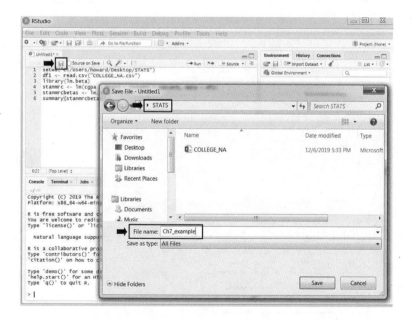

7.4 4. EXECUTE THE SCRIPT TO CONFIRM IT WORKS PROPERLY

After saving the modified script file, the next step is to execute it in order to determine if it runs without errors. To execute a script file, click on the **Source** button in the upper right of the Script editor window:

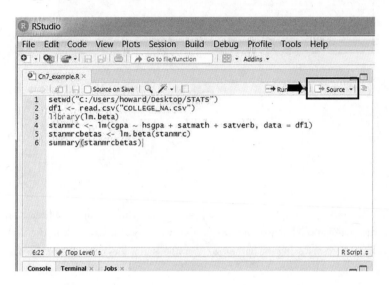

The result of executing the script is presented in the Console:

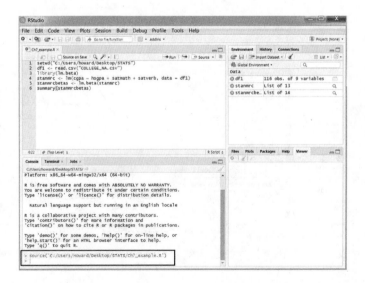

Looking in the Console, we see that clicking the **Source** button resulted in the command "`source('C:/Users/Howard/Desktop/STATS/Ch7_example.R')`" being pasted into the Console. The `source` command executes the file indicated in the parentheses, which in this example is the Ch7 _ example script file in the working directory. In essence, clicking the **Source** button is the same as typing the produced command in the Console and pressing the <Enter> key.

If the script file is free from errors, the R prompt (the > symbol) will appear in the line in the Console below the `source` command. However, any errors in the script will result in an error message. For example, what if we defined the data frame as *df11* in one of the commands rather than the correct `df1`? The consequences of this mistake are illustrated below:

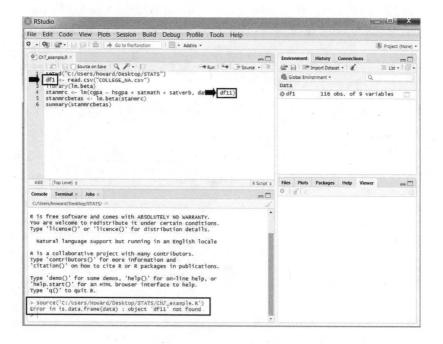

Looking at the above screen, the misspelled `df11` resulted in the error message, *Error in is.data.frame(data) : object 'df11' not found*. At this point we would hopefully be able to diagnose the error, make any needed changes to the script file, and then click the **Source** button again.

Clicking the **Source** button executes all of the commands in a script file. Although rare, there may be times you'll want to execute only a single command. To execute a single command in a script file, place the cursor anywhere in the desired command and either click the **Run** button (located to the left of the Source button) or press **CTLR + R** (Windows) or **command + enter** (Mac).

7.5 5. COPY AND PASTE THE SCRIPT INTO A MARKDOWN FILE

Once the script file runs correctly and without errors, we're ready to copy and paste the script into a markdown file in order to create a markdown document. The first thing we must do is create a new markdown file. To do this, we select **File | New File | R Markdown**. Once the new markdown file has been opened, we can provide a title for the markdown file and choose the desired output format (html, Word doc, or pdf). In this chapter, we will use the title, "Conducting analyses using this book: Intro" and knit the markdown file into a **Word** document:

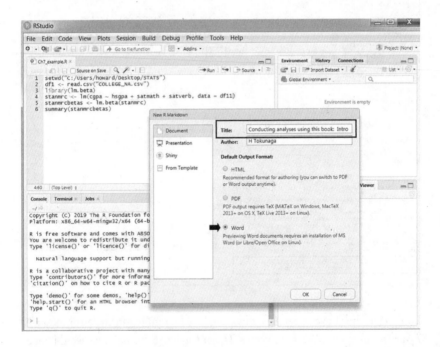

Next, we click on the tab with the name of the script file (in this case, **Ch7_example.R**), select all of the commands in the script by placing the cursor at the start of the first command and dragging over them and then copy the script of commands:

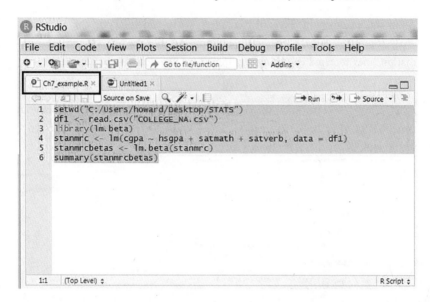

Once the script of commands has been copied, we move back to the markdown file by clicking on the tab of the **Untitled** markdown file. Next, we paste the copied script between two lines of back tick marks (```); the result of this is illustrated below:

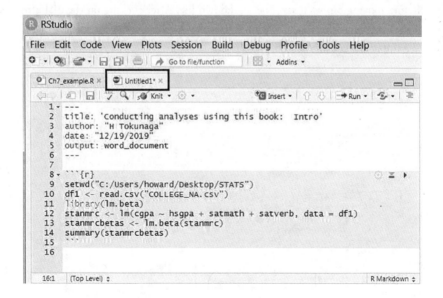

As in the examples in the earlier chapters, we've had the code chunk for this analysis replace <u>all</u> of the lines in the example file after the four Document information lines to avoid executing any unwanted code chunks or comments (e.g., `summary(cars)`, `plot(pressure)`).

As mentioned several times, the commands in a script must be located between two lines of three back tick marks (```` ```{r} ```` and ```` ``` ````). Below is what the script would look like if these two lines were <u>not</u> included:

```
1  ---
2  title: 'conducting analyses using this book:  Intro'
3  author: "H Tokunaga"
4  date: "12/19/2019"
5  output: word_document
6  ---
7
8  setwd("C:/Users/howard/Desktop/STATS")
9  df1 <- read.csv("COLLEGE_NA.csv")
10 library(lm.beta)
11 stanmrc <- lm(cgpa ~ hsgpa + satmath + satverb, data = df1)
12 stanmrcbetas <- lm.beta(stanmrc)
13 summary(stanmrcbetas)
14
```

Comparing this image with the one just above it, you can see that a script without the two lines of back tick marks is not shaded in light gray or blue. This implies that the commands in the script are treated as comments, which are not executed.

Before moving on, we'll save the markdown file. After clicking on the **diskette** icon and navigating to the working directory, we'll save the markdown file as "Example markdown file (Chapter 7)."

7.6 6. KNIT THE MARKDOWN FILE TO CREATE A MARKDOWN DOCUMENT

The next step is to knit the saved markdown file by clicking on the **Knit** (⚙) button and selecting the type of file to be created (html, pdf, Word). In this example, we will **Knit to Word:**

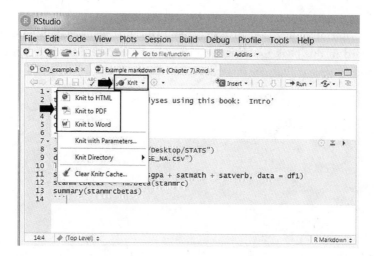

The Word markdown file for this example, which has the same name as the markdown file and is saved in the same directory as the markdown file, is presented below:

Conducting analyses using this book: Intro

H Tokunaga

12/19/2019

```
setwd("C:/Users/howard/Desktop/STATS")
df1 <- read.csv("COLLEGE_NA.csv")
library(lm.beta)
stanmrc <- lm(cgpa ~ hsgpa + satmath + satverb, data = df1)
stanmrcbetas <- lm.beta(stanmrc)
summary(stanmrcbetas)

##
## Call:
## lm(formula = cgpa ~ hsgpa + satmath + satverb, data = df1)
##
## Residuals:
##     Min      1Q  Median      3Q     Max
## -0.86954 -0.24337 -0.03368  0.23833 1.02097
##
## Coefficients:
##             Estimate Standardized Std. Error t value Pr(>|t|)
## (Intercept) 1.5757621    0.0000000  0.4623516   3.408 0.000976 ***
## hsgpa       0.0426038    0.0385536  0.1158545   0.368 0.713924
## satmath     0.0014147    0.3228847  0.0004594   3.079 0.002743 **
## satverb     0.0008351    0.1443145  0.0005713   1.462 0.147291
## ---
## Signif. codes:  0 '***' 0.001 '**' 0.01 '*' 0.05 '.' 0.1 ' ' 1
##
## Residual standard error: 0.378 on 91 degrees of freedom
##   (21 observations deleted due to missingness)
## Multiple R-squared:  0.1548, Adjusted R-squared:  0.1269
## F-statistic: 5.556 on 3 and 91 DF,  p-value: 0.001513
```

As in the earlier chapters, there are both similarities and differences between the output in the R markdown file and the SPSS output. Although both provide the same critical information (e.g., R^2 = .16, adjusted R^2 = .13, $F(3, 91)$ = 5.56, $p < .01$, betas for *hsgpa*, *satmath*, and *satverb* = .04 (t = .37, $p > .05$), .32 (t = 3.08, $p < .01$), and .14 (t = 1.46, $p > .05$), respectively), there are also differences in what information is provided by R and how this information is formatted.

* * * * *

This chapter introduced and discussed steps that can be followed in using scripts provided in this book to conduct statistical analyses. The next chapter uses a second example to illustrate these steps more succinctly.

Conducting Statistical Analyses Using this Book: A Detailed Example

Step	Command/Menu	Example
1. Start RStudio		

2. Copy and paste an example script into a script file		`setwd("e:/R output")`
		`df1 <- read.csv`
		`("COLLEGE _ NA.csv")`
		`library(lm.beta)`
		`stanmrc <- lm(cgpa~satmath`
		`+ satverb,data = df1)`
		`stanmrcbetas`
		`<- lm.beta(stanmrc)`
		`summary(stanmrcbetas)`

3. Modify the example script as needed for the desired statistical analysis		`setwd("C:/Users/howard/`
		`Desktop/STATS")`
		`df1 <- read.csv`
		`("COLLEGE _ NA.csv")`
		`library(lm.beta)`
		`stanmrc <- lm(cgpa ~ hsgpa`
		`+ satmath + satverb, data`
		`= df1)`
		`stanmrcbetas`
		`<- lm.beta(stanmrc)`
		`summary(stanmrcbetas)`

4. Execute the script to confirm it works properly	**Source** button in Script editor window	
5. Copy and paste the script into a markdown file	**File | New File | R Markdown**	
6. Knit the markdown file to create a markdown document	**Knit (⚙)**	

8

CONDUCTING STATISTICAL ANALYSES USING THIS BOOK: A BRIEF EXAMPLE

The previous chapter introduced steps that can be followed in using scripts provided in this book to conduct different statistical procedures. The purpose of this chapter is to use a second example to illustrate these steps more quickly.

* * * * *

The example in this chapter will be based on the following research situation: Data that have been collected from 119 people ($N = 119$) are in a CSV file named PSYCH_NA.csv (any missing data in this file have been converted into NAs). The PSYCH_NA.csv file has been placed in the working directory, which in this example will be a folder named "Thesis" on the Desktop. Part of the PSYCH_NA.csv file is provided below:

	A	B	C	D	E	F	G	H	I	J	K	L
1	fplan1	fplan2	fplan3	fplan4	fplan5	fplan6	instruct	faculty	relfac	tguide	tpsk	doagain
2	5	5	6	2	4	3	5.571429	4.375	2.25	2.666667	3.714286	2
3	4	4	4	3	4	4	4.142857	4.375	3.75	4.333333	2.928571	2
4	6	NA	6	5	4	6	4.285714	4.875	3.125	2.2	4	1
5	6	5	5	6	6	6	5.285714	5.75	4.375	3.5	3.857143	1
6	6	5	5	6	5	6	4.857143	5.375	4	3.2	3.785714	1
7	1	3	4	NA	4	3	5.142857	4.75	3.25	3	3.928571	2
8	4	2	2	5	3	3	4	6	2.125	1.4	2.571429	2
9	3	4	NA	3	3	4	4.142857	4.25	3.75	5	2.928571	2
10	4	5	6	4	5	6	5.714286	5.375	2.875	1	3.714286	1
11	6	3	2	6	4	6	4	3.875	3.625	2.5	3.142857	1

Imagine you wish to calculate the Cronbach's alpha measure of internal consistency (reliability) for six variables: *fplan1* to *fplan6*. Below is what this output may look like if it were performed using the RELIABILITY command in SPSS:

```
RELIABILITY
  /VARIABLES=fplan1 fplan2 fplan3 fplan4 fplan5 fplan6
  /SCALE('ALL VARIABLES') ALL
  /MODEL=ALPHA
  /STATISTICS=CORR
  /SUMMARY=TOTAL.
```

Reliability

Case Processing Summary

		N	%
Cases	Valid	116	97.5
	Excluded[a]	3	2.5
	Total	119	100.0

a. Listwise deletion based on all variables in the procedure.

Reliability Statistics

Cronbach's Alpha	Cronbach's Alpha Based on Standardized Items	N of Items
.837	.841	6

Item-Total Statistics

	Scale Mean if Item Deleted	Scale Variance if Item Deleted	Corrected Item-Total Correlation	Squared Multiple Correlation	Cronbach's Alpha if Item Deleted
fplan1	22.57	23.308	.668	.628	.798
fplan2	22.94	25.866	.708	.619	.798
fplan3	23.16	28.184	.340	.208	.861
fplan4	22.61	23.561	.690	.641	.794
fplan5	23.16	25.767	.626	.561	.809
fplan6	22.68	22.237	.697	.525	.792

Note that, in addition to the variables included in this analysis (*fplan1* to *fplan6*), the PSYCH_NA.csv file contains other variables, such as *instruct, faculty,* and *relfac.* This will need to be taken into consideration when conducting this analysis using R. It is also important to note that 116 of the 119 participants had no missing data among the six variables *fplan1* to *fplan6*; that is, three participants were not included in the SPSS analysis.

To conduct this analysis using R and RStudio, we'll follow the six steps introduced in Chapter 7:

1. Start RStudio

2. Copy and paste an example script into a script file

3. Modify the example script as needed for the desired statistical analysis

4. Execute the script to confirm it works properly

5. Copy and paste the script into a markdown file

6. Knit the markdown file to create a markdown document

As mentioned in Chapter 7, using the scripts in this book is based on several assumptions: (1) the data file has been prepared for use in R by saving the SPSS or Excel file as a CSV file, importing the CSV file into R and changing any missing data in the data file to NAs, and saving the data frame with NAs as a new CSV file in the working directory; (2) packages needed to conduct the statistical procedures in this book (`psych`, `ggplot2`, `phia`, `GPArotation`, `lm.beta`, `lmSupport`, `CCA`, `candisc`, and `gmodels`) have been downloaded and installed in R; and (3) the user of this chapter understands how to write and execute commands that define the working directory (`setwd`), read CSV files to create data frames (`read.csv`), and load packages into R (`library`)—refer to Chapters 5 and 6 for an explanation of these commands.

Below, we'll work through each of these steps in order to calculate our Cronbach's alpha and save the output of the analysis in a markdown document.

8.1 1. START RSTUDIO

8.2 2. COPY AND PASTE AN EXAMPLE SCRIPT INTO A SCRIPT FILE

The next step is to locate the appropriate example script in Appendix B (Statistical Procedures). For the example in this chapter, we can locate a script that calculates Cronbach's alpha by looking at the back of this book, where we find the statistical procedure, "Internal consistency (Cronbach's alpha)." Within this procedure, you'll find the following example script:

```
Example script
    setwd("e:/R output")
    df1 <- read.csv("EWB_NA.csv")
    library(psych)
    df11 <- subset(df1, ,select = c(EWB1, EWB2,
    EWB3,EWB4,EWB5))
    df11 <- na.omit(df11)
    alpha(df11)
```

The first three commands in this script that utilize the `setwd`, `read.csv`, and `library` functions were used in the previous chapters to define the working directory, read the modified CSV file to create a data frame, and load any needed packages. What's new in this chapter are the commands needed to conduct our desired analysis:

```
df11 <- subset(df1, ,select = c(EWB1, EWB2, EWB3, EWB4, EWB5))
df11 <- na.omit(df11)
alpha(df11)
```

Within "Internal consistency (Cronbach's alpha)" in Appendix B (Statistical Procedures), a brief explanation of the commands in the example script that conduct the desired analysis is provided:

```
Create new data frame that contains only the variables to be analyzed

    Command:    newdataframe <- subset(dataframe, ,select = c
                (variable, variable,...))

    Example:    df11 <- subset(df1, ,select = c(EWB1, EWB2,
                EWB3, EWB4, EWB5))

Remove anyone with NAs on any variable in the new data frame

    Command:    newdataframe <- na.omit(newdataframe)

    Example:    df11 <- na.omit(df11)

Run the alpha function to calculate Cronbach's alpha

    Command:    alpha(newdataframe)

    Example:    alpha(df11)
```

The first command creates a new data frame (df11) that consists of only the variables we want to include in the calculation of Cronbach's alpha (in the example script, this is EWB1, EWB2, EWB3, EWB4, EWB5). The second command removes (omits) anyone in the sample who has missing data on any of the variables in the new data frame; this command has been included because we've determined that the alpha function we're about to execute does not allow for any missing data in the data frame. The third command uses the alpha command to calculate Cronbach's alpha for the variables in the df11 data frame.

Once the example script has been identified, it can be pasted into the new script file. This is shown below:

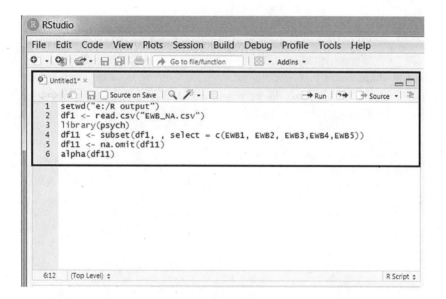

8.3 3. MODIFY THE EXAMPLE SCRIPT AS NEEDED FOR THE DESIRED STATISTICAL ANALYSIS

The next step is to modify the commands in the example script that's been pasted into the script file to meet the needs of the current situation. We've determined we need to make three modifications:

First, because the working directory in this example is the "Thesis" folder on the Desktop, we must change the first command from setwd("e:/R output") to setwd("C:/users/howard/ Desktop/Thesis"), where howard is the name of the author's Windows computer. As mentioned in the previous chapter, it's critical to indicate the proper working directory in the setwd command to avoid getting a *cannot change working directory* error message.

Second, in order to access the correct CSV file, we need to edit the df1 <- read.csv("EWB_NA.csv") command to df1 <- read. csv("PSYCH_NA.csv").

Third, in order to select the desired variables for this analysis, we must change the df11 <- subset(df1, ,select = c (EWB1,EWB2,EWB3,EWB4,EWB5)) command to df11 <- subset(df1, ,select = c(fplan1,fplan2,fplan3, fplan4,fplan5,fplan6)).

The modified script that accesses the Thesis working directory, imports the PSYCH_NA CSV file, loads the psych library, and calculates Cronbach's alpha for our six variables (fplan1 to fplan6) is presented below:

```
setwd("C:/users/howard/Desktop/Thesis")
df1 <- read.csv("PSYCH_NA.csv")
library(psych)
df11 <- subset(df1, ,select = c(fplan1,fplan2,fplan3,fplan4,
    fplan5,fplan6))
df11 <- na.omit(df11)
alpha(df11)
```

The script file that contains the modified script is illustrated below:

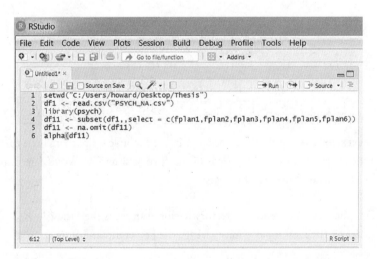

Before executing the script file, we'll save it in the working directory. For this example, we'll name the script file *Ch8_example*. The saving of the script file is illustrated below.

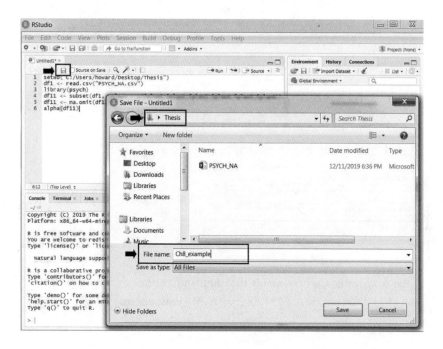

8.4 4. EXECUTE THE SCRIPT TO CONFIRM IT WORKS PROPERLY

The next step is to execute the modified script file in order to identify and resolve any errors that may occur. The script file is executed by clicking on the **Source** button in the upper-right of the Script editor window; doing so generates the command `source('C:/users/howard/Desktop/Ch8 _ example.R')` in the Console. If the script file is free from errors, the > R prompt appears in the next line of the Console. The script file and the results of the source command are presented below:

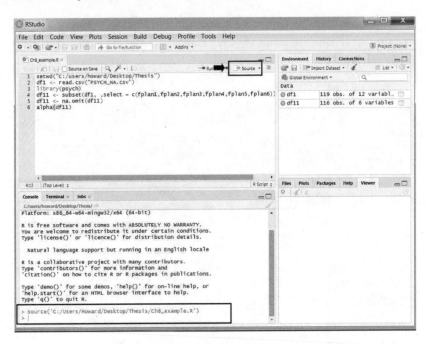

Looking in the Console, seeing the command `source('C:/users/howard/Desktop/Ch8 _ example.R')` indicates that the script runs without errors.

8.5 5. COPY AND PASTE THE SCRIPT INTO A MARKDOWN FILE

Once the script runs correctly, the next step is to paste the script into a markdown file. We create a new markdown file by selecting **File | New File | R Markdown**, providing a title for the markdown file, and choosing the desired output format (**html, pdf,** or **Word doc**). In this chapter, we will use the title, "Conducting analyses using this book: 2nd example," and knit the markdown file into a **Word** document:

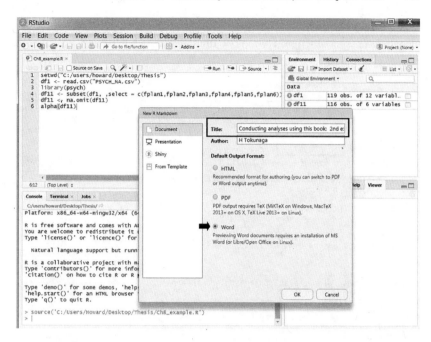

Next, we click on the tab with the name of the script file (**Ch8_example.R**), select all of the commands in the script, and copy the script of commands:

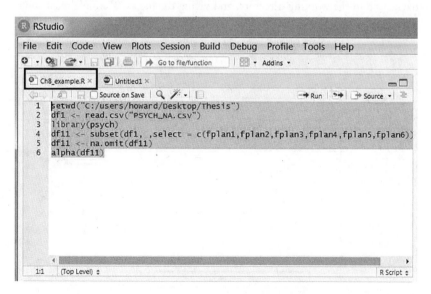

Next, we move back to the markdown file by clicking on the **Untitled** markdown file tab and paste the script between two lines of back tick marks (```):

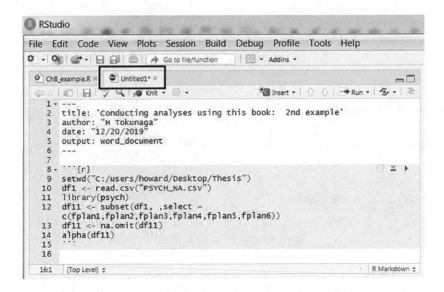

Before moving on, we'll save the markdown file by clicking on the **diskette** icon, navigating to the working directory, and saving the file as "Example markdown file (Chapter 8)."

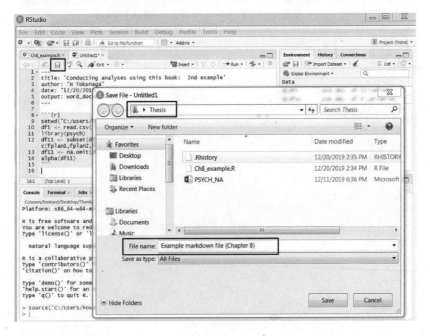

8.6 6. KNIT THE MARKDOWN FILE TO CREATE A MARKDOWN DOCUMENT

The next step is to knit the markdown file by clicking on **Knit** ( ) and selecting the type of file to be created (**html**, **pdf**, **Word**):

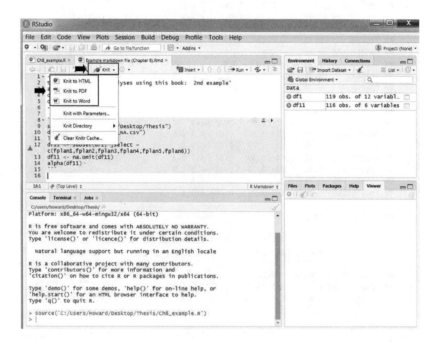

The markdown file for this example (created as a **Word** document) is presented below:

Conducting analyses using this book: 2nd example

H Tokunaga

12/20/2019

```
setwd("C:/users/howard/Desktop/Thesis")
df1 <- read.csv("PSYCH_NA.csv")
library(psych)
df11 <- subset(df1, ,select = c(fplan1,fplan2,fplan3,fplan4,fplan5,fplan6))
df11 <- na.omit(df11)
alpha(df11)
```

```
##
## Reliability analysis
## Call: alpha(x = df11)
##
##    raw_alpha std.alpha G6(smc) average_r S/N   ase mean   sd median_r
##       0.84      0.84    0.86      0.47 5.3 0.023  4.6 0.98     0.47
##
##  lower alpha upper    95% confidence boundaries
## 0.79 0.84 0.88
##
##  Reliability if an item is dropped:
##         raw_alpha std.alpha G6(smc) average_r S/N alpha se var.r med.r
## fplan1      0.80      0.81    0.81      0.46 4.2   0.030 0.027  0.46
## fplan2      0.80      0.79    0.80      0.44 3.9   0.029 0.039  0.42
## fplan3      0.86      0.86    0.87      0.56 6.4   0.020 0.014  0.53
## fplan4      0.79      0.80    0.81      0.45 4.1   0.030 0.025  0.48
## fplan5      0.81      0.81    0.82      0.46 4.3   0.028 0.038  0.49
## fplan6      0.79      0.80    0.83      0.45 4.0   0.031 0.035  0.46
##
##  Item statistics
##           n raw.r std.r r.cor r.drop mean  sd
## fplan1 116  0.79  0.77  0.74   0.67  4.9 1.4
## fplan2 116  0.79  0.82  0.79   0.71  4.5 1.1
## fplan3 116  0.53  0.54  0.39   0.34  4.3 1.3
## fplan4 116  0.80  0.78  0.76   0.69  4.8 1.4
## fplan5 116  0.74  0.76  0.72   0.63  4.3 1.2
## fplan6 116  0.82  0.80  0.75   0.70  4.7 1.5
##
## Non missing response frequency for each item
##         1    2    3    4    5    6 miss
## fplan1 0.05 0.05 0.04 0.15 0.26 0.45    0
## fplan2 0.03 0.03 0.08 0.30 0.45 0.12    0
## fplan3 0.05 0.06 0.10 0.29 0.34 0.16    0
## fplan4 0.03 0.04 0.09 0.18 0.22 0.43    0
## fplan5 0.03 0.07 0.09 0.30 0.42 0.09    0
## fplan6 0.06 0.07 0.06 0.12 0.26 0.43    0
```

Comparing the R markdown document for this analysis with the SPSS output provided at the start of this chapter both provide the same critical information (e.g., Cronbach's alpha (.84), the effects of deleting items on alpha). However, there are also differences between the two, perhaps most notably the inability to modify the formatting of decimal places on calculated statistics in R.

* * * * *

The chapters up to this point in this book have emphasized steps that can be taken to analyze data. Given that these data are contained in data frames created within R, the next chapter provides commands that perform common tasks with data frames and the variables within data frames.

Conducting Statistical Analyses Using This Book: A Brief Example

Step	Command/ Menu	Example
1. Start RStudio		

2. Copy and paste an example script into a script file		`setwd("e:/R output")`
		`df1 <- read.csv("EWB_NA.csv")`
		`library(psych)`
		`df11 <- subset(df1, ,select = c(EWB1,EWB2,EWB3,EWB4,EWB5))`
		`df11 <- na.omit(df11)`
		`alpha(df11)`

3. Modify the example script as needed for the desired statistical analysis		`setwd("C:/users/howard/Desktop/Thesis")`
		`df1 <- read.csv("PSYCH_NA.csv")`
		`library(psych)`
		`df11 <- subset(df1, ,select = c(fplan1,fplan2, fplan3,fplan4,fplan5,fplan6))`
		`df11 <- na.omit(df11)`
		`alpha(df11)`

4. Execute the script to confirm it works properly	**Source** button in Script editor window	
5. Copy and paste the script into a markdown file	**File	New File	R Markdown**	
6. Knit the markdown file to create a markdown document	**Knit (⚙)**	

9

WORKING WITH DATA FRAMES AND VARIABLES IN R

R is a powerful language that can be used to manipulate and analyze data. One of the primary mechanisms for working with data involves importing and modifying files of data to create what are called data frames. In earlier chapters of this book, we used the `read.csv` and `write.csv` functions to import CSV files saved from SPSS data files and Excel worksheets and to create data frames.

The purpose of this chapter is to provide a few commands that perform common tasks with data frames and the variables within data frames. The examples in these commands use a data frame named *df1*.

9.1 WORKING WITH DATA FRAMES

Display the Contents of a Data Frame

```
Command:    dataframe
Example:    df1
```

This command displays the contents (variables and data) in the data frame `df1`.

List the Number of Participants (Rows) in a Data Frame

```
Command:   nrow(dataframe)
Example:   nrow(df1)
```

This command lists the number of participants in the data frame df1.

List the Number of Variables (Columns) in a Data Frame

```
Command:   ncol(dataframe)
Example:   ncol(df1)
```

This command lists the number of variables in the data frame df1.

List the Names of the Variables in a Data Frame

```
Command:   names(dataframe)
Example:   names(df1)
```

This command lists the names of the variables in the data frame df1.

Refer to a Specific Variable in a Data Frame

```
Command:   dataframe$varname
Example:   df1$gender
```

This command refers to the variable gender in the data frame df1.

Remove a Variable From a Data Frame

```
Command:   dataframe$varname <- NULL
Example:   df1$var1 <- NULL
```

This command removes (deletes) the variable var1 from the data frame df1.

Sort the Rows in a Data Frame by a Variable

Command: *newdataframe* <- *dataframe*
            [order(dataframe*$varname*),**]**

Example: df11 <- df1[order(df1$gender),]

This command sorts (rearranges) the data in the data frame df1 by gender.

Create a New Data Frame With No Missing Data

Command: *newdataframe* <- **na.omit(***dataframe***)**

Example: df11 <- na.omit(df1)

This command removes (omits) anyone with any missing data in the data frame df1 (i.e., removes participants with 1+ NAs) and creates a new data frame with no missing data named df11.

Create a New Data Frame With Only Selected Variables From a Data Frame

Command: *newdataframe* <- **subset(***dataframe*, **,select = c (***variable, variable, variable...***))**

Example: df11 <- subset(df1, ,select = c(defp1, defp2, defp3))

This command selects the variables defp1, defp2, and defp3 from the data frame df1 and creates a new data frame with these three variables named df11.

Create a New Data Frame With Only Selected Cases From a Data Frame

Command: *newdataframe* <- **subset(***dataframe, variable* **==** **value)**

Example: df11 <- subset(df1, gender == 1)

This command selects those whose gender is equal to 1 in the data frame df1 and creates a new data frame with the selected cases named df11.

Save a Data Frame as a CSV File

Command: **write.csv(***newdataframe***, "***filename***.csv", row.
          names=FALSE)**

Example: write.csv(df11, "NEWDEFP.csv", row.
          names=FALSE)

This command saves the contents of the data frame df11 into a CSV file named NEWDEFP in the working directory. The argument row.names=FALSE is included to prevent R from adding a new first variable to the CSV file.

9.2 WORKING WITH VARIABLES

Convert Numeric Values of a Variable to String (Alphanumeric) Values

Command: *dataframe*$*varname* **<- factor
          (***dataframe***$***varname***,levels = c(***lowest
          value***,***highest value***),labels = c("***label***",
          "***label***"))**

Example: df1$gender <- factor(df1$gender,levels =
          c(1,2),labels c("Male", "Female"))

This command converts the numeric labels of the values of gender (1 and 2) to string labels ("Male" and "Female").

Convert a Numeric Variable into a String Variable (Factor)

Command: *dataframe*$*factor* **<- factor(***dataframe***$***numvar***,
          labels = c("***label***", "***label***"))**

Example: df1$group.f <- factor(df1$group, labels = c
          ("Yes", "No"))

This command creates the string variable group.f ("Yes", "No") from the numeric variable group that consists of the numeric values 1 and 2.

Note: A number of other ways variables may be modified or combined are provided in Appendix A (Data Transformations) of this book.

CONDUCTING STATISTICAL ANALYSES USING SPSS SYNTAX

The primary goal of this book is to illustrate how statistical analyses may be conducted using R and RStudio. As you've seen, we've tried to do this by showing how the same analysis may first be conducted in SPSS. In order to facilitate the comparison between SPSS and R, the purpose of this chapter is to briefly illustrate how statistical analyses may be conducted in SPSS using syntax commands.

Note: This book is based on Windows 64-bit version 25 of SPSS.

* * * * *

The example in this chapter will be based on the following research situation: You've collected data from 129 people (N = 129) on 11 variables measured on a 1–7 scale named *ABCD1* to *ABCD11* and saved the data in an SPSS data file named ABCD.sav. Part of the ABCD.sav file is provided below:

ABCD.sav [DataSet1] - IBM SPSS Statistics Data Editor

File Edit View Data Transform Analyze Graphs Utilities Extensions Window Help

	ABCD1	ABCD2	ABCD3	ABCD4	ABCD5	ABCD6	ABCD7	ABCD8	ABCD9	ABCD10	ABCD11
1	4	7	1	4	2	1	4	4	6	7	5
2	3	4	5	5	3	2	5	3	5	6	5
3	5	7	5	2	5	2	5	2	2	6	6
4	5	6	5	3	5	5	2	6	3	6	3
5	6	7	6	4	5	3	6	3	1	6	5
6	5	7	5	1	5	5	5	1	2	7	5
7	6	4	2	4	5	2	2	5	3	4	3
8	4	7	5	2	6	2	2	1	4	7	6

Imagine you wish to create a frequency distribution table for one variable: *ABCD1*. In this chapter, we'll first show how this analysis may be conducted using SPSS menus before illustrating how it may be conducted using SPSS syntax commands.

10.1 CONDUCTING ANALYSES IN SPSS USING MENU CHOICES

For a simple situation such as this, you could conduct this analysis using the SPSS menus. For this example, we can start the creation of frequency distribution tables by selecting **Analyze | Descriptive statistics | Frequencies:**

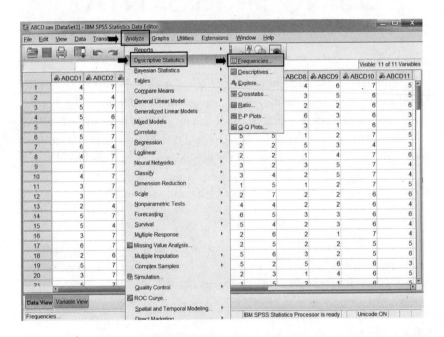

As with many of the statistical procedures in SPSS, a window now opens that shows all of the variables in the file. For this example, we click on the desired variable (ABCD1) and select it for analysis using the right arrow (→):

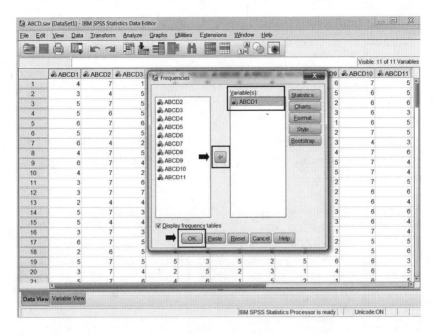

If so desired, we could customize this analysis using the other buttons in this window (**Statistics**, **Charts**, etc.). Regardless, the next step is to click **OK**, which generates an output file (which has a .spv extension):

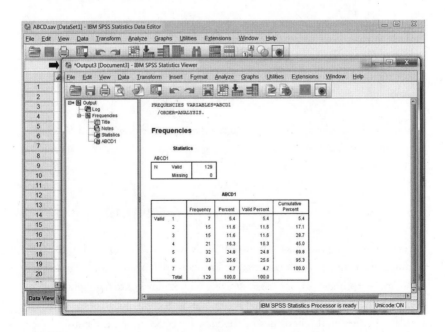

Looking at this output file, you'll see the following information has been provided above the results of the analysis:

FREQUENCIES VARIABLES=ABCD1
/ORDER=ANALYSIS.

These two lines represent the SPSS syntax command used to generate the output. SPSS syntax commands may be pasted into output files by clicking the **Edit** menu, selecting **Options**, clicking on the **Viewer** tab (**Edit | Options | Viewer**), and selecting "Display commands in the log."

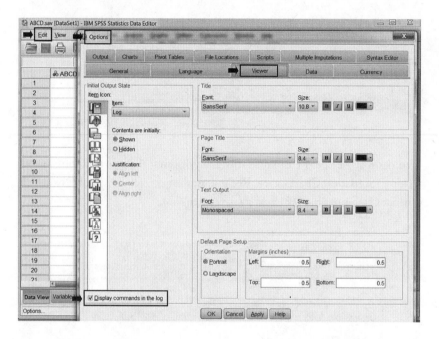

Looking at the Options window, you'll see that many settings within SPSS may be modified, such as font types and sizes, page margins, and page orientation.

10.2 CONDUCTING ANALYSES IN SPSS USING SYNTAX COMMANDS

In addition to using the menus, statistical analyses may be conducted in SPSS by writing and executing syntax commands. This book will utilize syntax rather than menus for two primary reasons. First, showing syntax allows us to highlight similarities and differences between SPSS and R commands. Second, not all of the statistical analyses discussed in this book can be conducted in SPSS using the menus.

In order to write and execute SPSS syntax commands, a syntax file (with the extension .sps) must be created. To open a new syntax file, click on the **File** menu, select **New**, and then select **Syntax**. This is illustrated below:

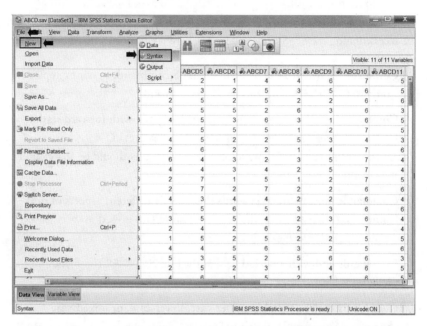

Starting a new syntax file opens a blank window named "Syntax1," which is an unsaved syntax file. Within this file, we'll type the commands needed to create a frequency distribution table for the variable ABCD1:

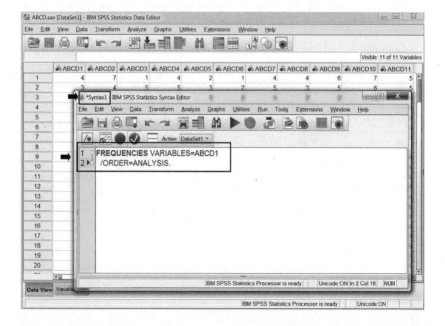

Writing SPSS Syntax Commands: Some Rules and Guidelines

Similar to R, there are rules and guidelines that need to be followed in writing SPSS syntax commands (below, we discuss how information about SPSS commands may be accessed using the SPSS Syntax Reference manual included with SPSS):

Commands start with the name of an SPSS command. In our example, the word FREQUENCIES represents an SPSS command.

Commands may include subcommands, indicated with forward slashes (/). The example in this chapter includes the subcommand /ORDER=ANALYSIS, which indicates that the variables should be analyzed in the order they were selected using the menus.

Commands may include keywords that specify different aspects of the command. In our example, the keyword VARIABLES is used to specify the variables included in the statistical analysis.

Commands end with a period (.). For the FREQUENCIES command, the period (.) is located after the word ANALYSIS.

Commands may be typed in upper-case, lower-case, or mixed-case characters. For example, the word "ABCD1" could have been typed as "abcd1" or "Abcd1."

Syntax files may include comments that start with an asterisk (*). For example, we could have included a comment in our syntax file, such as * Create a frequency distribution table for ABCD1.

Commands and comments may extend across lines; however, blank lines are not allowed within commands. In our example, the FREQUENCIES command consists of two lines, which were separated using the <Enter> key. However, we could not have included a blank line between the FREQUENCIES and /ORDER=ANALYSIS lines, as doing so would generate an error message, such as *"The first word in the line is not recognized as an SPSS Statistics command."*

SPSS syntax commands are color-coded. Different aspects of commands are indicated using different colors: command names (e.g., FREQUENCIES) are dark blue, subcommand names (e.g., /ORDER) are green, keywords (e.g., VARIABLES and ANALYSIS) are maroon, variable names are black, and comments are gray. Furthermore, any errors within commands are red or orange (e.g., if we had included a blank line between the FREQUENCIES and /ORDER=ANALYSIS lines, the word FREQUENCIES would be in red rather than blue).

Getting Information About SPSS Syntax Commands: The Syntax Reference Guide

SPSS commands have a large number of options and formatting requirements. To learn more about syntax commands, users can access the SPSS Syntax Reference guide within SPSS. To open the Syntax Reference guide, click on the **Help** menu, followed by **Command Syntax Reference**:

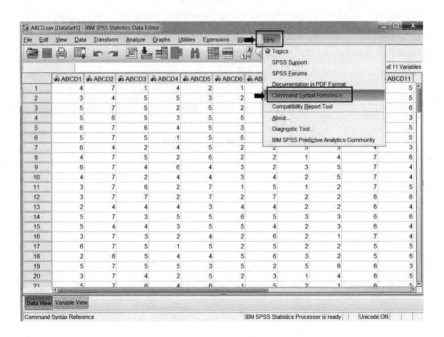

Next, the Syntax Reference guide, an extremely large pdf file, will open in a new window:

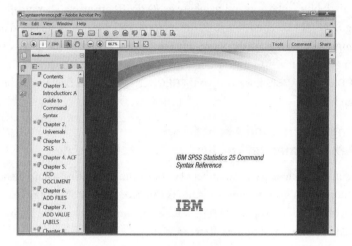

The column on the left side of this window lists all of the SPSS syntax commands. If we wanted assistance with the example in this chapter, we could scroll down the list of commands until we reach FREQUENCIES. We've provided part of the documentation for this command below; as you can see, the basic format for the command is provided, along with a description of any keywords and subcommands as well as examples of how the command may be written for different situations.

Chapter 107. FREQUENCIES

FREQUENCIES is available in Statistics Base Edition.

```
FREQUENCIES VARIABLES=varlist [varlist...]

[/FORMAT= [{NOTABLE }] [{AVALUE**}]
          {LIMIT(n)}   {DVALUE }
                       {AFREQ  }
                       {DFREQ  }

[/MISSING=INCLUDE]

[/BARCHART=[MINIMUM(n)] [MAXIMUM(n)] [{FREQ(n)   }]]
                                     {PERCENT(n)}

[/PIECHART=[MINIMUM(n)] [MAXIMUM(n)] [{FREQ   }] [{MISSING }]]
                                     {PERCENT}   {NOMISSING}

[/HISTOGRAM=[MINIMUM(n)] [MAXIMUM(n)] [{FREQ(n)  }] [{NONORMAL}] ]
                                                    {NORMAL }

[/GROUPED=varlist [{(width)       }]]
                  {(boundary list)}

[/NTILES=n]

[/PERCENTILES=value list]

[/STATISTICS=[DEFAULT] [MEAN] [STDDEV] [MINIMUM] [MAXIMUM]
             [SEMEAN] [VARIANCE] [SKEWNESS] [SESKEW] [RANGE]
             [MODE] [KURTOSIS] [SEKURT] [MEDIAN] [SUM] [ALL]
             [NONE]]

[/ORDER=[{ANALYSIS}] [{VARIABLE}]
```

** Default if subcommand is omitted or specified without keyword.

As you can imagine, the Syntax reference guide (which is over 2000 pages in length) is an extremely useful resource for writing syntax commands.

Executing SPSS Syntax Commands

SPSS syntax commands and comments may be executed by clicking on the **Run** menu located in the syntax file window:

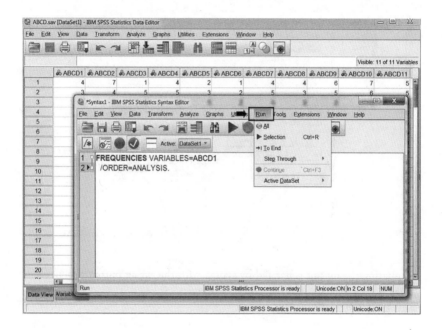

Within the **Run** menu, there are several choices regarding how commands may be executed. To execute all of the commands in the file, select **All**. To execute a single command, place the cursor anywhere in the desired command and click **Selection**. To execute multiple commands within the larger syntax file, place the cursor at the start of the first desired command, drag over the desired commands, and click **Selection**. Finally, to execute the commands starting from the current command to the final command in the file, place the cursor anywhere in the current command and click **To End**.

For the example in this chapter, we'll select **Run | All**; below is the output generated by executing the FREQUENCIES syntax command:

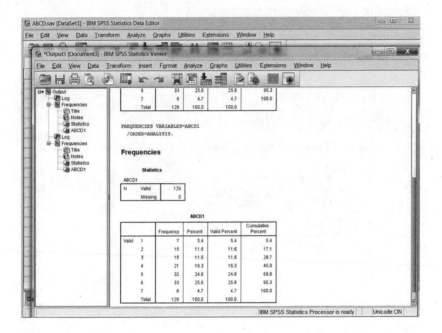

Comparing the output generated by syntax with the earlier output generated by menu choices, you see the two outputs are identical.

10.3 EDITING SPSS OUTPUT FILES

Once they've been created, SPSS output files may be edited and modified in a number of ways. In this section, we'll illustrate one method of selecting what parts of an output file to print and one method of setting the number of decimal places for calculated statistics.

Selecting Aspects of Output Files to be Printed

Even when an output file contains multiple analyses, it's possible to print only a subset of these analyses. For example, in this chapter we've created a frequency distribution table for the variable ABCD1 twice: once with menus and once with syntax. What if you only wanted to print the second output, the one from the syntax commands?

For this example, we'll "close" the output for the analysis we don't want to print. To do this, we'll work within the navigation window located to the left of the output. Looking at the above navigation window, you'll see there are two identical sets of "Logs" (which contain the syntax commands that were executed) and "Frequencies" (which contain the frequency distribution table for ABCD1). If we double-click on the "**Log**" and "**Frequencies**" for the first analysis (the one conducted using menus), they will no longer be displayed in the output file. This is demonstrated below:

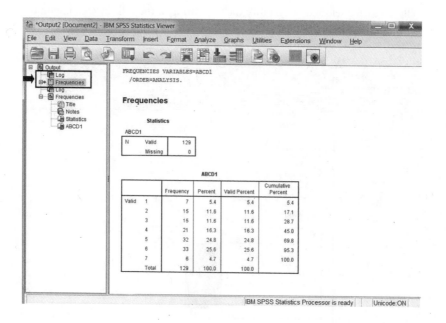

If you compare the above output file with the earlier one, you see that the frequency distribution table is only displayed once.

In addition to "closing" parts of output files, the navigation window can also be used to delete output or move output from one part of the output file to another.

Setting the Number of Decimal Places in Output Files

In addition to determining which parts of an output file to print, it's possible to change the formatting of the output. One common formatting change involves setting the number of decimal places for calculated statistics. For example, imagine that, in looking at the frequency distribution table for ABCD1, you want the percentage of the sample with each value of ABCD1 to be printed with two decimal places rather than one decimal place.

To edit an output, the first step is to select the output to be modified (in this example, the frequency distribution table for ABCD1) by double-clicking on it; this results in a dashed border (-----) appearing around the selected output. Next, we select the cells of the output to be modified (in this case, the "Valid Percent" of the values 1–7 of ABCD1) by clicking on the top cell and dragging to the other cells. The selected cells are dark in color (see the screen below). Once the desired cells have been selected, we modify the formatting of the cells by clicking on the **Format** menu, followed by **Cell Properties**:

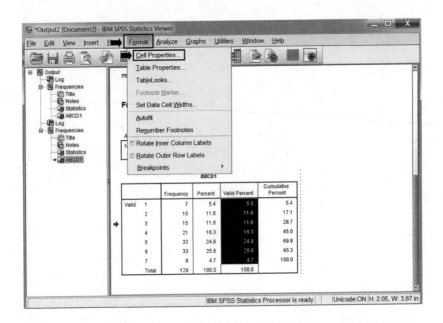

Within the **Cell Properties** window, we can change the number of decimal places by clicking on the **Format Value** tab and changing the **Decimals** from 1 to 2. This is illustrated below:

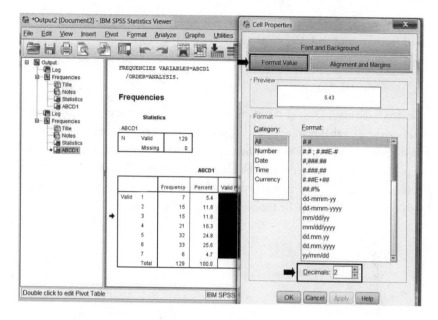

After clicking **OK**, the modified cells are displayed in the output:

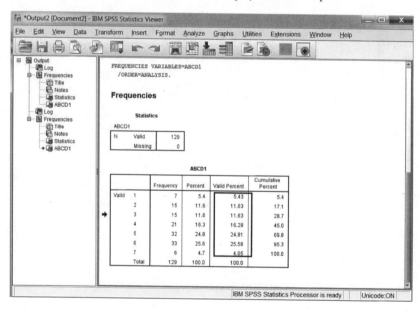

Looking at the above **Cell Properties** window, you'll see two other tabs: **Font and Background** and **Alignment and Margins**. Clicking on these tabs facilitates changes in other aspects of the cells of SPSS output tables.

* * * * *

Although the main focus of this book is on how to conduct statistical analyses, it is often the case that before these analyses may be conducted, the variables to be used in the analysis must be modified or transformed. For example, a researcher may wish to combine a set of variables into a single score. The next section of this book (Appendix A: Data Transformations) illustrates how a variety of common data transformations may be conducted using SPSS and R.

APPENDIX A:
DATA TRANSFORMATIONS

Researchers often modify and transform data they've collected and entered into a data file. For example, variables in a data set are combined to create a scale score, the number of groups for a variable is reduced to a smaller number of groups, or the many values of a continuous variable are collapsed into a small number of different categories.

The purpose of this appendix is to illustrate how a number of common data transformations may be performed using R. In order to build off users' SPSS knowledge and experience, we will first show how these transformations may be accomplished within SPSS using commands such as RECODE, COMPUTE, COUNT, and IF before showing how these transformations may be performed using R.

The data transformations in this appendix will be based on a hypothetical research situation. A researcher has collected data from 11 people on the 9 variables below:

Variable	Column	Valid values	Missing value
ID	1	1–11	–
ITEM1 to ITEM4	2–5	1 = A 2 = B 3 = C 4 = D 5 = E	9
GROUP	6	1 = White 2 = Blue 3 = Red 4 = Green 5 = Pink	9
INCOME	7	0–999999	–99999
SMOKE	8	1 = Yes 2 = No	9
DRINK	9	1 = Yes 2 = No	9

An SPSS syntax file that could be used to define the above variables and enter data for the sample of 11 participants on these variables is presented on the next page. The SPSS data file created by running the commands in the syntax file is also provided.

Looking at the SPSS data file, you see that several of the variables have missing data as assigned in the MISSING VALUES command in the SPSS syntax file. For example, ID #10 has a missing value of 9 for the variable ITEM4, and ID #9 has missing values of 9 for SMOKE and DRINK. Furthermore, some of the missing values of 9 and -99999 have been changed into the SPSS missing value of a period (.). For example, ID #2 has a system missing value for ITEM3. The numeric missing values have been changed into periods, which has been done to later illustrate how different types of missing data may be converted for use in R.

SPSS syntax file

```
DATA LIST   FREE
    /ID   ITEM1 to ITEM4   GROUP   INCOME   SMOKE   DRINK.
FORMATS ID (F3.0)   ITEM1 to ITEM4 (F1.0)   GROUP (F1.0)   INCOME (F6.0)
                SMOKE DRINK (F1.0).
VARIABLE WIDTH    ID to DRINK (5).
MISSING VALUES    ITEM1 to ITEM4 (9)   GROUP (9)   INCOME
                (-99999)   SMOKE DRINK (9).
VARIABLE LABELS   INCOME "Child's annual income"
                /SMOKE "Do you smoke?"
                /DRINK "Do you drink?".
VALUE LABELS   ITEM1 to ITEM4   1 "A"   2 "B"   3 "C"   4 "D"   5 "E"
                /GROUP   1 "White"   2 "Blue"   3 "Red"
                4 "Green"   5 "Pink"
                /SMOKE DRINK   1 "Yes"   2 "No".

BEGIN DATA.
   1   2   3   5   1   1    45,000   1   1
   2   3   4   9   1   1    27,500   1   2
   3   1   5   4   2   1   100,000   2   1
   4   5   4   1   2   1    33,000   2   2
   5   3   5   9   3   1    56,000   1   2
   6   2   4   3   3   2    18,000   2   9
   7   4   1   4   4   2    60,000   9   1
   8   9   5   9   4   3   -99,999   9   1
   9   3   4   3   5   4    48,000   9   9
  10   3   5   1   9   5    35,500   1   1
  11   4   9   9   9   9    50,000   9   9
END DATA.

EXECUTE.
```

SPSS data file

In order to perform the data transformations for this data using R, several of the steps discussed earlier in this book needed to be conducted on the data file:

First, the SPSS data file was saved in a CSV file named DATATRANS. CSV in the working directory (e:/R output); the **Write variable names to file** box was checked so that the variable names were included in the top row of the CSV file:

File | Save As | Comma delimited (*.csv) | *DATATRANS.CSV* | Save

Second, RStudio was started and the commands below were written and executed in the Console:

a. Define the working directory.

```
setwd("e:/R output")
```

b. Import CSV file to create a data frame.

```
df1 = read.csv("DATATRANS.csv")
```

c. Change any missing data in data frame to NA.

```
# Change periods (.) to NA
df1 [df1 == "."] <- NA
# Change 9 to NA for ITEM1 to ITEM4,
GROUP (columns 2-6)
df1[, 2:6][ df1[, 2:6] == 9] <- NA
# Change 9 to NA for SMOKE, DRINK (columns 8-9)
df1[, 8:9][ df1[, 8:9] == 9] <- NA
```

d. Save data frame with NAs as CSV file in the working directory.

```
write.csv(df1, "DATATRANS_NA.csv",row.names=FALSE)
```

e. Read the modified CSV file to create a data frame.

```
read.csv("DATATRANS_NA.csv")
```

To verify that the modified data frame is correct, the dataframe command (in this situation, df1) was executed in order to view the contents of the data frame. The results of executing these commands are provided below.

```
> setwd("e:/R output")
> df1 = read.csv("DATATRANS.csv")
>
> # change missing (9) for variables in columns 2-6 to NA
> df1[, 2:6][ df1[, 2:6] == 9] <- NA
> # change missing (.) for variables in columns 2-9 to NA
> df1[, 2:9][ df1[, 2:9] == "."] <- NA
> # change missing (9) for variables in columns 8-9 to NA
> df1[, 8:9][ df1[, 8:9] == 9] <- NA
>
> write.csv(df1, "DATATRANS_NA.csv")
>
> df1
    ï..ID ITEM1 ITEM2 ITEM3 ITEM4 GROUP INCOME SMOKE DRINK
1      1     2     3     5     1     1  45000     1     1
2      2     3     4    NA     1     1  27500     1     2
3      3     1     5     4     2     1 100000     2     1
4      4     5     4     1     2     1  33000     2     2
5      5     3     5    NA     3     1  56000     1     2
6      6     2     4     3     3     2  18000     2    NA
7      7     4     1     4     4     2  60000    NA     1
8      8    NA     5    NA     4     3     NA    NA     1
9      9     3     4     3     5     4  48000    NA    NA
10    10     3     5     1    NA     5  35500     1     1
11    11     4    NA    NA    NA    NA  50000    NA    NA
>
```

Comparing the data frame with the SPSS data file, you see that the missing values have been changed to NAs. Now that the modified data frame has been created and saved, the data transformations conducted on the following pages will be performed on the imported file DATATRANS_NA.CSV rather than the original DATATRANS.CSV file.

REVERSE SCORE A VARIABLE (RECODE)

EXAMPLE: Reverse score ITEM4 into a new variable NITEM4

SPSS: The RECODE command

Command:

```
RECODE variable (old-value = new-value) (old-value = new-value)... INTO
newvariable.
```

Example:

```
RECODE        ITEM4 (1 = 5) (2 = 4) (3 = 3) (4 = 2) (5 = 1) INTO NITEM4.
FORMATS       NITEM4 (F1.0).
EXECUTE.
```

R: The recode function

Command:

```
library(car)
dataframe$newvar<-recode(dataframe$var,"old-value=
new-value; old-value=new-value;...")
```

Example:

```
library(car)
df1$NITEM4 <- recode(df1$ITEM4,"1 = 5; 2 = 4; 3 = 3;
4 = 2; 5 = 1")
```

```
> setwd("e:/R output")
> df1 = read.csv("DATATRANS_NA.csv")
>
> library("car")
> df1$NITEM4 <- recode(df1$ITEM4,"1 = 5; 2 = 4; 3 = 3; 4 = 2; 5 = 1")
>
> df1
   ID ITEM1 ITEM2 ITEM3 ITEM4 GROUP INCOME SMOKE DRINK NITEM4
1   1     2     3     5     1     1  45000     1     1      5
2   2     3     4    NA     1     1  27500     1     2      5
3   3     1     5     4     2     1 100000     2     1      4
4   4     5     4     1     2     1  33000     2     2      4
5   5     3     5    NA     3     1  55000     2     2      3
6   6     2     4     3     3     2              NA     3
7   7     4     1     4     4     2  60000    NA     1      2
8   8    NA     5    NA     4     3     NA    NA     1      2
9   9     3     4     3     5     4  48000    NA    NA      1
10 10     3     5     1    NA     5  35500     1     1     NA
11 11     4    NA    NA    NA    NA  50000    NA    NA     NA
>
```

REDUCE THE NUMBER OF GROUPS IN A CATEGORICAL VARIABLE (RECODE)

EXAMPLE: Reduce the number of levels of GROUP from 5 levels to 2

SPSS: The RECODE command

Command:

```
RECODE variable (old-value = new-value) (old-value = new-value) ... INTO
newvariable.
```

Example:

```
RECODE      GROUP (1 = 1) (2 = 2) (3 = 2) (4 = 2) (5 = 2) INTO NGROUP.
FORMATS     NGROUP (F1.0).
EXECUTE.
```

R: The `recode` function

Command:

```
library(car)
dataframe$newvar <-recode(dataframe$var,"old-value = new-
value; old-value = new-value; ...")
```

Example:

```
library(car)
df1$NGROUP <- recode(df1$GROUP,"1 = 1; 2 = 2;
3 = 2; 4 = 2; 5 = 2")
```

```
> setwd("e:/R output")
> df1 = read.csv("DATATRANS_NA.csv")
>
> library("car")
> df1$NGROUP <- recode(df1$GROUP,"1 = 1; 2 = 2; 3 = 2; 4 = 2; 5 = 2")
>
> df1
   ID ITEM1 ITEM2 ITEM3 ITEM4 GROUP INCOME SMOKE DRINK NGROUP
1   1     2     3     5     1     1  45000     1     1      1
2   2     3     4    NA     1     1  27500     1     2      1
3   3     1     5     4     2     1 100000     2     1      1
4   4     5     4     1     2     1  33000     2     2      1
5   5     3     5    NA     3     1  5          2     1      1
6   6     2     4     3     3     2  18000     2    NA      2
7   7     4     1     4     4     2  60000    NA     1      2
8   8    NA     5    NA     4     3     NA    NA     1      2
9   9     3     4     3     5     4  48000    NA    NA      2
10 10     3     5     1    NA     5  35500     1     1      2
11 11     4    NA    NA    NA    NA  50000    NA    NA     NA
>
```

CREATE A CATEGORICAL VARIABLE FROM A CONTINUOUS VARIABLE (RECODE)

EXAMPLE: Group the values of INCOME into a new variable NINCOME (two groups)

SPSS: The RECODE command

Command:

> **RECODE *variable (range = new-value) (range = new-value) ...* INTO *newvariable.***

Example:

```
RECODE          INCOME (0 thru 49999 = 1) (50000 thru Hi = 2) INTO
                NINCOME.
FORMATS         NINCOME (F1.0).
VALUE LABELS    NINCOME 1 "< $50,000" 2 "$50,000+".
EXECUTE.
```

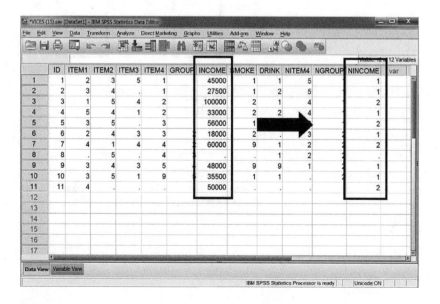

R: The `recode` function (Create a <u>numerical</u> categorical variable from a continuous variable)

Command:

```
library(car)
dataframe$newvar <- recode(dataframe$var,
"min:max = new-value; min:max = new-value; ...")
```

Example:

```
library(car)
df1$NGROUP <- recode(df1$INCOME,"lo:49999 = 1;
50000:hi = 2")
```

```
> setwd("e:/R output")
> df1 = read.csv("DATATRANS_NA.csv")
>
> library("car")
> df1$NINCOME <- recode(df1$INCOME,"lo:49999 = 1;  50000:hi = 2")
>
> df1
    ID ITEM1 ITEM2 ITEM3 ITEM4 GROUP INCOME SMOKE DRINK NINCOME
1   1      2     3     5     1         45000     1     1       1
2   2      3     4    NA     1         27500     1     2       1
3   3      1     5     4     2        100000     2     1       2
4   4      5     4     1     2         33000     2     2       1
5   5      3     5    NA     3         56000           2       2
6   6      2     4     3     3         18000          NA       1
7   7      4     1     4     4         60000    NA     1       2
8   8     NA     5    NA     4            NA    NA     1      NA
9   9      3     4     3     5         48000    NA    NA       1
10 10      3     5     1    NA         35500     1     1       1
11 11      4    NA    NA    NA    NA    50000    NA    NA       2
>
```

R: The `recode` function (Create a <u>string</u> categorical variable from a continuous variable)

Command:

```
library(car)
dataframe$groupingvar <- cut(dataframe$contvar,breaks=c
(min, cutpoint, max), labels=c("Label for Group1","Label
for Group2"))
```

Example:

```
library(car)
df1$NINCOME <- cut(df1$INCOME,breaks=c(0, 49999,
Inf),labels=c("< $50,000"," $50,000+"))
```

```
> setwd("e:/R output")
> df1 = read.csv("DATATRANS_NA.csv")
>
> df1$NINCOME <- cut(df1$INCOME,breaks=c(0, 49999, Inf),labels=c("< $50,000"," $50,000+"))
>
> df1
   ID ITEM1 ITEM2 ITEM3 ITEM4 GROUP INCOME SMOKE DRINK  NINCOME
1   1     2     3     5     1         45000     1       < $50,000
2   2     3     4    NA     1         27500     1       < $50,000
3   3     1     5     4     2        100000     2        $50,000+
4   4     5     4     1     2         33000     2       < $50,000
5   5     3     5    NA     3         56000              $50,000+
6   6     2     4     3     3         18000     2    NA < $50,000
7   7     4     1'    4     4         60000    NA        $50,000+
8   8    NA     5    NA     4            NA    NA          <NA>
9   9     3     4     3     5         48000    NA    NA < $50,000
10 10     3     5     1    NA         35500     1       < $50,000
11 11     4    NA    NA    NA    NA   50000    NA    NA  $50,000+
>
```

CREATE A VARIABLE FROM OTHER VARIABLES (COMPUTE)

EXAMPLE: Create the variable MITEM that is the mean of ITEM1 to ITEM4

SPSS: The COMPUTE command

Command:

```
COMPUTE    newvariable = expression.
```

Example:

```
COMPUTE ITEM = MEAN (ITEM1, ITEM2, ITEM3, ITEM4).
FORMATS MITEM (F3.2).
EXECUTE.
```

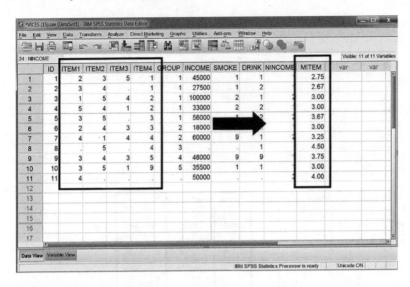

R: The `subset` and `rowMeans` functions

Command:

```
setofvariables <- subset(dataframe,select=c(var, var,
var,…) )
dataframe$newvar <- rowMeans(setofvariables, na.rm=TRUE )
```

Example:

```
items <- subset(df1,select=c(ITEM1,ITEM2,ITEM3,ITEM4) )
df1$MITEM <- rowMeans(items, na.rm=TRUE )
```

```
> setwd("e:/R output")
> df1 = read.csv("DATATRANS_NA.csv")
>
> items <- subset(df1,select=c(ITEM1,ITEM2,ITEM3,ITEM4) )
> df1$MITEM <- rowMeans(items, na.rm=TRUE )
>
> df1
    ID ITEM1 ITEM2 ITEM3 ITEM4 GROUP INCOME SMOKE DRINK    MITEM
1    1     2     3     5     1     1  45000     1          2.750000
2    2     3     4    NA     1     1  27500     1          2.666667
3    3     1     5     4     2     1 100000     2          3.000000
4    4     5     4     1     2     1  33000     2          3.000000
5    5     3     5    NA     3                 1          3.666667
6    6     2     4     3     3                 2    NA     3.000000
7    7     4     1     4     4     2  60000    NA          3.250000
8    8    NA     5    NA     4     3     NA    NA          4.500000
9    9     3     4     3     5     4  48000    NA    NA    3.750000
10  10     3     5     1    NA     5  35500     1          3.000000
11  11     4    NA    NA    NA    NA  50000    NA    NA    4.000000
>
```

CREATE A VARIABLE
FROM OTHER VARIABLES
(MINIMUM NUMBER OF
VALID VALUES) (COMPUTE)

EXAMPLE: Create the variable MITEM that is the mean of ITEM1 to ITEM4 (at least three valid values)

SPSS: The COMPUTE command

Command:

> **COMPUTE**   *newvariable* = **MEAN.#** *(variables)*

Example:

```
COMPUTE     MITEM2 = MEAN.3 (ITEM1, ITEM2, ITEM3, ITEM4).
FORMATS     MITEM2 (F3.2).
EXECUTE.
```

R: The `apply`, `subset`, `ifelse` and `rowMeans` functions

Command:

```
# count number of valid responses
dataframe$numvalid <- apply(dataframe[startcol:endcol],
1, function(x) sum(!is.na(x)))
# calculate score for those w/min # valid values,
otherwise assign NA
setofvariables <- subset(dataframe,select=c(var, var,
var,…) )
dataframe$newvar <- ifelse(dataframe$numvalid >= #,
dataframe$newvar <- rowMeans(setofvariables,
na.rm=TRUE),NA)
```

Example:

```
# count number of valid responses
df1$item.nvalid <- apply(df1[2:5], 1, function(x) sum(!is.
na(x)))
# calculate MITEM2 for those with 3+ valid values,
otherwise assign NA
items <- subset(df1,select=c(ITEM1,ITEM2,ITEM3,ITEM4) )
df1$MITEM2 <- ifelse(df1$item.nvalid >= 3,df1$MITEM2
<- rowMeans(items, na.rm=TRUE),NA)
```

```
> setwd("e:/R output")
> df1 = read.csv("DATATRANS_NA.csv")
>
> #  count the number of valid responses
> df1$item.nvalid <- apply(df1[2:5], 1, function(x) sum(!is.na(x)))
> # calculate MITEM2 for those with 3+ valid values, otherwise assign NA
> items <- subset(df1,select=c(ITEM1,ITEM2,ITEM3,ITEM4) )
> df1$MITEM2  <- ifelse(df1$item.nvalid >= 3, df1$MITEM2 <- rowMeans(items, na.rm=TRUE ), NA)
> #  remove # valid variable from data frame
> df1$item.nvalid <- NULL
>
> df1
```

	ID	ITEM1	ITEM2	ITEM3	ITEM4	GROUP	INCOME	SMOKE	DRINK	MITEM2
1	1	2	3	5	1	1	45000	1		2.750000
2	2	3	4	NA	1	1	27500	1		2.666667
3	3	1	5	4	2	1	100000	2		3.000000
4	4	5	4	1	2	1	33000	2		3.000000
5	5	3	5	NA	3	1				3.666667
6	6	2	4	3	3	2			NA	3.000000
7	7	4	1	4	4	2	60000	NA		3.250000
8	8	NA	5	NA	4	3	NA	NA		NA
9	9	3	4	3	5	4	48000	NA	NA	3.750000
10	10	3	5	1	NA	5	35500	1		3.000000
11	11	4	NA	NA	NA	NA	50000	NA		NA

```
>
```

CREATE A VARIABLE FROM OCCURRENCES OF VALUES OF OTHER VARIABLES (COUNT)

EXAMPLE: Count the number of vices (i.e., SMOKE and DRINK = 1 (yes))

SPSS: The COUNT command

Command:

```
COUNT    newvariable = variables (value).
```

Example:

```
COUNT                NVICES = SMOKE DRINK (1).
FORMATS              NVICES (F1.0).
VARIABLE LABELS      NVICES "Number of vices (0-2)".
EXECUTE.
```

R: The `apply` function

Command:

```
dataframe$newvar <- apply(dataframe[startcol:endcol],
1, function(x) length(which(x==value)))
```

Example:

```
df1$NVICES <- apply(df1[8:9], 1, function(x) length(which
(x==1)))
```

```
> setwd("e:/R output")
> df1 = read.csv("DATATRANS_NA.csv")
>
> df1$NVICES <- apply(df1[8:9], 1, function(x) length(which(x==1)))
>
> df1
   ID ITEM1 ITEM2 ITEM3 ITEM4 GROUP INCOME SMOKE DRINK NVICES
1   1     2     3     5     1     1  45000     1     1      2
2   2     3     4    NA     1     1  27500     1     2      1
3   3     1     5     4     2     1 100000     2     1      1
4   4     5     4     1     2     1  33000     2     2      0
5   5     3     5    NA     3     1  56000     1     2      1
6   6     2     4     3     3     2  18000     2    NA      0
7   7     4     1     4     4     2  60000    NA     1      1
8   8    NA     5    NA     4     3     NA    NA     1      1
9   9     3     4     3     5     4  48000    NA    NA      0
10 10     3     5     1    NA     5  35500     1     1      2
11 11     4    NA    NA    NA    NA  50000    NA    NA      0
>
```

PERFORM DATA TRANSFORMATIONS WHEN CONDITIONS ARE MET (IF)

EXAMPLE: Create groups based on combinations of SMOKE and DRINK (Yes, No)

SPSS: The IF command

Command:

IF (*something is true*) target-variable = *expression or numeric value*.

Example:

```
IF (SMOKE eq 1 and DRINK eq 1) SDCOMB = 1.
IF (SMOKE eq 1 and DRINK eq 2) SDCOMB = 2.
IF (SMOKE eq 2 and DRINK eq 1) SDCOMB = 2.
IF (SMOKE eq 2 and DRINK eq 2) SDCOMB = 3.
FORMATS SDCOMB (F1.0).
VALUE LABELS SDCOMB    1 "Both smoke and drink" 2 "Either smoke or drink"
                       3 "Neither smoke nor drink".
EXECUTE.
```

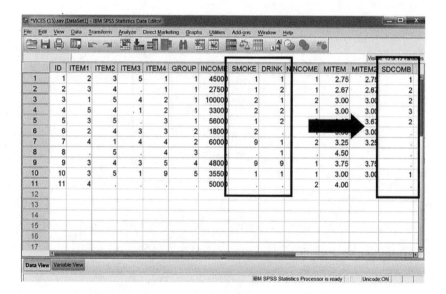

R: The `ifelse` function

Command:

```
dataframe$newvar <- ifelse((expression1),
outcome_if_expression1_true, ifelse(expression2),
outcome_if_expression2_true, ... ,
outcome_if_all_expressions_false)
```

Example:

```
df1$SDCOMB <- ifelse((df1$SMOKE == 1) & (df1$DRINK == 1),
df1$SDCOMB <- 1, ifelse((df1$SMOKE == 1) & (df1$DRINK == 2),
df1$SDCOMB <- 2, ifelse((df1$SMOKE == 2) & (df1$DRINK == 1),
df1$SDCOMB <- 2, ifelse((df1$SMOKE == 2) & (df1$DRINK == 2),
df1$SDCOMB <- 3, NA))))
```

```
> setwd("e:/R output")
> df1 = read.csv("DATATRANS_NA.csv")
>
> df1$SDCOMB <- ifelse((df1$SMOKE == 1) & (df1$DRINK == 1), df1$SDCOMB <- 1, ifelse((d
f1$SMOKE == 1) & (df1$DRINK == 2), df1$SDCOMB <- 2, ifelse((df1$SMOKE == 2) & (df1$DRIN
K == 1), df1$SDCOMB <- 2, ifelse((df1$SMOKE == 2) & (df1$DRINK == 2), df1$SDCOMB <- 3, N
A))))
>
> df1
```

	ID	ITEM1	ITEM2	ITEM3	ITEM4	GROUP	INCOME	SMOKE	DRINK	SDCOMB
1	1	2	3	5	1	1	45000	1	1	1
2	2	3	4	NA	1	1	27500	1	2	2
3	3	1	5	4	2	1	100000	2	1	2
4	4	5	4	1	2	1	33000	2	2	3
5	5	3	5	NA	3	1	56000	1	2	2
6	6	2	4	3	3	2	18000	2	NA	NA
7	7	4	1	4	4	2	60000	NA	1	NA
8	8	NA	5	NA	4	3	NA	NA	1	NA
9	9	3	4	3	5	4	48000	NA	NA	NA
10	10	3	5	1	NA	5	35500	1	1	1
11	11	4	NA	NA	NA	NA	50000	NA	NA	NA

```
>
```

PERFORM DATA TRANSFORMATIONS UNDER SPECIFIED CONDITIONS (DO IF/END IF)

EXAMPLE: Count occurrences across set of variables for those with no missing data

SPSS: The DO IF/END IF commands

Command:

DO IF *expression.*
Desired data transformation commands (i.e., RECODE, COMPUTE, IF, COUNT).
END IF.

Example:

```
COUNT MVICES = SMOKE DRINK (MISSING).
DO IF (MVICES EQ 0).
COUNT NVICES2 = SMOKE DRINK (1).
FORMATS NVICES2 (F1.0).
VARIABLE LABELS NVICES2 "# vices (0-2), those with zero missing data".
END IF.
EXECUTE.
```

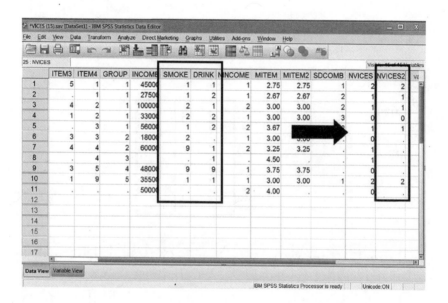

R: The `apply` and `ifelse` functions

Command:

```
# count the number of missing responses
dataframe$nummissing <- apply(dataframe[startcol:endcol], 1,
function(x) sum(is.na(x)))
# calculate new var for those with no missing, otherwise
assign NA
dataframe$newvar <- ifelse((expression),
outcomeifexpressiontrue, outcomeifexpressionfalse)
```

Example:

```
# count the number of missing responses
df1$MVICES <- apply(df1[8:9], 1, function(x) sum(is.na(x)))
# calculate NVICES2 for those with no missing, otherwise
assign NA
df1$NVICES2 <- ifelse((df1$MVICES == 0), df1$NVICES2 <-
apply(df1[8:9], 1, function(x) length(which(x==1))), NA)
```

```
> setwd("e:/R output")
> df1 = read.csv("DATATRANS_NA.csv")
>
> # count the number of missing responses
> df1$MVICES <- apply(df1[8:9], 1, function(x) sum(is.na(x)))
> # calculate NVICES2 for those with no missing data, otherwise assign NA
> df1$NVICES2 <- ifelse((df1$MVICES == 0), df1$NVICES2 <- apply(df1[8:9], 1, function(x
) length(which(x==1))), NA)
> # remove # missing variable from data frame
> df1$MVICES <- NULL
>
> df1
      ID ITEM1 ITEM2 ITEM3 ITEM4 GROUP INCOME SMOKE DRINK NVICES2
1   1     2     3     5     1     1   45000     1     1       2
2   2     3     4    NA     1     1   27500     1     2       1
3   3     1     5     4     2     1  100000     2     1       1
4   4     5     4     1     2     1   33000     2     2       0
5   5     3     5    NA     3     1   56000     1     2       1
6   6     2     4     3     3     2   18000     2    NA      NA
7   7     4     1     4     4     2   60000    NA     1      NA
8   8    NA     5    NA     4     3     NA    NA     1      NA
9   9     3     4     3     5     4   48000    NA    NA      NA
10 10     3     5     1    NA     5   35500     1     1       2
11 11     4    NA    NA    NA    NA   50000    NA    NA      NA
>
```

PERFORM DATA TRANSFORMATIONS UNDER DIFFERENT SPECIFIED CONDITIONS (DO IF/ELSE IF/END IF)

EXAMPLE: Create the variable MITEM3 differently for different incomes

SPSS: The DO IF/ELSE IF/END IF commands

Command:

```
DO IF expression.
Desired data transformation commands (i.e., RECODE, COMPUTE, IF, COUNT).
ELSE IF.
Desired data transformation commands (i.e., RECODE, COMPUTE, IF, COUNT).
END IF.
```

Example:

```
* Multiply MITEM by 10 for those whose INCOME = 1.
DO IF (NINCOME EQ 1).
COMPUTE MITEM3 = MITEM x 10.
* Multiply MITEM by 100 for those whose INCOME = 2.
ELSE IF (NINCOME EQ 2). .
COMPUTE MITEM3 = MITEM x 100.
END IF.
EXECUTE.
```

R: The `ifelse` function

Command:

```
dataframe$newvar <-             ifelse((expression1),
outcomeifexpression1true,       ifelse(expression2),
outcomeifexpression2true,       ... ,
outcomeifexpressionsfalse)
```

Example:

```
df1$MITEM3 <- ifelse((df1$NINCOME == 1), df1$MITEM3 <-
df1$MITEM * 10, ifelse((df1$NINCOME == 2), df1$MITEM3 <-
df1$MITEM * 100, NA))
```

```
> df1$MITEM3  <- ifelse((df1$NINCOME == 1), df1$MITEM3  <- df1$MITEM * 10, ifelse((df1$
NINCOME == 2), df1$MITEM3  <- df1$MITEM * 100, NA))
>
> df1
   ID ITEM1 ITEM2 ITEM3 ITEM4 GROUP INCOME SMOKE DRINK NINCOME    MITEM    MITEM3
1   1    2    3    5    1    1  45000    1    1        1 2.750000   27.50000
2   2    3    4   NA    1    1  27500    1    2        1 2.666667   26.66667
3   3    1    5    4    2    1 100000    2    1        2 3.000000  300.00000
4   4    5    4    1    2    1  33000    2    2        1 3.000000   30.00000
5   5    3    5   NA    3    1  56000    1    2        2 3.666667  366.66667
6   6    2    4    3    3    2  18000    2   NA        1 3.000000   30.00000
7   7    4    1    4    4    2  60000   NA    1        2 3.250000  325.00000
8   8   NA    5   NA    4    3     NA   NA    1       NA 4.500000        NA
9   9    3    4    3    5    4  48000   NA   NA        1 3.750000   37.50000
10 10    3    5    1   NA    5  35500    1    1        1 3.000000   30.00000
11 11    4   NA   NA   NA   NA  50000   NA   NA        2 4.000000  400.00000
> |
```

USE NUMERIC FUNCTIONS IN DATA TRANSFORMATIONS (ABS, RND, TRUNC, SQRT)

EXAMPLE: Calculate absolute, rounded, truncated, and square root value of Variable X

SPSS: The ABS, RND, TRUNC, and SQRT functions

Command:

COMPUTE	*newvariable = function (expression)*

Example:

```
* Absolute value.
COMPUTE      ABSX = ABS(X).
* Round.
COMPUTE      RNDX = RND(X).
* Truncate.
COMPUTE      TRUNCX = TRUNC(X).
* Square root.
COMPUTE      SQRTX = SQRT(X).
EXECUTE.
```

R: The `abs`, `rnd`, `trunc`, and `sqrt` functions

Command:

```
dataframe$newvar <- numericfunction(dataframe$oldvar)
```

Example:

```
# absolute value
df1$ABSX <- abs(df1$x)
# round to zero decimal places
df1$RNDX <- rnd(df1$x, digits = 0)
# truncate
df1$TRUNCX <- trunc(df1$x)
# square root
df1$SQRTX <- sqrt(df1$x
```

```
> setwd("e:/R output")
> df1 = read.csv("functions.csv")
>
> #    absolute value
> df1$ABSX <- abs(df1$x)
>
> #    round to 0 decimal places
> df1$ROUNDX <- round(df1$x,digits = 0)
>
> #    truncate
> df1$TRUNCX <- trunc(df1$x)
>
> #    square root
> df1$SQRTX <- sqrt(df1$x)
Warning message:
In sqrt(df1$x) : NaNs produced
>
> df1
    ï..id     x ABSX ROUNDX TRUNCX      SQRTX
1       1 -2.00 2.00     -2     -2        NaN
2       2 -1.75 1.75     -2     -1        NaN
3       3 -1.50 1.50     -2     -1        NaN
4       4 -1.25 1.25     -1     -1        NaN
5       5 -1.00 1.00     -1     -1        NaN
6       6  0.00 0.00      0      0   0.000000
7       7  1.00 1.00      1      1   1.000000
8       8  1.25 1.25      1      1   1.118034
9       9  1.50 1.50      2      1   1.224745
10     10  1.75 1.75      2      1   1.322876
11     11  2.00 2.00      2      2   1.414214
```

APPENDIX B:
STATISTICAL PROCEDURES

This appendix provides scripts that can be used to conduct a variety of statistical procedures. Similar to Appendix A (Data Transformations), each statistical procedure will be illustrated two ways: using SPSS and then using R. It is our hope that by relying on your training in statistics and previous experience with SPSS, you'll be able to extract the desired information from the R output.

The data analyses conducted in this appendix will utilize different CSV files. Information about the cases and variables in these files is provided below:

CSV file name	N	Variables	Valid values
EWB_NA	115	EWB1 to EWB5	1–7
		AGE	1–99
COLLEGE_NA	116	id	1–116
		cgpa	0.00–4.00
		hsgpa	0.00–4.00
		satmath	200–800
		satverb	200–800
		sshada	0–50
		sshawm	0–50
		sshata	0–50
		sshaea	0–50
PSYCH_NA	119	fplan1 to fplan6	1–6
		instruct	1.00–6.00
		faculty	1.00–6.00

(Continued)

(Continued)

CSV file name	N	Variables	Valid values
		relfac	1.00–6.00
		tguide	1.00–6.00
		tpsk	1.00–6.00
		doagain	1–2
MISC_NA	141	id	1–141
	113	gender	1–2
	113	defp	1.00–5.00
	141	riskgain	1–8
	141	riskloss	1–8
	141	moneyr	1.00–5.00
	141	ncateg	1–3
	141	age	0–99
	141	nage	1–2
	38	income	0–999,999
	17	ageatdeath	0–105
TREND_NA	32	FACTORA	1–4
		DEPVAR	1–25
SINGLEWS_NA	8	TIME1 to TIME4	1–20
TWOFACTORBS_NA	36	FACTORA	1–2
		FACTORB	1–3
		DEPVAR	1–10
TWOMIXED_NA	30	BETWEEN	1–3
		TIME1 to TIME4	10–40
TWOFACTORWS_NA	3	a1b1	1–15
		a1b2	1–15
		a1b3	1–15
		a2b1	1–15

CSV file name	*N*	Variables	Valid values
		a2b2	1–15
		a2b3	1–15
THREEFACTORBS_NA	48	FACTORA	1–2
		FACTORB	1–3
		FACTORC	1–2
		DEPVAR	1–50
ABCD_NA	129	ABCD1 to ABCD11	1–7

DESCRIPTIVE STATISTICS (ALL VARIABLES)

EXAMPLE: Calculate descriptive statistics for all variables in a data set

SPSS: The FREQUENCIES command

```
FREQUENCIES VARIABLES=EWB1 EWB2 EWB3 EWB4 EWB5 age
  /FORMAT=NOTABLE
  /STATISTICS=STDDEV RANGE MINIMUM MAXIMUM MEAN MEDIAN MODE SKEWNESS SESKEW KURTOSIS SEKURT
  /ORDER=ANALYSIS.
```

Frequencies

Statistics

		EWB1	EWB2	EWB3	EWB4	EWB5	age
N	Valid	115	111	112	110	113	115
	Missing	0	4	3	5	2	0
Mean		5.41	5.86	4.72	5.90	4.55	21.37
Median		6.00	6.00	5.00	6.00	5.00	21.00
Mode		6	6	6	6	3	21
Std. Deviation		1.235	.830	1.502	.938	1.575	1.519
Skewness		-1.394	-1.086	-.343	-1.224	-.084	2.967
Std. Error of Skewness		.226	.229	.228	.230	.227	.226
Kurtosis		1.567	2.389	-.992	2.476	-1.010	15.329
Std. Error of Kurtosis		.447	.455	.453	.457	.451	.447
Range		5	4	6	5	6	13
Minimum		2	3	1	2	1	18
Maximum		7	7	7	7	7	31

R: The `describe` function in the `psych` package

Calculate descriptive statistics for all variables in data frame

Command: **describe(*dataframe*, type=2)**

Note: **type=2** calculates skewness/kurtosis the same way as SPSS

Example: describe(df1, type=2)

Example script:
```
setwd("e:/R output")
df1 <- read.csv("EWB_NA.csv")
library(psych)
describe(df1, type=2)
```

```
> setwd("e:/R output")
> df1 <- read.csv("EWB_NA.csv")
> library("psych")
> describe(df1,type=2)
     vars   n  mean    sd median trimmed   mad min max range  skew kurtosis   se
X       1 115 58.00 33.34     58   58.00 43.00   1 115   114  0.00    -1.20 3.11
EWB1    2 115  5.41  1.23      6    5.57  0.00   2   7     5 -1.39     1.57 0.12
EWB2    3 111  5.86  0.83      6    5.91  0.00   3   7     4 -1.09     2.39 0.08
EWB3    4 112  4.72  1.50      5    4.78  1.48   1   7     6 -0.34    -0.99 0.14
EWB4    5 110  5.90  0.94      6    6.01  0.00   2   7     5 -1.22     2.48 0.09
EWB5    6 113  4.55  1.58      5    4.56  1.48   1   7     6 -0.08    -1.01 0.15
AGE     7 115 21.37  1.52     21   21.19  0.00  18  31    13  2.97    15.33 0.14
>
```

DESCRIPTIVE STATISTICS (SELECTED VARIABLES)

EXAMPLE: Calculate descriptive statistics for *EWB1* and *EWB2*

SPSS: The FREQUENCIES command

```
FREQUENCIES VARIABLES=EWB1 EWB2
  /FORMAT=NOTABLE
  /STATISTICS=STDDEV RANGE MINIMUM MAXIMUM MEAN MEDIAN MODE SKEWNESS SESKEW KURTOSIS SEKURT
  /ORDER=ANALYSIS.
```

Frequencies

Statistics

		EWB1	EWB2
N	Valid	115	111
	Missing	0	4
Mean		5.41	5.86
Median		6.00	6.00
Mode		6	6
Std. Deviation		1.235	.830
Skewness		-1.394	-1.086
Std. Error of Skewness		.226	.229
Kurtosis		1.567	2.389
Std. Error of Kurtosis		.447	.455
Range		5	4
Minimum		2	3
Maximum		7	7

R: The describe function in the psych package

Create a new data frame containing selected variables

Command: *newdataframe* <- **subset(***dataframe*, **,select =c(***variable*, *variable...*)**)**

Example: df11 <- subset(df1, ,select = c(EWB1, EWB2))

Calculate descriptive statistics for the variables in the new data frame

Command: **describe(***newdataframe*,**type=2)**

Note: **type=2** calculates skewness/kurtosis the same way as SPSS

Example: describe(df11,type=2)

Example script:
```
setwd("e:/R output")
df1 <- read.csv("EWB_NA.csv")
library(psych)
df11 <- subset(df1, ,select = c(EWB1, EWB2))
describe(df11,type=2)
```

```
> setwd("e:/R output")
> df1 <- read.csv("EWB_NA.csv")
> library("psych")
> df11 <- subset(df1, , select = c(EWB1, EWB2))
> describe(df11,type=2)
       vars   n mean   sd median trimmed mad min max range  skew kurtosis   se
EWB1      1 115 5.41 1.23      6    5.57   0   2   7     5 -1.39     1.57 0.12
EWB2      2 111 5.86 0.83      6    5.91   0   3   7     4 -1.09     2.39 0.08
```

DESCRIPTIVE STATISTICS (SELECTED VARIABLES) BY GROUP

EXAMPLE: Calculate descriptive statistics for *DEFP* by *NCATEG* (three groups)

SPSS: The MEANS command

```
MEANS TABLES=defp BY ncateg
  /CELLS=COUNT MEAN STDDEV MIN MAX RANGE SKEW KURT SEMEAN.
```

Means

Report

defp

ncateg	N	Mean	Std. Deviation	Minimum	Maximum	Range	Skewness	Kurtosis	Std. Error of Mean
1 Disagree	40	2.9844	.70749	1.22	4.72	3.50	.136	.727	.11186
2 Unsure	38	2.9774	.45375	1.94	3.83	1.89	-.331	-.581	.07361
3 Agree	35	3.0584	.66237	1.78	4.72	2.94	.543	.526	.11196
Total	113	3.0050	.61384	1.22	4.72	3.50	.248	.841	.05774

R: The `describeBy` function in the `psych` package

Calculate descriptive statistics for the variables in the new data frame by sub-samples (groups)

Command: **describeBy(***dataframe$variable***,** *dataframe$grpvar***, type = 2)**

Note: **type=2** calculates skewness/kurtosis the same way as SPSS

dataframe$variable = dependent variable

dataframe$grpvar = grouping variable

Example: describeBy (df1$defp, df1$ncateg, type = 2)

Example script:
```
setwd("e:/R output")
df1 <- read.csv("MISC_NA.csv")
library(psych)
describeBy (df1$defp, df1$ncateg, type = 2)
```

```
> setwd("e:/R output")
> df1 <- read.csv("MISC_NA.csv")
> library("psych")
> describeBy (df1$defp, df1$ncateg, type = 2)

 Descriptive statistics by group
group: 1
    vars  n mean   sd median trimmed  mad  min  max range skew kurtosis   se
X1     1 40 2.98 0.71   3.06    2.97 0.66 1.22 4.72   3.5 0.14     0.73 0.11
-------------------------------------------------------------------------
group: 2
    vars  n mean   sd median trimmed  mad  min  max range  skew kurtosis   se
X1     1 38 2.98 0.45   3.08    2.99 0.37 1.94 3.83  1.89 -0.33    -0.58 0.07
-------------------------------------------------------------------------
group: 3
    vars  n mean   sd median trimmed  mad  min  max range skew kurtosis   se
X1     1 35 3.06 0.66   3.11    3.02 0.66 1.78 4.72  2.94 0.54     0.53 0.11
```

FREQUENCY DISTRIBUTION TABLE

EXAMPLE: Create a frequency distribution table for *EWB1*

SPSS: The FREQUENCIES command

```
FREQUENCIES VARIABLES=EWB1
   /ORDER=ANALYSIS.
```

Frequencies

Statistics

EWB1

N	Valid	115
	Missing	0

EWB1

		Frequency	Percent	Valid Percent	Cumulative Percent
Valid	2 Disagree	6	5.2	5.2	5.2
	3 Slightly disagree	8	7.0	7.0	12.2
	4 Neither agree/disagree	1	.9	.9	13.0
	5 Slightly agree	30	26.1	26.1	39.1
	6 Agree	58	50.4	50.4	89.6
	7 Strongly agree	12	10.4	10.4	100.0
	Total	115	100.0	100.0	

R: The `table` function in the `psych` package

Create frequency distribution table

Command: **transform(table(*dataframe*$*variable*), cumFreq=
cumsum(Freq), pct = prop.table(Freq)*100)**

Note: **cumFreq = cumsum(Freq)** = cumulative
frequencies

pct = prop.table(Freq)*100) = percentage for
each value

Example: transform(table(df1$EWB1), cumFreq = cumsum
(Freq), pct = prop.table(Freq)*100)

Example script:

```
setwd("e:/R output")
df1 <- read.csv("EWB_NA.csv")
library(psych)
transform(table(df1$EWB1), cumFreq = cumsum(Freq),
pct = prop.table(Freq)*100)
```

```
> setwd("e:/R output")
> df1 <- read.csv("EWB_NA.csv")
> library("psych")
> transform(table(df1$EWB1), cumFreq = cumsum(Freq), pct = prop.table(Freq)*100)
  Var1 Freq cumFreq        pct
1    2    6       6  5.2173913
2    3    8      14  6.9565217
3    4    1      15  0.8695652
4    5   30      45 26.0869565
5    6   58     103 50.4347826
6    7   12     115 10.4347826
```

HISTOGRAM

EXAMPLE: Create a histogram for *age*

R: The geom _ histogram function within the ggplot2 package

Create a histogram

Command: **ggplot(**_dataframe_**, aes(**_variable_**)) + geom_ histogram(color = "**_color_**", fill = "**_color_**", binwidth = #) + ggtitle("**_title_**") + labs(x="**_label_**", y="**_label_**") + theme_bw()**

Note: _color_ = color of border of bars and inside of bars

= width of bars (adjust depending on # values of variable)

title = title above histogram

label = label for axis (X and Y)

theme_bw() = removes gray background of histogram

Example: ggplot(df1, aes(AGE)) + geom_ histogram(color = "black", fill = "gray", binwidth = 1) + ggtitle("Age of participants") + labs(x="Age (in years)", y="f") + theme_bw()

Example script:
```
setwd("e:/R output")
df1 <- read.csv("EWB_NA.csv")
library(ggplot2)
ggplot(df1, aes(AGE)) + geom_histogram(color =
"black", fill = "gray", binwidth =1) + ggtitle("Age
of participants") + labs(x="Age (in years)", y="f") +
theme_bw()
```

```
> setwd("e:/R output")
> df1 <- read.csv("EWB_NA.csv")
> library("ggplot2")
> ggplot(df1, aes(AGE)) + geom_histogram(color = "black", fill = "gray", binwidth = 1) +
  ggtitle("Age of participants") + labs(x="Age (in years)", y="f") + theme_bw()
```

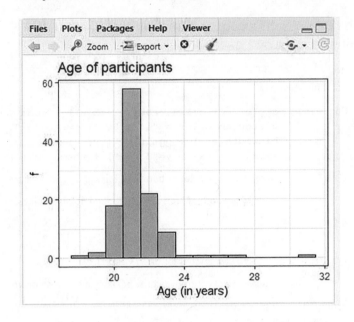

t-TEST FOR ONE MEAN

EXAMPLE: Test the difference between a sample mean and a hypothesized population mean ($\mu = 78$)

SPSS: The T-TEST command

```
T-TEST
  /TESTVAL=78
  /MISSING=ANALYSIS
  /VARIABLES=ageatdeath
  /CRITERIA=CI(.95).
```

T-Test

One-Sample Statistics

	N	Mean	Std. Deviation	Std. Error Mean
ageatdeath	17	84.00	8.008	1.942

One-Sample Test

	Test Value = 78					
					95% Confidence Interval of the Difference	
	t	df	Sig. (2-tailed)	Mean Difference	Lower	Upper
ageatdeath	3.089	16	.007	6.000	1.88	10.12

R: The `describe` and `t.test` functions in the `psych` package

Calculate descriptive statistics for the variable

    Command: **describe(`dataframe$var`)**

    Example: describe (df1$ageatdeath)

Conduct the *t*-test for one mean

    Command: **t.test(`dataframe$var`, mu = #)**

                    Note: **mu** = # = value of hypothesized population mean

    Example: t.test (df1$ageatdeath, mu = 78)

Example script:
```
setwd("e:/R output")
df1 <- read.csv("MISC_NA.csv")
library(psych)
describe (df1$ageatdeath)
t.test(df1$ageatdeath, mu = 78)
```

```
> setwd("e:/R output")
> df1 <- read.csv("MISC_NA.csv")
> library("psych")
> describe (df1$ageatdeath)
   vars  n  mean   sd median trimmed  mad min max range  skew kurtosis   se
X1    1 17 84.12 8.04     84   84.13 5.93  68 100    32 -0.03    -0.54 1.95
> t.test(df1$ageatdeath, mu = 78)

        One Sample t-test

data:  df1$ageatdeath
t = 3.138, df = 16, p-value = 0.006353
alternative hypothesis: true mean is not equal to 78
95 percent confidence interval:
 79.98486 88.25043
sample estimates:
mean of x
 84.11765
```

CONFIDENCE INTERVAL FOR THE MEAN

EXAMPLE: Calculate a confidence interval for the mean for the variable *income*

SPSS: The T-TEST command

```
T-TEST
  /TESTVAL=0
  /MISSING=ANALYSIS
  /VARIABLES=income
  /CRITERIA=CI(.95).
```

T-Test

One-Sample Statistics

	N	Mean	Std. Deviation	Std. Error Mean
income	38	64508.84	14523.922	2356.091

One-Sample Test

	Test Value = 0					
					95% Confidence Interval of the Difference	
	t	df	Sig. (2-tailed)	Mean Difference	Lower	Upper
income	27.380	37	.000	64508.842	59734.95	69282.74

R: The describe and t.test functions in the psych package

Calculate descriptive statistics for the variable

    Command: **describe(dataframe$var)**

    Example: describe (df1$income)

Calculate the confidence interval for the mean

    Command: **t.test(dataframe$var, mu = 0)**

    Example: t.test(df1$income, mu = 0)

Example script:
```
setwd("e:/R output")
df1 <- read.csv("MISC_NA.csv")
library(psych)
describe (df1$income)
t.test(df1$income, mu = 0)
```

```
> setwd("e:/R output")
> df1 <- read.csv("MISC_NA.csv")
> library("psych")
> describe (df1$income)
   vars  n    mean       sd median  trimmed      mad   min   max range  skew kurtosis
X1    1 38 64508.84 14523.92  65000 64749.62 13602.85 31000 93300 62300 -0.12    -0.59
      se
X1 2356.09
> t.test(df1$income, mu = 0)

        One Sample t-test

data:  df1$income
t = 27.38, df = 37, p-value < 2.2e-16
alternative hypothesis: true mean is not equal to 0
95 percent confidence interval:
 59734.95 69282.74
sample estimates:
mean of x
 64508.84
```

T-TEST FOR INDEPENDENT MEANS

EXAMPLE: Conduct *t*-test for independent means (IV: *gender(1,2)*; DV: *defp*)

SPSS: The T-TEST command

```
T-TEST GROUPS=gender(1 2)
  /MISSING=ANALYSIS
  /VARIABLES=defp
  /CRITERIA=CI(.95).
```

T-Test

Group Statistics

	gender	N	Mean	Std. Deviation	Std. Error Mean
defp	1 Male	56	2.9095	.65589	.08765
	2 Female	57	3.0988	.55947	.07410

Independent Samples Test

		Levene's Test for Equality of Variances		t-test for Equality of Means						
		F	Sig.	t	df	Sig. (2-tailed)	Mean Difference	Std. Error Difference	95% Confidence Interval of the Difference Lower	95% Confidence Interval of the Difference Upper
defp	Equal variances assumed	2.296	.133	-1.651	111	.101	-.18928	.11461	-.41640	.03783
	Equal variances not assumed			-1.649	107.690	.102	-.18928	.11478	-.41679	.03823

R: The `describeBy` and `t.test` functions in the `psych` package

Calculate descriptive statistics for each group

    Command: **describeBy(***dataframe***$***depvar***,** ***dataframe***$***indvar***)**

    Example: describeBy (df1$defp, df1$gender)

Conduct the *t*-test for independent means

    Command: **t.test(***dataframe***$***depvar*** ~ ***dataframe***$***indvar*,** **var.equal=TRUE, paired=FALSE)**

                      Note: **var.equal=TRUE** = assumed homogeneity of variance

                      paired=FALSE = independent samples

    Example: t.test(df1$defp ~ df1$gender, var. equal=TRUE, paired=FALSE)

Example script:
```
setwd("e:/R output")
df1 <- read.csv("MISC_NA.csv")
library(psych)
describeBy (df1$defp, df1$gender)
t.test(df1$defp ~ df1$gender, var.equal=TRUE,
paired=FALSE)
```

```
> setwd("e:/R output")
> df1 <- read.csv("MISC_NA.csv")
> library("psych")
> describeBy (df1$defp, df1$gender)

 Descriptive statistics by group
group: 1
   vars  n mean   sd median trimmed  mad  min  max range skew kurtosis   se
X1    1 56 2.91 0.66   2.88    2.89 0.64 1.22 4.72   3.5 0.34     0.59 0.09
------------------------------------------------------------------------
group: 2
   vars  n mean   sd median trimmed  mad  min  max range skew kurtosis   se
X1    1 57  3.1 0.56   3.12    3.09 0.48 1.89 4.67  2.78 0.28     0.71 0.07
> t.test(df1$defp ~ df1$gender, var.equal=TRUE, paired=FALSE)

        Two Sample t-test

data:  df1$defp by df1$gender
t = -1.6515, df = 111, p-value = 0.1015
alternative hypothesis: true difference in means is not equal to 0
95 percent confidence interval:
 -0.41639771  0.03783276
sample estimates:
mean in group 1 mean in group 2
       2.909489        3.098771
```

T-TEST FOR DEPENDENT MEANS (REPEATED-MEASURES T-TEST)

EXAMPLE: Conduct *t*-test for dependent means (IV: Situation*(riskgain, riskloss)*; DV: *score*)

SPSS: The T-TEST command

```
T-TEST PAIRS=riskgain WITH riskloss (PAIRED)
  /CRITERIA=CI(.9500)
  /MISSING=ANALYSIS.
```

T-Test

Paired Samples Statistics

		Mean	N	Std. Deviation	Std. Error Mean
Pair 1	riskgain	1.70	137	1.592	.136
	riskloss	4.88	137	2.029	.173

Paired Samples Correlations

		N	Correlation	Sig.
Pair 1	riskgain & riskloss	137	.092	.288

Paired Samples Test

		Paired Differences							
					95% Confidence Interval of the Difference				
		Mean	Std. Deviation	Std. Error Mean	Lower	Upper	t	df	Sig. (2-tailed)
Pair 1	riskgain - riskloss	-3.182	2.462	.210	-3.598	-2.766	-15.13	136	.000

R: The `describe` and `t.test` functions in the *psych* package

> Create new data frame that contains only the two variables to be analyzed
>
> Command: `newdataframe <- subset(dataframe,,select = c(variable, variable))`
>
> Example: `df11 <- subset(df1,,select = c(riskgain,riskloss))`
>
> Remove anyone with NAs on any variable in the new data frame
>
> Command: `newdataframe <- na.omit(newdataframe)`
>
> Example: `df11 <- na.omit(df11)`

(Continued)

(Continued)

Calculate descriptive statistics for the two variables

   Command: **describe(***newdataframe***)**

   Example: describe(df11)

Run the t.test function to conduct *t*-test for dependent means

   Command: **t.test(***newdataframe***$var1,** *newdataframe***$var2,**
               var.equal=TRUE, paired=TRUE)

               Note: **var.equal=TRUE** = assumed homogeneity of
                     variance

               paired=TRUE = dependent samples

   Example: t.test(df11$riskgain, df11$riskloss, var.
               equal=TRUE, paired=TRUE)

Example script:
```
setwd("e:/R output")
df1 <- read.csv("MISC_NA.csv")
library(psych)
df11 <- subset(df1,,select = c(riskgain,riskloss))
df11 <- na.omit(df11)
describe(df11)
t.test(df11$riskgain, df11$riskloss, var.equal=TRUE,
paired=TRUE)
```

```
> setwd("e:/R output")
> df1 <- read.csv("MISC_NA.csv")
> library("psych")
> df11 <- subset(df1, , select = c(riskgain,riskloss))
> df11 <- na.omit(df11)
> describe (df11)
         vars   n mean   sd median trimmed  mad min max range  skew kurtosis   se
riskgain    1 137 1.70 1.59      1     1.5 1.48   0   8     8  1.19     1.66 0.14
riskloss    2 137 4.88 2.03      5     5.0 2.97   0   8     8 -0.49    -0.61 0.17
> t.test(df11$riskgain, df11$riskloss, var.equal=TRUE, paired=TRUE)

        Paired t-test

data:  df11$riskgain and df11$riskloss
t = -15.129, df = 136, p-value < 2.2e-16
alternative hypothesis: true difference in means is not equal to 0
95 percent confidence interval:
 -3.598468 -2.766495
sample estimates:
mean of the differences
              -3.182482
```

ONE-WAY ANOVA AND TUKEY POST-HOC COMPARISONS

EXAMPLE: Conduct one-way ANOVA and Tukey post-hocs (IV: *ncateg* (3 groups); DV: *moneyr*)

SPSS: The ONEWAY command

```
ONEWAY moneyr BY ncateg
  /STATISTICS DESCRIPTIVES
  /MISSING ANALYSIS
  /POSTHOC=TUKEY ALPHA(0.05).
```

Oneway

Descriptives

moneyr

	N	Mean	Std. Deviation	Std. Error	95% Confidence Interval for Mean		Minimum	Maximum
					Lower Bound	Upper Bound		
1 CONTROL	67	3.3390	.76924	.09398	3.1514	3.5267	1.86	4.86
2 CREDIT - LIFE EVENTS	39	2.8901	.73171	.11717	2.6529	3.1273	1.00	4.14
3 CREDIT - NO LIFE EVENTS	34	2.7437	.74171	.12720	2.4849	3.0025	1.57	4.43
Total	140	3.0694	.79243	.06697	2.9370	3.2018	1.00	4.86

ANOVA

moneyr

	Sum of Squares	df	Mean Square	F	Sig.
Between Groups	9.731	2	4.865	8.595	.000
Within Groups	77.554	137	.566		
Total	87.285	139			

Post Hoc Tests

Multiple Comparisons

Dependent Variable: moneyr

Tukey HSD

(I) ncateg	(J) ncateg	Mean Difference (I-J)	Std. Error	Sig.	95% Confidence Interval	
					Lower Bound	Upper Bound
1 CONTROL	2 CREDIT - LIFE EVENTS	.44891*	.15154	.010	.0898	.8080
	3 CREDIT - NO LIFE EVENTS	.59532*	.15843	.001	.2199	.9707
2 CREDIT - LIFE EVENTS	1 CONTROL	-.44891*	.15154	.010	-.8080	-.0898
	3 CREDIT - NO LIFE EVENTS	.14641	.17654	.685	-.2719	.5647
3 CREDIT - NO LIFE EVENTS	1 CONTROL	-.59532*	.15843	.001	-.9707	-.2199
	2 CREDIT - LIFE EVENTS	-.14641	.17654	.685	-.5647	.2719

*. The mean difference is significant at the 0.05 level.

R: The `factor`, `describeBy`, `aov`, and `TukeyHSD` functions in the `psych` package

Create new data frame that contains only the variables to be analyzed

Command: `newdataframe <- subset(dataframe,,select = c(variable, variable))`

Example: `df11 <- subset(df1,,select = c(ncateg,moneyr))`

Remove anyone with NAs on any variable in the new data frame

Command: `newdataframe <- na.omit(newdataframe)`

Example: `df11 <- na.omit(df11)`

Convert a numeric independent variable to a factor (if IV is a numeric variable)

Command: `newdataframe$factor <- factor(newdataframe$numvar, labels = c("label", "label", "label"...))`

   Note: `newdataframe$factor` = name of factor

   `newdataframe$numvar` = numeric independent variable

   `label` = label to level of factor based on numeric independent variable

Example: `df11$ncateg.f <- factor(df11$ncateg, labels = c("Control", "Life events", "No life events"))`

Calculate descriptive statistics for each group

Command: `describeBy(newdataframe$depvar, newdataframe$factor)`

Example: `describeBy (df11$moneyr, df11$ncateg.f)`

Conduct one-way ANOVA

Command: `result <- aov(newdataframe$depvar ~ newdataframe$factor, data = newdataframe)`

   `summary(result)`

Example: `oneway <- aov(moneyr ~ ncateg.f, data = df11)`

   `summary(oneway)`

Conduct post-hoc comparisons between groups

Command: `TukeyHSD (result)`

   Note: `result` = result of analysis created by aov function

Example: `TukeyHSD(oneway)`

Example script:

```
setwd("e:/R output")
df1 <- read.csv("MISC_NA.csv")
library(psych)
df11 <- subset(df1, ,select = c(ncateg,moneyr))
df11 <- na.omit(df11)
df11$ncateg.f <- factor(df11$ncateg, labels =
c("Control", "Life events", "No life events"))
describeBy (df11$moneyr, df11$ncateg.f)
oneway <- aov(moneyr ~ ncateg.f, data = df11)
summary(oneway)
TukeyHSD(oneway)
```

```
> setwd("e:/R output")
> df1 <- read.csv("MISC_NA.csv")
> library("psych")
> df11 <- subset(df1, , select = c(ncateg,moneyr))
> df11 <- na.omit(df11)
> df11$ncateg.f <- factor(df11$ncateg, labels = c("Control", "Life events", "No life events"))
> describeBy (df11$moneyr, df11$ncateg.f)

Descriptive statistics by group
group: Control
   vars  n mean   sd median trimmed  mad  min  max range  skew kurtosis   se
X1    1 67 3.34 0.77   3.43    3.35 0.85 1.86 4.86     3 -0.17    -0.81 0.09
--------------------------------------------------------------------
group: Life events
   vars  n mean   sd median trimmed  mad min  max range  skew kurtosis   se
X1    1 39 2.89 0.73   2.86    2.91 0.85   1 4.14  3.14 -0.16    -0.33 0.12
--------------------------------------------------------------------
group: No life events
   vars  n mean   sd median trimmed  mad  min  max range skew kurtosis   se
X1    1 34 2.74 0.74   2.79    2.71 0.95 1.57 4.43  2.86 0.32    -0.84 0.13
> oneway <- aov(moneyr ~ ncateg.f, data = df11)
> summary(oneway)
             Df Sum Sq Mean Sq F value   Pr(>F)
ncateg.f      2   9.73   4.865   8.595 0.000304 ***
Residuals   137  77.55   0.566
---
Signif. codes:  0 '***' 0.001 '**' 0.01 '*' 0.05 '.' 0.1 ' ' 1
> TukeyHSD(oneway)
  Tukey multiple comparisons of means
    95% family-wise confidence level

Fit: aov(formula = moneyr ~ ncateg.f, data = df11)

$ncateg.f
                               diff        lwr         upr     p adj
Life events-Control      -0.4489093 -0.8079759 -0.08984272 0.0100117
No life events-Control   -0.5953217 -0.9707056 -0.21993786 0.0007356
No life events-Life events -0.1464124 -0.5647062  0.27188139 0.6854801
```

ONE-WAY ANOVA AND TREND ANALYSIS

EXAMPLE: Conduct one-way ANOVA and trend analysis (IV: *DEPVAR*; DV: *FACTORA*)

SPSS: The ONEWAY command

```
ONEWAY DEPVAR BY FACTORA
  /POLYNOMIAL=2
  /STATISTICS DESCRIPTIVES
  /MISSING ANALYSIS.
```

Oneway

Descriptives

DEPVAR

	N	Mean	Std. Deviation	Std. Error	95% Confidence Interval for Mean		Minimum	Maximum
					Lower Bound	Upper Bound		
1 Time 1	8	6.00	2.777	.982	3.68	8.32	3	11
2 Time 2	8	6.75	2.816	.996	4.40	9.10	4	11
3 Time 3	8	9.75	3.770	1.333	6.60	12.90	5	15
4 Time 4	8	15.50	3.928	1.389	12.22	18.78	10	21
Total	32	9.50	4.964	.878	7.71	11.29	3	21

ANOVA

DEPVAR

			Sum of Squares	df	Mean Square	F	Sig.
Between Groups	(Combined)		447.000	3	149.000	13.161	.000
	Linear Term	Contrast	396.900	1	396.900	35.057	.000
		Deviation	50.100	2	25.050	2.213	.128
	Quadratic Term	Contrast	50.000	1	50.000	4.416	.045
		Deviation	.100	1	.100	.009	.926
Within Groups			317.000	28	11.321		
Total			764.000	31			

R: The `factor`, `describeBy`, `cbind`, `contrasts`, and `aov` functions in the `psych` package

Create new data frame that contains only the two variables to be analyzed

Command: `newdataframe <- subset(dataframe, ,select = c(variable, variable))`

Example: `df11 <- subset(df1, ,select = c(FACTORA,DEPVAR))`

Remove anyone with NAs on any variable in the new data frame

Command: `newdataframe <- na.omit(newdataframe)`

Example: `df11 <- na.omit(df11)`

Convert a numeric independent variable to a factor (if IV is a numeric variable)

Command: `newdataframe$factor <- factor`
            `(newdataframe$numvar, labels = c("label",`
            `"label", "label"...))`

Note: `newdataframe$factor` = name of factor

`newdataframe$numvar` = numeric independent variable

`label` = label to level of factor based on numeric independent variable

Example: `df11$FACTORA.f <- factor(df11$FACTORA,`
            `labels = c("Time 1","Time 2","Time 3",`
            `"Time 4"))`

Calculate descriptive statistics for each group

Command: **describeBy(**`newdataframe$depvar`,
            `newdataframe$factor`**)**

Example: `describeBy (df11$DEPVAR, df11$FACTORA.f)`

Provide coefficients needed to conduct trend analyses and create matrix of comparisons

Command: `trend <- c(# # #...)`
            `matrix <- cbind(trend, trend, trend...)`
            contrasts (`newdataframe$factor`**) <-** `matrix`
            NOTE: # = coefficient

Example: `linear <- c(-3, -1, 1, 3)`
            `quadratic <- c(1, -1, -1, 1)`
            `cubic <- c(-1, 3, -3, 1)`
            `matrix <- cbind(linear, quadratic, cubic)`
            `contrasts(df11$FACTORA.f) <- matrix`

Conduct one-way ANOVA and trend analysis

Command: `result <- aov(newdataframe$depvar ~`
            `newdataframe$factor, data = newdataframe)`
            summary(`result`**)**
            `summary(result, split=list(newdataframe`
            `$depvar =list("trend"=1, "trend" = 2,`
            `"trend"=3...)))`

Example: `oneway <- aov(DEPVAR ~ FACTORA.f, data = df11)`
            `summary(oneway)`
            `summary(oneway, split=list(FACTORA.f =list`
            `("Linear "=1,"Quadratic"=2, "Cubic"=3)))`

Example script:
```
setwd("e:/R output")
df1 <- read.csv("TREND_NA.csv")
library(psych)
df11 <- subset(df1, ,select = c(FACTORA,DEPVAR))
df11 <- na.omit(df11)
df11$FACTORA.f <- factor(df11$FACTORA, labels =
c("Time1","Time2","Time3","Time4"))
describeBy (df11$DEPVAR, df11$FACTORA.f)
linear <- c(-3, -1, 1, 3)
quadratic <- c(1, -1, -1, 1)
cubic <- c(-1, 3, -3, 1)
matrix <- cbind(linear, quadratic, cubic)
contrasts(df11$FACTORA.f) <- matrix
oneway <- aov(DEPVAR ~ FACTORA.f, data = df11)
summary(oneway)
summary(oneway, split=list(FACTORA.f =list
("Linear"=1,"Quadratic"=2, "Cubic"=3)))
```

```
> setwd("e:/R output")
> df1 <- read.csv("TREND_NA.csv")
> library(psych)
> df11 <- subset(df1, ,select = c(FACTORA,DEPVAR))
> df11 <- na.omit(df11)
> df11$FACTORA.f <- factor(df11$FACTORA, labels = c("Time1","Time2","Time3","Time4"))
> describeBy (df11$DEPVAR, df11$FACTORA.f)

 Descriptive statistics by group
group: Time1
   vars n mean   sd median trimmed  mad min max range skew kurtosis   se
X1    1 8  6 2.78      5       6 2.22   3  11     8 0.63    -1.27 0.98
-----------------------------------------------------------------
group: Time2
   vars n mean   sd median trimmed  mad min max range skew kurtosis se
X1    1 8 6.75 2.82    5.5    6.75 2.22   4  11     7 0.39    -1.81  1
-----------------------------------------------------------------
group: Time3
   vars n mean   sd median trimmed  mad min max range skew kurtosis   se
X1    1 8 9.75 3.77    9.5    9.75 4.45   5  15    10 0.11    -1.83 1.33
-----------------------------------------------------------------
group: Time4
   vars n mean   sd median trimmed  mad min max range skew kurtosis   se
X1    1 8 15.5 3.93     15    15.5 4.45  10  21    11 0.09     -1.7 1.39


> linear <- c(-3, -1,  1, 3)
> quadratic <- c(1, -1, -1, 1)
> cubic <- c(-1, 3, -3, 1)
> matrix <- cbind(linear, quadratic, cubic)
> contrasts(df11$FACTORA.f) <- matrix
> oneway <- aov(DEPVAR ~ FACTORA.f, data = df11)
> summary(oneway)
            Df Sum Sq Mean Sq F value  Pr(>F)
FACTORA.f    3    447  149.00   13.16 1.52e-05 ***
Residuals   28    317   11.32
---
Signif. codes:  0 '***' 0.001 '**' 0.01 '*' 0.05 '.' 0.1 ' ' 1
> summary(oneway, split=list(FACTORA.f =list("Linear"=1,"Quadratic"=2, "Cubic"=3)))
                    Df Sum Sq Mean Sq F value   Pr(>F)
FACTORA.f            3  447.0   149.0  13.161 1.52e-05 ***
  FACTORA.f: Linear  1  396.9   396.9  35.057 2.26e-06 ***
  FACTORA.f: Quadratic 1  50.0    50.0   4.416   0.0447 *
  FACTORA.f: Cubic   1    0.1     0.1   0.009   0.9258
Residuals           28  317.0    11.3
---
Signif. codes:  0 '***' 0.001 '**' 0.01 '*' 0.05 '.' 0.1 ' ' 1
```

SINGLE-FACTOR WITHIN-SUBJECTS (REPEATED MEASURES) ANOVA

EXAMPLE: Conduct repeated measures ANOVA (IV: Situation*(TIME1* to *TIME4)*; DV: *score*)

Note: This example assumes the data file resembles the one below (one line per participant):

TIME1	TIME2	TIME3	TIME4
10	13	9	4
10	11	9	6
13	18	20	13
6	5	3	3
6	8	9	5
8	13	10	7
11	10	9	7
2	5	7	5

SPSS: The MANOVA command

```
DESCRIPTIVES TIME1 TIME2 TIME3 TIME4 .
```

Descriptives

Descriptive Statistics

	N	Minimum	Maximum	Mean	Std. Deviation
TIME1	8	2	13	8.25	3.495
TIME2	8	5	18	10.38	4.406
TIME3	8	3	20	9.50	4.781
TIME4	8	3	13	6.25	3.059
Valid N (listwise)	8				

```
MANOVA
      TIME1  TIME2  TIME3  TIME4
      /WSFACTOR  TIME(4)
      /ERROR = WITHIN
      /NOPRINT = SIGNIF(MULTIV)
      /WSDESIGN   TIME  .
```

Manova

```
* * * * * * * * * * * * * * * * A n a l y s i s   o f   V a r i a n c e -- Design  1 * * * * * * * * * * * * * *

Tests involving 'TIME' Within-Subject Effect.

AVERAGED.Tests of Significance for TIME using UNIQUE sums of squares
Source of Variation         SS      DF      MS       F  Sig of F

WITHIN CELLS              76.41     21     3.64
TIME                     76.84      3    25.61     7.04    .002

- - - - - - - - - - - - - - - - - - - - - - - - - - - - - - - - - - - - - - - - - - - - - -
```

R: The `stack`, `rep`, `colnames`, `describeBy`, and `aov` functions in the `psych` package

Create new data frame that contains only the levels of the within-subjects variable

Command: `newdataframe <- subset(dataframe,,select = c(variable, variable, variable...))`

Example: `df11 <- subset(df1,,select = c(TIME1,TIME2,TIME3,TIME4))`

Remove anyone with NAs on any variable in the new data frame

Command: `newdataframe <- na.omit(newdataframe)`

Example: `df11 <- na.omit(df11)`

If the data frame has all levels of the within-subjects factor in the same row, (a) rearrange the data frame so that each row contains <u>one</u> level of the within-subjects factor, (b) create a "subject" variable, and (c) add names of variables to data frame.

Command: `newdataframe =stack(newdataframe)`
`nsubjects = #`
`nlevels = #`
`newdataframe =data.frame(recall= newdataframe, subj=factor(rep(paste("subj", 1:nsubjects, sep=""), nlevels)))`
`colnames(newdataframe) = c("labelDV","labelIV","subject")`
NOTE: **nsubjects =** `#` = number of participants
nlevels = `#` = number of levels of within-subjects factor

Example: `df11=stack(df11)`
`nsubjects= 8`
`nlevels= 4`
`df11=data.frame(recall= df11, subj=factor(rep(paste ("subj", 1:nsubjects, sep=""), nlevels)))`
`colnames(df11) = c("DEPVAR","FACTORA","subject")`

Calculate descriptive statistics for the levels of the within-subjects variable

Command: **describeBy(***newdataframe***$***depvar***,**
            *newdataframe***$***factor***)**

Example: describeBy (df11$DEPVAR, df11$FACTORA)

Conduct repeated measures ANOVA

Command: *result* = **aov (***newdataframe***$***depvar* ~
            *newdataframe***$***factor* + **Error (subject/**
            *newdataframe***$***factor***) , data=** *newdataframe***)**
            summary (*result***)**

Example: singlewf = aov(DEPVAR ~ FACTORA +
            Error(subject/FACTORA), data= df11)
            summary(singlewf)

Example script:
```
setwd("e:/R output")
df1 <- read.csv("SINGLEWS_NA.csv")
library(psych)
df11 <- subset(df1,,select = c(TIME1,TIME2,
TIME3,TIME4))
df11 <- na.omit(df11)
df11=stack(df11)
nsubjects= 8
nlevels= 4
df11=data.frame(recall= df11, subj=factor
(rep(paste("subj", 1:nsubjects, sep=""), nlevels)))
colnames(df11) = c("DEPVAR","FACTORA","subject")
describeBy (df11$DEPVAR, df11$FACTORA)
singlewf = aov(DEPVAR ~ FACTORA + Error(subject/
FACTORA), data= df11)
summary(singlewf)
```

```
> setwd("e:/R output")
> df1 <- read.csv("SINGLEWS_NA.csv")
> library(psych)
> df11 <- subset(df1,,select = c(TIME1,TIME2,TIME3,TIME4))
> df11 <- na.omit(df11)
> df11=stack(df11)
> nsubjects= 8
> nlevels= 4
> df11=data.frame(recall= df11, subj=factor(rep(paste("subj", 1:nsubjects, sep=""), nl
evels)))
> colnames(df11) = c("DEPVAR","FACTORA","subject")
> describeBy (df11$DEPVAR, df11$FACTORA)
```

```
 Descriptive statistics by group
group: TIME1
   vars n mean   sd median trimmed  mad min max range  skew kurtosis   se
X1    1 8 8.25 3.49      9    8.25 3.71   2  13    11 -0.38    -1.19 1.24
-----------------------------------------------------------------
group: TIME2
   vars n  mean   sd median trimmed  mad min max range skew kurtosis   se
X1    1 8 10.38 4.41   10.5   10.38 3.71   5  18    13 0.23    -1.28 1.56
-----------------------------------------------------------------
group: TIME3
   vars n mean   sd median trimmed  mad min max range skew kurtosis   se
X1    1 8  9.5 4.78      9     9.5 0.74   3  20    17 0.99     0.34 1.69
-----------------------------------------------------------------
group: TIME4
   vars n mean   sd median trimmed  mad min max range skew kurtosis   se
X1    1 8 6.25 3.06    5.5    6.25 2.22   3  13    10 1.13     0.17 1.08
```

```
> singlewf = aov(DEPVAR ~ FACTORA + Error(subject/FACTORA), data= df11)
> summary(singlewf)
```

```
Error: subject
          Df Sum Sq Mean Sq F value Pr(>F)
Residuals  7  370.5   52.92

Error: subject:FACTORA
          Df Sum Sq Mean Sq F value  Pr(>F)
FACTORA    3  76.84  25.615    7.04 0.00187 **
Residuals 21  76.41   3.638
---
Signif. codes:  0 '***' 0.001 '**' 0.01 '*' 0.05 '.' 0.1 ' ' 1
```

TWO-FACTOR BETWEEN-SUBJECTS ANOVA

EXAMPLE: Conduct two-way between-subjects ANOVA (IVs: *FACTORA*, *FACTORB*; DV: *DEPVAR*) (2 × 3 design)

SPSS: The MEANS and MANOVA command

MEANS DEPVAR by FACTORA by FACTORB .

Means

Report

DEPVAR

FACTORA	FACTORB	Mean	N	Std. Deviation
1 A1	1 B1	4.83	6	1.169
	2 B2	7.67	6	1.211
	3 B3	7.00	6	1.414
	Total	6.50	18	1.724
2 A2	1 B1	5.17	6	1.169
	2 B2	7.17	6	1.169
	3 B3	9.00	6	.894
	Total	7.11	18	1.906
Total	1 B1	5.00	12	1.128
	2 B2	7.42	12	1.165
	3 B3	8.00	12	1.537
	Total	6.81	36	1.818

MANOVA
    DEPVAR by FACTORA (1,2) FACTORB (1,3)
    /ERROR = WITHIN
    /DESIGN .

Manova

* A n a l y s i s   o f   V a r i a n c e -- Design   1 * * * * * * * * * * * * *

Tests of Significance for DEPVAR using UNIQUE sums of squares

Source of Variation	SS	DF	MS	F	Sig of F
WITHIN CELLS	41.83	30	1.39		
FACTORA	3.36	1	3.36	2.41	.131
FACTORB	60.72	2	30.36	21.77	.000
FACTORA BY FACTORB	9.72	2	4.86	3.49	.044
(Model)	73.81	5	14.76	10.59	.000
(Total)	115.64	35	3.30		

R-Squared =   .638
Adjusted R-Squared = .578

- -

R: The factor, describeBy, and aov functions within the psych package

Create new data frame that contains only the variables to be analyzed

Command: *newdataframe* <- subset(*dataframe*,,select =
           c(*variable, variable, variable*))

Example: df11 <- subset(df1,,select =
           c(FACTORA,FACTORB,DEPVAR))

(Continued)

(Continued)

Remove anyone with NAs on any variable in the new data frame

Command: *newdataframe* <- **na.omit**(*newdataframe*)

Example: df11 <- na.omit(df11)

Convert a numeric independent variable to a factor (if IV is a numeric variable)

Command: *newdataframe$factor* <-
factor(*newdataframe$numvar*, **labels =**
c("*label*", "*label*", "*label*"...))
Note: *newdataframe$factor* = name of factor
newdataframe$numvar = numeric independent
variable
label = label to level of factor based on numeric
independent variable

Example: df11$FACTORA.f <- factor(df11$FACTORA,labels
= c("A1","A2"))
df11$FACTORB.f <- factor(df11$FACTORB,labels
= c("B1","B2","B3"))

Calculate descriptive statistics for the main effects and interaction

Command: **describeBy**(*newdataframe$depvar*,
list(*newdataframe$factor*,
newdataframe$factor))
describeBy(*newdataframe$depvar*,
newdataframe$factor)
describeBy(*newdataframe$depvar*,
newdataframe$factor)

Example: describeBy (df11$DEPVAR, list(df11$FACTORA.f,
df11$FACTORB.f))
describeBy (df11$DEPVAR, df11$FACTORA.f)
describeBy (df11$DEPVAR, df11$FACTORB.f)

Conduct two-way between-subjects ANOVA

Command: *result* <- **aov**(*newdataframe$depvar* ~
newdataframe$factor * *newdataframe$factor*,
data = *newdataframe*)
summary(*result*)

Example: twoway <- aov(DEPVAR ~ FACTORA.f * FACTORB.f,
data =df11)
summary(twoway)

Example script:

```
setwd("e:/R output")
df1 <- read.csv("TWOFACTORBS_NA.csv")
library(psych)
df11 <- subset(df1,,select =
c(FACTORA,FACTORB,DEPVAR))
df11 <- na.omit(df11)
df11$FACTORA.f <- factor(df11$FACTORA,labels = c
("A1","A2"))
df11$FACTORB.f <- factor(df11$FACTORB,labels = c
("B1","B2","B3"))
describeBy (df11$DEPVAR,list(df11$FACTORA.f,
df11$FACTORB.f))
describeBy (df11$DEPVAR,df11$FACTORA.f)
describeBy (df11$DEPVAR,df11$FACTORB.f)
twoway <- aov(DEPVAR ~ FACTORA.f * FACTORB.f,
data = df11)
summary(twoway)
```

```
> setwd("e:/R output")
> df1 <- read.csv("TWOFACTORBS_NA.csv")
> library(psych)
> df11 <- subset(df1,,select = c(FACTORA,FACTORB,DEPVAR))
> df11 <- na.omit(df11)
> df11$FACTORA.f <- factor(df11$FACTORA,labels = c("A1","A2"))
> df11$FACTORB.f <- factor(df11$FACTORB,labels = c("B1","B2","B3"))
> describeBy (df11$DEPVAR, list(df11$FACTORA.f, df11$FACTORB.f))

Descriptive statistics by group
: A1
: B1
   vars n mean   sd median trimmed  mad min max range skew kurtosis   se
X1    1 6 4.83 1.17      5    4.83 1.48   3   6     3 -0.37    -1.62 0.48
-----------------------------------------------------------------
: A2
: B1
   vars n mean   sd median trimmed  mad min max range skew kurtosis   se
X1    1 6 5.17 1.17      5    5.17 1.48   4   7     3  0.37    -1.62 0.48
-----------------------------------------------------------------
: A1
: B2
   vars n mean   sd median trimmed  mad min max range skew kurtosis   se
X1    1 6 7.67 1.21    7.5    7.67 1.48   6   9     3 -0.04    -1.88 0.49
-----------------------------------------------------------------
: A2
: B2
   vars n mean   sd median trimmed  mad min max range skew kurtosis   se
X1    1 6 7.17 1.17      7    7.17 1.48   6   9     3  0.37    -1.62 0.48
-----------------------------------------------------------------
```

```
------------------------------------------------------------------
: A1
: B2
     vars n mean   sd median trimmed  mad min max range  skew kurtosis   se
X1      1 6 7.67 1.21    7.5    7.67 1.48   6   9     3 -0.04    -1.88 0.49
------------------------------------------------------------------
: A2
: B2
     vars n mean   sd median trimmed  mad min max range skew kurtosis   se
X1      1 6 7.17 1.17      7    7.17 1.48   6   9     3 0.37    -1.62 0.48
------------------------------------------------------------------
: A1
: B3
     vars n mean   sd median trimmed  mad min max range skew kurtosis   se
X1      1 6    7 1.41      7       7 1.48   5   9     4    0    -1.58 0.58
------------------------------------------------------------------
: A2
: B3
     vars n mean   sd median trimmed  mad min max range skew kurtosis   se
X1      1 6    9 0.89      9       9 1.48   8  10     2    0    -1.96 0.37
```

```
> describeBy (df11$DEPVAR, df11$FACTORA.f)
group: A1
      vars  n mean   sd median trimmed  mad min max range  skew kurtosis   se
X1       1 18  6.5 1.72    6.5    6.56 2.22   3   9     6 -0.16    -0.91 0.41
------------------------------------------------------------------------
group: A2
      vars  n mean   sd median trimmed  mad min max range skew kurtosis   se
X1       1 18 7.11 1.91      7    7.12 2.22   4  10     6 -0.1    -1.27 0.45
> describeBy (df11$DEPVAR, df11$FACTORB.f)
group: B1
      vars  n mean   sd median trimmed  mad min max range skew kurtosis   se
X1       1 12    5 1.13      5       5 1.48   3   7     4    0    -1.05 0.33
------------------------------------------------------------------------
group: B2
      vars  n mean   sd median trimmed  mad min max range skew kurtosis   se
X1       1 12 7.42 1.16      7     7.4 1.48   6   9     3 0.18    -1.58 0.34
------------------------------------------------------------------------
group: B3
      vars  n mean   sd median trimmed  mad min max range  skew kurtosis   se
X1       1 12    8 1.54      8     8.1 1.48   5  10     5 -0.41       -1 0.44
```

```
> df11$FACTORA.f <- factor(df11$FACTORA, labels = c("A1", "A2"))
> df11$FACTORB.f <- factor(df11$FACTORB, labels = c("B1", "B2", "B3"))
> twoway <- aov(DEPVAR ~ FACTORA.f * FACTORB.f, data = df11)
> summary(twoway)
                  Df Sum Sq Mean Sq F value   Pr(>F)
FACTORA.f          1   3.36   3.361   2.410   0.1310
FACTORB.f          2  60.72  30.361  21.773 1.44e-06 ***
FACTORA.f:FACTORB.f 2   9.72   4.861   3.486   0.0435 *
Residuals         30  41.83   1.394
---
Signif. codes:  0 '***' 0.001 '**' 0.01 '*' 0.05 '.' 0.1 ' ' 1
```

TWO-FACTOR BETWEEN-SUBJECTS ANOVA (SIMPLE EFFECTS)

EXAMPLE: Conduct simple effects of *FACTORB* at each level of *FACTORA*

SPSS: The MANOVA command

```
MANOVA
   DEPVAR by FACTORA (1,2) FACTORB (1,3)
   /ERROR = WITHIN
   /DESIGN    FACTORB within FACTORA(1)    FACTORB within FACTORA(2) .
```

Manova

```
* * * * * * * * * * * * * * * * * * A n a l y s i s   o f   V a r i a n c e -- Design  1 * * * * * * * * * * * *

Tests of Significance for DEPVAR using UNIQUE sums of squares
Source of Variation        SS      DF      MS        F   Sig of F

WITHIN CELLS             41.83     30    1.39
FACTORB WITHIN FACTO     26.33      2   13.17     9.44     .001
RA(1)
FACTORB WITHIN FACTO     44.11      2   22.06    15.82     .000
RA(2)
```

- -

R: The `factor`, `aov` and `testInteractions` functions and the `psych` and `phia` packages

Create new data frame that contains only the variables to be analyzed

Command: `newdataframe <- subset(dataframe,,select = c(variable, variable, variable))`

Example: `df11 <- subset(df1,,select = c(FACTORA,FACTORB,DEPVAR))`

Remove anyone with NAs on any variable in the new data frame

Command: `newdataframe <- na.omit(newdataframe)`

Example: `df11 <- na.omit(df11)`

Convert a numeric independent variable to a factor (if IV is a numeric variable)

Command: `newdataframe$factor <- factor(newdataframe$numvar, labels = c("label", "label", "label"...))`

Example: `df11$FACTORA.f <- factor(df11$FACTORA, labels = c("A1","A2"))`

`df11$FACTORB.f <- factor(df11$FACTORB, labels = c("B1","B2","B3"))`

(Continued)

(Continued)

Conduct two-way between-subjects ANOVA

Command: *result* **<- aov(***newdataframe$depvar* ~
newdataframe$factor * *newdataframe$factor*,
data = *newdataframe***)**

Example: twoway <- aov(DEPVAR ~ FACTORA.f * FACTORB.f,
data = df11)

Conduct simple effects analyses

Command: **testInteractions(***result*, **fixed=**"*newdataframe
$factor*", **across=**"*newdataframe$factor*",
adjustment="none")

Example: testInteractions(twoway, fixed="FACTORA.f",
across="FACTORB.f", adjustment="none")

Example script:

```
setwd("e:/R output")
df1 <- read.csv("TWOFACTORBS_NA.csv")
library(psych)
library(phia)
df11 <- subset(df1, ,select = c(FACTORA,FACTORB,DEP-
VAR))
df11 <- na.omit(df11)
df11$FACTORA.f <- factor(df11$FACTORA,
labels = c("A1","A2"))
df11$FACTORB.f <- factor(df11$FACTORB,
labels = c("B1","B2","B3"))
twoway <- aov(DEPVAR ~ FACTORA.f * FACTORB.f,
data = df11)
testInteractions(twoway, fixed="FACTORA.f",
across="FACTORB.f", adjustment="none")
```

```
> setwd("e:/R output")
> df1 <- read.csv("TWOFACTORBS_NA.csv")
> library(psych)
> library(phia)
> df11 <- subset(df1, ,select = c(FACTORA,FACTORB,DEPVAR))
> df11 <- na.omit(df11)
> df11$FACTORA.f <- factor(df11$FACTORA, labels = c("A1","A2"))
> df11$FACTORB.f <- factor(df11$FACTORB, labels = c("B1","B2","B3"))
> twoway <- aov(DEPVAR ~ FACTORA.f * FACTORB.f, data = df11)
> testInteractions(twoway, fixed="FACTORA.f", across="FACTORB.f", adjustment="none")
F Test:
P-value adjustment method: none
           FACTORB.f1 FACTORB.f2 Df Sum of Sq      F    Pr(>F)
A1           -2.1667    0.66667   2    26.333  9.4422 0.0006596 ***
A2           -3.8333   -1.83333   2    44.111 15.8167 2.04e-05  ***
Residuals                        30    41.833
---
Signif. codes:  0 '***' 0.001 '**' 0.01 '*' 0.05 '.' 0.1 ' ' 1
>
```

TWO-FACTOR BETWEEN-SUBJECTS ANOVA (SIMPLE COMPARISONS)

EXAMPLE: Compare levels of *FACTORB* within level *A1* of *FACTORA*

SPSS: The MANOVA command

```
MANOVA
   DEPVAR by FACTORA (1,2) FACTORB (1,3)
   /ERROR = WITHIN
   /CONTRAST(FACTORB)  =  SPECIAL ( 1   1   1
                                    1  -1   0
                                    0   1  -1)
   /DESIGN   FACTORB(1) within FACTORA(1)    FACTORB(2) within FACTORA(1) .
```

Manova

```
* * * * * * * * * * * * * * * * * * A n a l y s i s   o f   V a r i a n c e -- Design  1 * * * * * * * * * * * *

Tests of Significance for DEPVAR using UNIQUE sums of squares
Source of Variation        SS      DF     MS       F   Sig of F

WITHIN CELLS             41.83     30    1.39
FACTORB(1) WITHIN FA     24.08      1   24.08   17.27    .000
CTORA(1)
FACTORB(2) WITHIN FA      1.33      1    1.33     .96    .336
CTORA(1)

- - - - - - - - - - - - - - - - - - - - - - - - - - - - - - - - - - - - - -
```

R: The `factor`, `list`, `aov` and `testInteractions` functions in the `psych` and `phia` packages

Create new data frame that contains only the variables to be analyzed

Command: `newdataframe <- subset(dataframe,,select = c(variable, variable, variable))`

Example: `df11 <- subset(df1,,select = c(FACTORA,FACTORB,DEPVAR))`

Remove anyone with NAs on any variable in the new data frame

Command: `newdataframe <- na.omit(newdataframe)`

Example: `df11 <- na.omit(df11)`

Convert a numeric independent variable to a factor (if IV is a numeric variable)

Command: `newdataframe$factor <- factor(newdataframe$numvar, labels = c("label", "label", "label"...))`

Example: `df11$FACTORA.f <- factor(df11$FACTORA, labels = c("A1","A2"))`

`df11$FACTORB.f <- factor(df11$FACTORB, labels = c("B1","B2","B3"))`

Conduct two-way between-subjects ANOVA

Command: `result <- aov(newdataframe$depvar ~ newdataframe$factor * newdataframe$factor, data = newdataframe)`

Example: `twoway <- aov(DEPVAR ~ FACTORA.f * FACTORB.f, data = df11)`

Provide coefficients needed to conduct simple comparisons

Command: `comp <- list(newdataframe$factor = c(# # #...) )`

Note: # = coefficient

Example: `b1_vs_b2 <- list(FACTORB.f = c(1, -1, 0))`

`b2_vs_b3 <- list(FACTORB.f = c(0, 1, -1))`

Conduct simple comparisons analyses

Command: `testInteractions(result, custom=c(comp), fixed="newdataframe$factor", adjustment="none")`

Example: `testInteractions(twoway, custom=c(b1_vs_b2), fixed="FACTORA.f", adjustment="none")`

Example script:

```
setwd("e:/R output")
df1 <- read.csv("TWOFACTORBS_NA.csv")
library(psych)
library(phia)
df11 <- subset(df1, ,select =
c(FACTORA,FACTORB,DEPVAR))
df11 <- na.omit(df11)
df11$FACTORA.f <- factor(df11$FACTORA,
labels = c("A1","A2"))
df11$FACTORB.f <- factor(df11$FACTORB,
labels = c("B1","B2","B3"))
twoway <- aov(DEPVAR ~ FACTORA.f * FACTORB.f,
data = df11)
b1_vs_b2 <- list(FACTORB.f = c(1, -1, 0))
b2_vs_b3 <- list(FACTORB.f = c(0, 1, -1))
testInteractions(twoway, custom=c(b1_vs_b2),
fixed="FACTORA.f", adjustment="none")
testInteractions(twoway, custom=c(b2_vs_b3),
fixed="FACTORA.f", adjustment="none")
```

```
> setwd("e:/R output")
> df1 <- read.csv("TWOFACTORBS_NA.csv")
> library(psych)
> library(phia)
> df11 <- subset(df1, ,select = c(FACTORA,FACTORB,DEPVAR))
> df11 <- na.omit(df11)
> df11$FACTORA.f <- factor(df11$FACTORA, labels = c("A1","A2"))
> df11$FACTORB.f <- factor(df11$FACTORB, labels = c("B1","B2","B3"))
> twoway <- aov(DEPVAR ~ FACTORA.f * FACTORB.f, data = df11)
> b1_vs_b2 <- list(FACTORB.f = c(1, -1, 0))
> b2_vs_b3 <- list(FACTORB.f = c(0, 1, -1))
> testInteractions(twoway, custom=c(b1_vs_b2), fixed="FACTORA.f", adjustment="none")
F Test:
P-value adjustment method: none
                  value Df Sum of Sq        F    Pr(>F)
A1 : FACTORB.f1 -2.8333  1    24.083 17.2709 0.0002484 ***
A2 : FACTORB.f1 -2.0000  1    12.000  8.6056 0.0063663 **
Residuals               30    41.833
---
Signif. codes:  0 '***' 0.001 '**' 0.01 '*' 0.05 '.' 0.1 ' ' 1
> testInteractions(twoway, custom=c(b2_vs_b3), fixed="FACTORA.f", adjustment="none")
F Test:
P-value adjustment method: none
                  value Df Sum of Sq        F   Pr(>F)
A1 : FACTORB.f1  0.66667  1     1.333 0.9562 0.33597
A2 : FACTORB.f1 -1.83333  1    10.083 7.2311 0.01159 *
Residuals                30    41.833
---
Signif. codes:  0 '***' 0.001 '**' 0.01 '*' 0.05 '.' 0.1 ' ' 1
```

TWO-FACTOR BETWEEN-SUBJECTS ANOVA (MAIN COMPARISONS)

EXAMPLE: Compare levels of *FACTORB*

SPSS: The MANOVA command

```
MANOVA
   DEPVAR by FACTORA (1,2) FACTORB (1,3)
   /ERROR = WITHIN
   /CONTRAST(FACTORB)  =  SPECIAL ( 1   1   1
                                     1  -1   0
                                     0   1  -1)
   /DESIGN   FACTORB(1)   FACTORB(2)  .
```

Manova

```
* * * * * * * * * * * * * * * * * A n a l y s i s   o f   V a r i a n c e -- Design   1 * * * * * * * * * * * * * *

Tests of Significance for DEPVAR using UNIQUE sums of squares
Source of Variation        SS  .   DF       MS        F  Sig of F

WITHIN CELLS            41.83       30     1.39
FACTORB(1)              35.04        1    35.04     25.13    .000
FACTORB(2)               2.04        1     2.04      1.46    .236

- - - - - - - - - - - - - - - - - - - - - - - - - - - - - - - - - - - - - - - - - - - -
```

R: The `factor`, `list`, `aov` and `testInteractions` functions in the `psych` and `phia` packages

Create new data frame that contains only the variables to be analyzed

Command: `newdataframe <- subset(dataframe,,select = c(variable, variable, variable))`

Example: `df11 <- subset(df1,,select = c(FACTORA,FACTORB,DEPVAR))`

Remove anyone with NAs on any variable in the new data frame

Command: `newdataframe <- na.omit(newdataframe)`

Example: `df11 <- na.omit(df11)`

Convert a numeric independent variable to a factor (if IV is a numeric variable)

Command: `newdataframe$factor <- factor (newdataframe$numvar, labels = c("label", "label", "label"...))`

Example: `df11$FACTORA.f <- factor(df11$FACTORA, labels = c("A1","A2"))`

                 `df11$FACTORB.f <- factor(df11$FACTORB, labels = c("B1","B2","B3"))`

Conduct two-way between-subjects ANOVA

Command: `result <- aov(newdataframe$depvar ~`
`newdataframe$factor * newdataframe$factor,`
`data = newdataframe)`

Example: `twoway <- aov(DEPVAR ~ FACTORA.f * FACTORB.f,`
`data = df11)`

Provide coefficients needed to conduct main comparisons

Command: `comp <- list(newdataframe$factor = c(# #`
`#...) )`

Note: # = coefficient

Example: `b1_vs_b2 <- list(FACTORB.f = c(1, -1, 0))`

`b2_vs_b3 <- list(FACTORB.f = c(0, 1, -1))`

Conduct main comparisons

Command: `testInteractions(result, custom=c(comp),`
`adjustment="none")`

Example: `testInteractions(twoway, custom=c(b1_vs_`
`b2), adjustment="none")`

Example script:
```
setwd("e:/R output")
df1 <- read.csv("TWOFACTORBS_NA.csv")
library(psych)
library(phia)
df11 <- subset(df1, ,select =
c(FACTORA,FACTORB,DEPVAR))
df11 <- na.omit(df11)
df11$FACTORA.f <- factor(df11$FACTORA,
labels = c("A1","A2"))
df11$FACTORB.f <- factor(df11$FACTORB,
labels = c("B1","B2","B3"))
twoway <- aov(DEPVAR ~ FACTORA.f * FACTORB.f,
data = df11)
b1_vs_b2 <- list(FACTORB.f = c(1, -1, 0))
b2_vs_b3 <- list(FACTORB.f = c(0, 1, -1))
testInteractions(twoway, custom=c(b1_vs_b2),
adjustment="none")
testInteractions(twoway, custom=c(b2_vs_b3),
adjustment="none")
```

```
> setwd("e:/R output")
> df1 <- read.csv("TWOFACTORBS_NA.csv")
> library(psych)
> library(phia)
> df11 <- subset(df1, ,select = c(FACTORA,FACTORB,DEPVAR))
> df11 <- na.omit(df11)
> df11$FACTORA.f <- factor(df11$FACTORA, labels = c("A1","A2"))
> df11$FACTORB.f <- factor(df11$FACTORB, labels = c("B1","B2","B3"))
> twoway <- aov(DEPVAR ~ FACTORA.f * FACTORB.f, data = df11)
> b1_vs_b2 <- list(FACTORB.f = c(1, -1,  0))
> b2_vs_b3 <- list(FACTORB.f = c(0,  1, -1))
> testInteractions(twoway, custom=c(b1_vs_b2), adjustment="none")
F Test:
P-value adjustment method: none
             Value Df Sum of Sq     F    Pr(>F)
FACTORB.f1 -2.4167  1    35.042 25.13 2.246e-05 ***
Residuals           30    41.833
---
Signif. codes:  0 '***' 0.001 '**' 0.01 '*' 0.05 '.' 0.1 ' ' 1
> testInteractions(twoway, custom=c(b2_vs_b3), adjustment="none")
F Test:
P-value adjustment method: none
              Value Df Sum of Sq      F Pr(>F)
FACTORB.f1 -0.58333  1     2.042 1.4641 0.2357
Residuals            30    41.833
```

TWO-FACTOR MIXED FACTORIAL ANOVA

EXAMPLE: Conduct ANOVA for one between-subjects factor (*BETWEEN*) and one within-subjects factor (*WITHIN*) (3 × 4 design)

SPSS: The MEANS and MANOVA command

Note: This example assumes (a) the data file resembles the one below (one line per participant) and (b) the groups that make up the between-subjects factor are the same size (in this example, three groups with $n = 10$).

BETWEEN	TIME1	TIME2	TIME3	TIME4
1	30	26	25	15
1	23	22	20	10
1	26	21	20	17
1	20	17	21	13
1	31	27	25	18
1	23	22	26	16
1	29	25	24	13
1	33	29	30	24
1	26	28	25	18
1	21	19	23	15
2	22	23	29	18
2	22	21	27	18

```
COMPUTE  TIME = MEAN(TIME1, TIME2, TIME3, TIME4) .
EXECUTE  .
MEANS  TIME1  TIME2  TIME3 TIME4   TIME  by BETWEEN .
```

Means

Report

BETWEEN		TIME1	TIME2	TIME3	TIME4	TIME
1 Group 1	Mean	26.20	23.60	23.90	15.90	22.4000
	N	10	10	10	10	10
	Std. Deviation	4.442	4.006	3.071	3.784	3.39157
2 Group 2	Mean	23.10	21.90	27.00	22.40	23.6000
	N	10	10	10	10	10
	Std. Deviation	3.143	2.923	3.055	5.232	2.64102
3 Group 3	Mean	21.40	20.00	27.40	19.50	22.0750
	N	10	10	10	10	10
	Std. Deviation	4.377	3.333	4.742	4.223	3.41168
Total	Mean	23.57	21.83	26.10	19.27	22.6917
	N	30	30	30	30	30
	Std. Deviation	4.384	3.649	3.916	5.078	3.12918

```
MANOVA
    TIME1  TIME2  TIME3 TIME4  by BETWEEN (1,3)
    /WSFACTOR  TIME(4)
    /NOPRINT = SIGNIF(MULTIV)
    /ERROR = WITHIN
    /DESIGN  .
```

Manova

```
* * * * * * * * * * * * * * * * * *Analysis  of  Variance -- Design  1 * * * * * * * * * * * *

Tests of Between-Subjects Effects.

Tests of Significance for T1 using UNIQUE sums of squares
Source of Variation         SS      DF       MS       F  Sig of F

WITHIN CELLS             1084.23    27     40.16
BETWEEN                    51.62     2     25.81     .64     .534

- - - - - - - - - - - - - - - - - - - - - - - - - - - - - - - - - - - - - - - - - - - - - - - - - - - -


* * * * * * * * * * * * * * * * * *Analysis  of  Variance -- Design  1 * * * * * * * * * * * *

Tests involving 'TIME' Within-Subject Effect.

AVERAGED Tests of Significance for TIME using UNIQUE sums of squares
Source of Variation         SS      DF       MS       F  Sig of F

WITHIN CELLS              583.08    81      7.20
TIME                     745.49     3    248.50    34.52    .000
BETWEEN BY TIME          417.18     6     69.53     9.66    .000

- - - - - - - - - - - - - - - - - - - - - - - - - - - - - - - - - - - - - - - - - - - - - - - - - - - .
```

R: The `factor`, `describeBy`, and `aov` functions in the `psych` package

Create new data frame that contains only the variables to be analyzed

Command: *newdataframe* <- **subset(***dataframe*, **,select = c(***variable*, *variable*, *variable...***))**

Example: df11 <- subset(df1, ,select = c(TIME1,TIME2,TIME3,TIME4))

Remove anyone with NAs on any variable in the new data frame

Command: *newdataframe* <- **na.omit(***newdataframe***)**

Example: df11 <- na.omit(df11)

If the data frame has all levels of the within-subjects factor in the same row, (a) rearrange the data frame so that each row contains <u>one</u> level of the within-subjects factor, (b) create a "subject" variable, and (c) add names of variables to data frame.

Command: *newdataframe* =**stack(***newdataframe*]
nlevelsw= #
ngroup= #
ntotal= #
newdataframe =**data.frame(recall=**
newdataframe, **subj=factor(rep(paste("subj",**
1:nsubjects,sep=""), nlevels)))
newdataframe =**data.frame(recall=**
newdataframe$*BSfactor*
=**factor(rep(c("***label***", "***label***",
"***label***"...), c(***ngroup*, *ngroup*,
ngroup,...***)))**,subj=factor(rep(paste("subj",
1:ntotal, sep=""), nlevelsw)))
colnames(*newdataframe***)=**
c("*DV***","***WSfactor***","***BSfactor***","subject")**
NOTE: **nlevelsw=** # = number of levels of within-subjects factor
ngroup= # = number in each group (between-subjects factor)
ntotal= # = total number of participants

Example: df11=stack(df11)
nlevelsw= 4
ngroup= 10
ntotal= 30
df11 =data.frame(recall= df11,
BETWEEN=factor(rep(c("Group1",
"Group2","Group3"),c(ngroup,ngroup,
ngroup))),subj=factor(rep(paste("subj",
1:ntotal, sep=""), nlevelsw)))

colnames(df11) = c("DEPVAR","WITHIN",
"BETWEEN","subject")

Calculate descriptive statistics for the main effects and interaction

Command: **describeBy(**`newdataframe`**$DV,**
list(`newdataframe`**$BSfactor,**
`newdataframe`**$WSfactor)**
describeBy(`newdataframe`**$DV,** `newdataframe`
$BSfactor)
describeBy(`newdataframe`**$DV,** `newdataframe`
$WSfactor)

Example: describeBy (df11$DEPVAR, list(df11$BETWEEN,
df11$WITHIN))
describeBy (df11$DEPVAR, df11$BETWEEN)
describeBy (df11$DEPVAR, df11$WITHIN)

Conduct the two-factor mixed factorial ANOVA

Command: `result` **<- aov(**`newdataframe`**$DV**
~ `newdataframe`**$BSfactor** *****
`newdataframe`**$WSfactor + Error(subject/**
`newdataframe`**$WSfactor), data =**`newdataframe`**)**
summary(`result`**)**

Example: mixed = aov(DEPVAR ~ BETWEEN * WITHIN +
Error(subject/WITHIN), data=df11)
summary(mixed)

Example script:

```
setwd("e:/R output")
df1 <- read.csv("TWOMIXED_NA.csv")
library(psych)
df11 <- subset(df1, ,select = c(TIME1,TIME2,TIME3,TIME4))
df11 <- na.omit(df11)
df11=stack(df11)
nlevelsw= 4
ngroup= 10
ntotal= 30
df11 =data.frame(recall= df11, BETWEEN=factor
(rep(c("Group1", "Group2","Group3"),
c(ngroup,ngroup,ngroup))),subj=factor
(rep(paste("subj", 1:ntotal, sep=""), nlevelsw)))

colnames(df11) = c("DEPVAR","WITHIN",
"BETWEEN","subject")
```

(Continued)

(Continued)

```
describeBy (df11$DEPVAR, list(df11$BETWEEN,
df11$WITHIN))
describeBy (df11$DEPVAR, df11$BETWEEN)
describeBy (df11$DEPVAR, df11$WITHIN)
mixed = aov(DEPVAR ~ BETWEEN * WITHIN + Error(subject/
WITHIN), data= df11)
summary(mixed)
```

```
> setwd("e:/R output")
> df1 <- read.csv("TWOMIXED_NA.csv")
> library(psych)
> df11 <- subset(df1, ,select = c(TIME1,TIME2,TIME3,TIME4))
> df11 <- na.omit(df11)
> df11=stack(df11)
> nlevelsw= 4
> ngroup= 10
> ntotal= 30
> df11 =data.frame(recall= df11, BETWEEN=factor(rep(c("Group1", "Group2","Group3"),c(n
group,ngroup,ngroup))),subj=factor(rep(paste("subj", 1:ntotal, sep=""), nlevelsw)))
> colnames(df11) = c("DEPVAR","WITHIN","BETWEEN","subject")

> mixed = aov(DEPVAR ~ BETWEEN * WITHIN + Error(subject/WITHIN), data= df11)
> summary(mixed)

Error: subject
          Df Sum Sq Mean Sq F value Pr(>F)
BETWEEN    2   51.6   25.81   0.643  0.534
Residuals 27 1084.2   40.16

Error: subject:WITHIN
               Df Sum Sq Mean Sq F value   Pr(>F)
WITHIN          3  745.5  248.50  34.521 1.79e-14 ***
BETWEEN:WITHIN  6  417.2   69.53   9.659 5.28e-08 ***
Residuals      81  583.1    7.20
---
Signif. codes:  0 '***' 0.001 '**' 0.01 '*' 0.05 '.' 0.1 ' ' 1
```

TWO-FACTOR WITHIN-SUBJECTS ANOVA

EXAMPLE: Conduct ANOVA for two within-subjects factors (*WSfactor1* and *WSfactor2*)) (2 × 3 design)

Note: This example assumes the data file resembles the one below (one line per participant):

a1b1	a1b2	a1b3	a2b1	a2b2	a2b3
8	12	9	15	10	7
20	15	8	11	9	4
6	10	4	9	6	5

SPSS: The MEANS and MANOVA command

```
COMPUTE  A1 = MEAN(a1b1, a1b2, a1b3) .
COMPUTE  A2 = MEAN(a2b1, a2b2, a2b3) .
COMPUTE  B1 = MEAN(a1b1, a2b1) .
COMPUTE  B2 = MEAN(a1b2, a2b2) .
COMPUTE  B3 = MEAN(a1b3, a2b3) .
EXECUTE  .
DESCRIPTIVES  A1  A2  B1  B2  B3.
```

Descriptives

Descriptive Statistics

	N	Minimum	Maximum	Mean	Std. Deviation
A1	3	6.33	11.00	9.1111	2.45704
A2	3	6.67	10.67	8.4444	2.03670
B1	3	7.00	11.50	9.6667	2.36291
B2	3	8.00	12.00	10.3333	2.08167
B3	3	4.50	8.50	6.3333	2.02073
Valid N (listwise)	3				

```
MANOVA
   a1b1 a1b2 a1b3 a2b1 a2b2 a2b3
   /WSFACTOR  WSFACTORA(2)  WSFACTORB(3)
   /NOPRINT = SIGNIF(MULTIV)
   /WSDESIGN  .
```

Manova

```
- - - - - - - - - - - - - - - - - - - - - - - - - - - - - - - - - - - - - - - - - - - - - - - -
Cell Means and Standard Deviations
Variable .. a1b1

                               Mean  Std. Dev.       N   95 percent Conf. Interval

For entire sample             7.667    2.517         3     1.415    13.918

- - - - - - - - - - - - - - - - - - - - - - - - - - - - - - - - - - - - - - - - - - - - - - - -
Variable .. a1b2

                               Mean  Std. Dev.       N   95 percent Conf. Interval

For entire sample            12.333    2.517         3     6.082    18.585

- - - - - - - - - - - - - - - - - - - - - - - - - - - - - - - - - - - - - - - - - - - - - - - -
Variable .. a1b3

                               Mean  Std. Dev.       N   95 percent Conf. Interval

For entire sample             7.333    3.055         3     -.256    14.922

- - - - - - - - - - - - - - - - - - - - - - - - - - - - - - - - - - - - - - - - - - - - - - - -
Variable .. a2b1

                               Mean  Std. Dev.       N   95 percent Conf. Interval

For entire sample            11.667    3.055         3     4.078    19.256

- - - - - - - - - - - - - - - - - - - - - - - - - - - - - - - - - - - - - - - - - - - - - - - -
Variable .. a2b2

                               Mean  Std. Dev.       N   95 percent Conf. Interval

For entire sample             8.333    2.082         3     3.162    13.504

- - - - - - - - - - - - - - - - - - - - - - - - - - - - - - - - - - - - - - - - - - - - - - - -
Variable .. a2b3

                               Mean  Std. Dev.       N   95 percent Conf. Interval

For entire sample             5.333    1.528         3     1.539     9.128
```

```
* * * * * * * * * * * * * * * * * *Analysis   of   Variance -- Design   1 * * * * * * * * * * * *
```

Tests of Between-Subjects Effects.

Tests of Significance for T1 using UNIQUE sums of squares

Source of Variation	SS	DF	MS	F	Sig of F
WITHIN CELLS	48.78	2	24.39		
CONSTANT	1386.89	1	1386.89	56.87	.017

- -

```
* * * * * * * * * * * * * * * * * *Analysis   of   Variance -- Design   1 * * * * * * * * * * * *
```

Tests involving 'WSFACTORA' Within-Subject Effect.

Tests of Significance for T2 using UNIQUE sums of squares

Source of Variation	SS	DF	MS	F	Sig of F
WITHIN CELLS	12.33	2	6.17		
WSFACTORA	2.00	1	2.00	.32	.626

- -

```
* * * * * * * * * * * * * * * * * *Analysis   of   Variance -- Design   1 * * * * * * * * * * * *
```

Tests involving 'WSFACTORB' Within-Subject Effect.

AVERAGED Tests of Significance for MEAS.1 using UNIQUE sums of squares

Source of Variation	SS	DF	MS	F	Sig of F
WITHIN CELLS	7.22	4	1.81		
WSFACTORB	55.11	2	27.56	15.26	.013

- -

```
* * * * * * * * * * * * * * * * * *Analysis   of   Variance -- Design   1 * * * * * * * * * * * *
```

Tests involving 'WSFACTORA BY WSFACTORB' Within-Subject Effect.

AVERAGED Tests of Significance for MEAS.1 using UNIQUE sums of squares

Source of Variation	SS	DF	MS	F	Sig of F
WITHIN CELLS	7.67	4	1.92		
WSFACTORA BY WSFACTORB	52.00	2	26.00	13.57	.017

- -

R: The `factor`, `describeBy`, and `aov` functions within the `psych` package

Create new data frame that contains only the variables to be analyzed

> Command: `newdataframe <- subset(dataframe, ,select = c(variable, variable, variable...))`
>
> Example: `df11 <- subset(df1,,select = c(a1b1,a1b2,a1b3,a2b1,a2b2,a2b3))`

Remove anyone with NAs on any variable in the new data frame

> Command: `newdataframe <- na.omit(newdataframe)`
>
> Example: `df11 <- na.omit(df11)`

If the data frame has all combinations of the within-subjects factors in the same row, (a) rearrange the data frame so that each row contains <u>one</u> combination of the within-subjects factors, (b) create a "subject" variable, and (c) add names of variables to data frame.

Command: *newdataframe* =**stack**(*newdataframe*)
ncases= #
nobs= #
newdataframe =**data.frame**(**recall=**
newdataframe, **subj=factor**(**rep**(**paste**("subj",
1: **ncases, sep=**""), **nobs**)), *WSfactor1*
=**factor**(**rep**(**rep**(**c**("*label*","*label*",…),
c(*ncases* * #, *ncases* *#,*…*)))), *WSfactor2*
=**factor**(**rep**(**c**("*label*","*label*",…), **c**(*ncases*,
ncases, …))))
colnames(*newdataframe*) =
c("*DV*","*ABCOMB*","**subject**",
"*WSfactor1*", "*WSfactor2*")
Note: **ncases =** # = total number of participants
  nobs = # = number observations for each participant

Example: df11=stack(df11)
ncases= 3
nobs= 6
df11=data.frame(recall=df11,subj=factor
(rep(paste("subj", 1:
ncases, sep=""), nobs)),
WSFACTORA=factor(rep(rep(c("A1","A2"),
c(ncases*3, ncases *3)))),WSFACTORB=
factor(rep(c("B1","B2","B3"), c(ncases,
ncases, ncases))))
colnames(df11) = c("DEPVAR","ABCOMB",
"subject", "WSFACTORA", "WSFACTORB")

Calculate descriptive statistics for the main effects and interaction

Command: **describeBy**(*newdataframe$DV*,
list(*newdataframe$WSfactor1*,
newdataframe$WSfactor2)
describeBy(*newdataframe$DV*,
newdataframe$WSfactor1)
describeBy(*newdataframe$DV*,
newdataframe$WSfactor2)

(Continued)

(Continued)

```
Example:    describeBy (df11$DEPVAR, list
            (df11$WSFACTORA,df11$WSFACTORB))
            describeBy (df11$DEPVAR,df11$WSFACTORA)
            describeBy (df11$DEPVAR,df11$WSFACTORB)
```

Conduct two-factor within-subjects ANOVA

```
Command:    result <- aov(newdataframe$DV ~
            newdataframe$WSfactor1 *
            newdataframe$WSfactor2 + Error(subject/
            (newdataframe$WSfactor1 *
            newdataframe$WSfactor2), data =
            newdataframe)
            summary(result)

Example:    twowithin= aov(DEPVAR ~ WSFACTORA * WSFACTORB
            + Error(subject/(WSFACTORA * WSFACTORB)),
            data=df11)
            summary(twowithin)
```

Example script:

```
setwd("e:/R output")
df1 <- read.csv("TWOFACTORWS_NA.csv")
library(psych)
df11 <- subset(df1,,select = c(a1b1,a1b2,a1b3,a2b1,a2b
2,a2b3))
df11 <- na.omit(df11)
df11=stack(df11)
ncases= 3
nobs= 6
df11=data.frame(recall=df11,subj=factor(rep(paste("subj",
1: ncases, sep=""), nobs)), WSFACTORA=factor
(rep(rep(c("A1","A2"), c(ncases*3, ncases
*3)))),WSFACTORB=factor(rep(c("B1","B2","B3"), c(ncases,
ncases, ncases))))
colnames(df11) = c("DEPVAR","ABCOMB","subject",
"WSFACTORA","WSFACTORB")
describeBy (df11$DEPVAR, list(df11$WSFACTORA,
df11$WSFACTORB))
describeBy (df11$DEPVAR, df11$WSFACTORA)
describeBy (df11$DEPVAR, df11$WSFACTORB)
twowithin= aov(DEPVAR ~ WSFACTORA * WSFACTORB +
Error(subject/(WSFACTORA * WSFACTORB)), data=df11)
summary(twowithin)
```

```
> setwd("e:/R output") .
> df1 <- read.csv("ANOVA_NA.csv")
> library("psych")
> df11 <- subset(df1, , select = c(a1b1,a1b2,a1b3,a2b1,a2b2,a2b3))
> df11 <- na.omit(df11)
> df11 =stack(df11)
> ncases= 3
> nobs= 6
> df11=data.frame(recall=df11,subj=factor(rep(paste("subj", 1: ncases, sep=""), nobs)),WSFACTORA=factor(rep(rep
(c("A1","A2"), c(ncases *3, ncases *3)))),WSFACTORB=factor(rep(rep(c("B1","B2","B3"), c(ncases, ncases, ncases))))
> colnames(df11) = c("DEPVAR","ABCOMB","subject", "WSFACTORA","WSFACTORB")
> describeBy (df11$DEPVAR, list(df11$WSFACTORA, df11$WSFACTORB))

 Descriptive statistics by group
: A1
: B1
    vars n mean   sd median trimmed  mad min max range  skew kurtosis   se
X1     1 3 7.67 2.52      8    7.67 2.97   5  10     5 -0.13    -2.33 1.45
-------------------------------------------------------------------------
: A2
: B1
    vars n  mean   sd median trimmed  mad min max range skew kurtosis   se
X1     1 3 11.67 3.06     11   11.67 2.97   9  15     6 0.21    -2.33 1.76
-------------------------------------------------------------------------
: A1
: B2
    vars n  mean   sd median trimmed  mad min max range skew kurtosis   se
X1     1 3 12.33 2.52     12   12.33 2.97  10  15     5 0.13    -2.33 1.45
-------------------------------------------------------------------------
: A2
: B2
    vars n mean   sd median trimmed  mad min max range  skew kurtosis  se
X1     1 3 8.33 2.08      9    8.33 1.48   6  10     4 -0.29    -2.33 1.2
-------------------------------------------------------------------------
: A1
: B3
    vars n mean   sd median trimmed  mad min max range  skew kurtosis   se
X1     1 3 7.33 3.06      8    7.33 2.97   4  10     6 -0.21    -2.33 1.76
-------------------------------------------------------------------------
: A2
: B3
    vars n mean   sd median trimmed  mad min max range skew kurtosis   se
X1     1 3 5.33 1.53      5    5.33 1.48   4   7     3 0.21    -2.33 0.88

> describeBy (df11$DEPVAR, df11$WSFACTORB)

 Descriptive statistics by group
group: B1
    vars n mean   sd median trimmed  mad min max range skew kurtosis   se
X1     1 6 9.67 3.33    9.5    9.67 2.22   5  15    10 0.22    -1.24 1.36
-------------------------------------------------------------------------
group: B2
    vars n  mean   sd median trimmed  mad min max range skew kurtosis   se
X1     1 6 10.33 3.01     10   10.33 2.22   6  15     9 0.14     -1.3 1.23
-------------------------------------------------------------------------
group: B3
    vars n mean   sd median trimmed  mad min max range skew kurtosis   se
X1     1 6 6.33 2.42      6    6.33 2.97   4  10     6 0.31    -1.78 0.99
> twowithin= aov(DEPVAR ~ WSFACTORA * WSFACTORB + Error(subject/(WSFACTORA * WSFACTORB)), data=df11)
> summary(twowithin)

Error: subject
          Df Sum Sq Mean Sq F value Pr(>F)
Residuals  2  48.78   24.39

Error: subject:WSFACTORA
          Df Sum Sq Mean Sq F value Pr(>F)
WSFACTORA  1   2.00   2.000   0.324  0.626
Residuals  2  12.33   6.167

Error: subject:WSFACTORB
          Df Sum Sq Mean Sq F value Pr(>F)
WSFACTORB  2  55.11  27.556   15.26 0.0134 *
Residuals  4   7.22   1.806
---
Signif. codes:  0 '***' 0.001 '**' 0.01 '*' 0.05 '.' 0.1 ' ' 1

Error: subject:WSFACTORA:WSFACTORB
                    Df Sum Sq Mean Sq F value Pr(>F)
WSFACTORA:WSFACTORB  2  52.00  26.000   13.56 0.0165 *
Residuals            4   7.67   1.917
---
Signif. codes:  0 '***' 0.001 '**' 0.01 '*' 0.05 '.' 0.1 ' ' 1
```

THREE-FACTOR
BETWEEN-SUBJECTS ANOVA

EXAMPLE: Conduct three-way between-subjects ANOVA (IVs: *FACTORA*, *FACTORB*, *FACTORC*; DV: *DEPVAR*) (2 × 3 × 2 design)

SPSS: The MEANS and MANOVA command

```
MEANS  DEPVAR by FACTORA by FACTORB by FACTORC .
```

Means

Report

DEPVAR

FACTORA	FACTORB	FACTORC	Mean	N	Std. Deviation
1 A1	1 B1	1 C1	10.00	4	5.888
		2 C2	20.00	4	4.967
		Total	15.00	8	7.348
	2 B2	1 C1	18.00	4	4.761
		2 C2	27.00	4	5.715
		Total	22.50	8	6.845
	3 B3	1 C1	20.00	4	6.055
		2 C2	41.00	4	4.163
		Total	30.50	8	12.212
	Total	1 C1	16.00	12	6.782
		2 C2	29.33	12	10.174
		Total	22.67	24	10.857
2 A2	1 B1	1 C1	7.50	4	3.873
		2 C2	10.00	4	4.546
		Total	8.75	8	4.132
	2 B2	1 C1	7.00	4	4.163
		2 C2	14.75	4	3.594
		Total	10.88	8	5.489
	3 B3	1 C1	15.00	4	5.099
		2 C2	16.75	4	4.113
		Total	15.87	8	4.390
	Total	1 C1	9.83	12	5.524
		2 C2	13.83	12	4.745
		Total	11.83	24	5.435
Total	1 B1	1 C1	8.75	8	4.803
		2 C2	15.00	8	6.928
		Total	11.88	16	6.602
	2 B2	1 C1	12.50	8	7.191
		2 C2	20.88	8	7.900
		Total	16.69	16	8.483
	3 B3	1 C1	17.50	8	5.831
		2 C2	28.88	8	13.517
		Total	23.19	16	11.646
	Total	1 C1	12.92	24	6.820
		2 C2	21.58	24	11.088
		Total	17.25	48	10.105

```
MANOVA
    DEPVAR by FACTORA (1,2) FACTORB (1,3) FACTORC (1,2)
    /ERROR = WITHIN
    /DESIGN  .
```

Manova

```
* * * * * * * * * * * * * * * * * * *A n a l y s i s   o f   V a r i a n c e -- Design  1 * * * * * * * * * *
```

```
Tests of Significance for DEPVAR using UNIQUE sums of squares
Source of Variation         SS      DF      MS        F   Sig of F

WITHIN CELLS             832.50      36    23.13
FACTORA                 1408.33       1  1408.33    60.90    .000
FACTORB                 1031.38       2   515.69    22.30    .000
FACTORC                  901.33       1   901.33    38.98    .000
FACTORA BY FACTORB       144.04       2    72.02     3.11    .057
FACTORA BY FACTORC       261.33       1   261.33    11.30    .002
FACTORB BY FACTORC        53.04       2    26.52     1.15    .329
FACTORA BY FACTORB B     167.04       2    83.52     3.61    .037
Y FACTORC

(Model)                 3966.50      11   360.59    15.59    .000
(Total)                 4799.00      47   102.11

R-Squared =         .827
Adjusted R-Squared =  .774
```

R: The `factor`, `describeBy`, and `aov` functions and the `psych` package

Create new data frame that contains only the variables to be analyzed

Command: `newdataframe <- subset(dataframe,,select = c(variable, variable, variable, variable))`

Example: `df11 <- subset(df1,,select = c(FACTORA,FACTORB,FACTORC,DEPVAR))`

Remove anyone with NAs on any variable in the new data frame

Command: `newdataframe <- na.omit(newdataframe)`

Example: `df11 <- na.omit(df11)`

Convert a numeric independent variable to a factor (if IV is a numeric variable)

Command: `newdataframe$factor <- factor (newdataframe$numvar, labels = c("label", "label", "label"...))`

Note: `newdataframe$factor` = name of factor

`newdataframe$numvar` = numeric independent variable

`label` = label to level of factor based on numeric independent variable

Example: `df11$FACTORA.f <- factor(df11$FACTORA, labels = c("A1","A2"))`

`df11$FACTORB.f <- factor(df11$FACTORB, labels = c("B1","B2","B3"))`

`df11$FACTORC.f <- factor(df11$FACTORC, labels = c("C1","C2"))`

Calculate descriptive statistics for the main effects and interactions

Command: `describeBy(newdataframe$depvar, list(newdataframe$factor, newdataframe$factor, newdataframe$factor)) describeBy(newdataframe$depvar, list(newdataframe$factor, newdataframe$factor)) describeBy(newdataframe$depvar, newdataframe$factor)`

(Continued)

(Continued)

Example: describeBy (df11$DEPVAR,
             list(df11$FACTORA.f, df11$FACTORB.f,
             df11$FACTORC.f))
             describeBy (df11$DEPVAR,
             list(df11$FACTORA.f,df11$FACTORB.f))
             describeBy (df11$DEPVAR,
             list(df11$FACTORA.f,df11$FACTORC.f))
             describeBy (df11$DEPVAR,
             list(df11$FACTORB.f,df11$FACTORC.f))
             describeBy (df11$DEPVAR, df11$FACTORA.f)
             describeBy (df11$DEPVAR, df11$FACTORB.f)
             describeBy (df11$DEPVAR, df11$FACTORC.f)

Conduct three-way between-subjects ANOVA

Command: **result <- aov(**newdataframe$depvar ~
             newdataframe$factor * newdataframe$factor
             *newdataframe$factor, **data =** newdataframe**)**
             summary(result**)**

Example: threeway <- aov(DEPVAR ~ FACTORA.f * FACTORB.f
             * FACTORC.f, data =df11)
             summary(threeway)

Example script:
```
setwd("e:/R output")
df1 <- read.csv("THREEFACTORBS_NA.csv")
library(psych)
df11 <- subset(df1,,select =
c(FACTORA,FACTORB,FACTORC,DEPVAR))
df11 <- na.omit(df11)
df11$FACTORA.f <- factor(df11$FACTORA,
labels = c("A1","A2"))
df11$FACTORB.f <- factor(df11$FACTORB,
labels = c("B1","B2","B3"))
df11$FACTORC.f <- factor(df11$FACTORC,
labels = c("C1","C2"))
```

```
describeBy (df11$DEPVAR, list(df11$FACTORA.f,
df11$FACTORB.f, df11$FACTORC.f))
describeBy (df11$DEPVAR, list(df11$FACTORA.f,
df11$FACTORB.f))
describeBy (df11$DEPVAR, list(df11$FACTORA.f,
df11$FACTORC.f))
describeBy (df11$DEPVAR, list(df11$FACTORB.f,
df11$FACTORC.f))
describeBy (df11$DEPVAR, df11$FACTORA.f)
describeBy (df11$DEPVAR, df11$FACTORB.f)
describeBy (df11$DEPVAR, df11$FACTORC.f)
threeway <- aov(DEPVAR ~ FACTORA.f * FACTORB.f *
FACTORC.f, data = df11)
summary(threeway)
```

```
> setwd("e:/R output")
> df1 <- read.csv("THREEFACTORBS_NA.csv")
> library(psych)
> df11 <- subset(df1,,select = c(FACTORA,FACTORB,FACTORC,DEPVAR))
> df11 <- na.omit(df11)
> df11$FACTORA.f <- factor(df11$FACTORA, labels = c("A1","A2"))
> df11$FACTORB.f <- factor(df11$FACTORB, labels = c("B1","B2","B3"))
> df11$FACTORC.f <- factor(df11$FACTORC, labels = c("C1","C2"))

> threeway <- aov(DEPVAR ~ FACTORA.f * FACTORB.f * FACTORC.f, data =  df11)
> summary(threeway)
                          Df Sum Sq Mean Sq F value   Pr(>F)
FACTORA.f                  1 1408.3  1408.3  60.901 2.98e-09 ***
FACTORB.f                  2 1031.4   515.7  22.300 5.01e-07 ***
FACTORC.f                  1  901.3   901.3  38.977 3.29e-07 ***
FACTORA.f:FACTORB.f        2  144.0    72.0   3.114  0.05656 .
FACTORA.f:FACTORC.f        1  261.3   261.3  11.301  0.00185 **
FACTORB.f:FACTORC.f        2   53.0    26.5   1.147  0.32897
FACTORA.f:FACTORB.f:FACTORC.f 2 167.0    83.5   3.612  0.03720 *
Residuals                 36  832.5    23.1
---
Signif. codes:  0 '***' 0.001 '**' 0.01 '*' 0.05 '.' 0.1 ' ' 1
>
```

PEARSON CORRELATION (ONE CORRELATION)

EXAMPLE: Calculate the correlation between *EWB1* and *EWB2*

SPSS: The CORRELATIONS command

```
CORRELATIONS
  /VARIABLES=EWB1 EWB2
  /PRINT=TWOTAIL NOSIG
  /MISSING=PAIRWISE.
```

Correlations

Correlations

		EWB1	EWB2
EWB1	Pearson Correlation	1	.388[**]
	Sig. (2-tailed)		.000
	N	115	111
EWB2	Pearson Correlation	.388[**]	1
	Sig. (2-tailed)	.000	
	N	111	111

**. Correlation is significant at the 0.01 level (2-tailed).

R: The cor.test function

Calculate the Pearson correlation between two variables

Command: **cor.test(~** *variable1* **+** *variable2***,na. action="na.exclude",** **data =** *dataframe***)**

Note: **na.action="na.exclude"** excludes those with missing data

Example: cor.test(~ EWB1 +EWB2,na.action="na. exclude", data =df1)

Example script:
```
setwd("e:/R output")
df1 <- read.csv("EWB_NA.csv")
cor.test(~ EWB1 +EWB2,na.action="na.exclude", data =df1)
```

```
> setwd("e:/R output")
> df1 <- read.csv("EWB_NA.csv")
> cor.test(~ EWB1 +EWB2,na.action="na.exclude", data = df1)

        Pearson's product-moment correlation

data:  EWB1 and EWB2
t = 4.397, df = 109, p-value = 2.562e-05
alternative hypothesis: true correlation is not equal to 0
95 percent confidence interval:
 0.2174781 0.5357694
sample estimates:
      cor
0.3881373
```

PEARSON CORRELATION (CORRELATION MATRIX)

EXAMPLE: Calculate Pearson correlations between *EWB1* and *EWB4*

SPSS: The CORRELATIONS command

Pairwise deletion (/MISSING=PAIRWISE)

```
CORRELATIONS
 /VARIABLES=EWB1 EWB2 EWB3 EWB4
 /PRINT=TWOTAIL NOSIG
 /MISSING=PAIRWISE.
```

Correlations

Correlations

		EWB1	EWB2	EWB3	EWB4
EWB1	Pearson Correlation	1	.388**	.393**	.187
	Sig. (2-tailed)		.000	.000	.050
	N	115	111	112	110
EWB2	Pearson Correlation	.388**	1	.418**	.366**
	Sig. (2-tailed)	.000		.000	.000
	N	111	111	108	106
EWB3	Pearson Correlation	.393**	.418**	1	.115
	Sig. (2-tailed)	.000	.000		.240
	N	112	108	112	107
EWB4	Pearson Correlation	.187	.366**	.115	1
	Sig. (2-tailed)	.050	.000	.240	
	N	110	106	107	110

**. Correlation is significant at the 0.01 level (2-tailed).

Listwise deletion (/MISSING=LISTWISE)

```
CORRELATIONS
 /VARIABLES=EWB1 EWB2 EWB3 EWB4
 /PRINT=TWOTAIL NOSIG
 /MISSING=LISTWISE.
```

Correlations

Correlations[b]

		EWB1	EWB2	EWB3	EWB4
EWB1	Pearson Correlation	1	.320**	.344**	.169
	Sig. (2-tailed)		.001	.000	.088
EWB2	Pearson Correlation	.320**	1	.386**	.345**
	Sig. (2-tailed)	.001		.000	.000
EWB3	Pearson Correlation	.344**	.386**	1	.124
	Sig. (2-tailed)	.000	.000		.211
EWB4	Pearson Correlation	.169	.345**	.124	1
	Sig. (2-tailed)	.088	.000	.211	

**. Correlation is significant at the 0.01 level (2-tailed).

b. Listwise N=103

R: The `corr.test` function in the `psych` package

Pairwise deletion

Create a new data frame with only selected variables

Command: `newdataframe <- subset(dataframe,,select = c(variable, variable,...))`

Example: `df11 <- subset(df1,,select = c(EWB1, EWB2, EWB3, EWB4))`

Calculate Pearson correlations between the selected variables

Command: `corr.test(newdataframe)`

Example: `corr.test(df11)`

Example script:
```
setwd("e:/R output")
df1 <- read.csv("EWB_NA.csv")
library(psych)
df11 <- subset(df1,,select = c(EWB1, EWB2, EWB3, EWB4))
corr.test(df11)
```

```
> setwd("e:/R output")
> df1 <- read.csv("EWB_NA.csv")
> library("psych")
> df11 <- subset(df1, , select = c(EWB1, EWB2, EWB3, EWB4))
> corr.test(df11)
Call:corr.test(x = df11)
Correlation matrix
     EWB1 EWB2 EWB3 EWB4
EWB1 1.00 0.39 0.39 0.19
EWB2 0.39 1.00 0.42 0.37
EWB3 0.39 0.42 1.00 0.11
EWB4 0.19 0.37 0.11 1.00
Sample Size
     EWB1 EWB2 EWB3 EWB4
EWB1  115  111  112  110
EWB2  111  111  108  106
EWB3  112  108  112  107
EWB4  110  106  107  110
Probability values (Entries above the diagonal are adjusted for multiple tests.)
     EWB1 EWB2 EWB3 EWB4
EWB1 0.00    0 0.00 0.10
EWB2 0.00    0 0.00 0.00
EWB3 0.00    0 0.00 0.24
EWB4 0.05    0 0.24 0.00
```

Listwise deletion

Create a new data frame with only selected variables

> Command: *newdataframe* **<- subset(***dataframe***,,select = c(***variable, variable, variable...***))**

> Example: df11 <- subset(df1,,select = c(EWB1, EWB2, EWB3, EWB4))

Remove anyone with NAs on any variable in the new data frame

> Command: *newdataframe* **<- na.omit(***newdataframe***)**

> Example: df11 <- na.omit(df11)

Calculate Pearson correlations between the selected variables

> Command: **corr.test(***newdataframe***)**

> Example: corr.test(df11)

Example script:
```
setwd("e:/R output")
df1 <- read.csv("EWB_NA.csv")
library(psych)
df11 <- subset(df1,,select = c(EWB1, EWB2, EWB3,
EWB4))
df11 <- na.omit(df11)
corr.test(df11)
```

```
> setwd("e:/R output")
> df1 <- read.csv("EWB_NA.csv")
> library("psych")
> df11 <- subset(df1, , select = c(EWB1, EWB2, EWB3, EWB4))
> df11 <- na.omit(df11)
> corr.test(df11)
Call:corr.test(x = df11)
Correlation matrix
     EWB1 EWB2 EWB3 EWB4
EWB1 1.00 0.32 0.34 0.17
EWB2 0.32 1.00 0.39 0.35
EWB3 0.34 0.39 1.00 0.12
EWB4 0.17 0.35 0.12 1.00
Sample Size
[1] 103
Probability values (Entries above the diagonal are adjusted for multiple tests.)
     EWB1 EWB2 EWB3 EWB4
EWB1 0.00    0 0.00 0.18
EWB2 0.00    0 0.00 0.00
EWB3 0.00    0 0.00 0.21
EWB4 0.09    0 0.21 0.00
```

SCATTERPLOT

EXAMPLE: Create a scatterplot between *satmath* and *cgpa*

R: The geom _ point function in the ggplot2 package

Create a scatterplot between two variables

Command: Command: **ggplot(***dataframe***, aes(x=***X variable***,
y=***Y variable***)) + geom_point(shape=1) +
ggtitle("***title***") + xlim(***min X, max X***)
+ ylim(***min Y, max Y***) + labs(x="***label***",
y="***label***") + theme_bw()**
Note: ***title*** = title above scatterplot
      label = label for axis (X and Y)
      theme_bw() = removes gray background of histogram

Example: ggplot(df1, aes(x=satmath, y=cgpa)) +
geom_point(shape=1) +ggtitle("SAT Math and
college GPA") + xlim(200, 800) + ylim(0,4) +
labs(x="SAT Math",y="College GPA") + theme_bw()

Example script:
```
setwd("e:/R output")
df1 <- read.csv("COLLEGE_NA.csv")
library(ggplot2)
ggplot(df1, aes(x=satmath, y=cgpa)) + geom_
point(shape=1) +ggtitle("SAT Math and college
GPA") + xlim(200, 800) + ylim(0,4) + labs(x="SAT
Math",y="College GPA") + theme_bw()
```

```
> setwd("e:/R output")
> df1 <- read.csv("COLLEGE_NA.csv")
> library("ggplot2")
> ggplot(df1, aes(x=satmath, y=cgpa)) + geom_point(shape=1) +ggtitle("SAT Math and
college GPA") + xlim(200, 800) + ylim(0, 4) + labs(x="SAT Math",y="College GPA")
+ theme_bw()
```

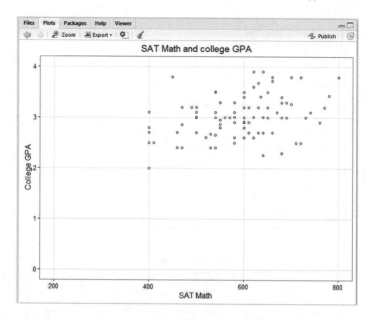

INTERNAL CONSISTENCY (CRONBACH'S ALPHA)

EXAMPLE: Calculate Cronbach's alpha for *EWB1* to *EWB5*

SPSS: The RELIABILITY command

```
RELIABILITY
  /VARIABLES=EWB1 EWB2 EWB3 EWB4 EWB5
  /SCALE('ALL VARIABLES') ALL
  /MODEL=ALPHA
  /STATISTICS=DESCRIPTIVE
  /SUMMARY=TOTAL.
```

Reliability

Case Processing Summary

		N	%
Cases	Valid	102	88.7
	Excluded[a]	13	11.3
	Total	115	100.0

a. Listwise deletion based on all variables in
   the procedure.

Reliability Statistics

Cronbach's Alpha	N of Items
.583	5

Item Statistics

	Mean	Std. Deviation	N
EWB1	5.38	1.227	102
EWB2	5.82	.776	102
EWB3	4.71	1.446	102
EWB4	5.87	.951	102
EWB5	4.45	1.577	102

Item-Total Statistics

	Scale Mean if Item Deleted	Scale Variance if Item Deleted	Corrected Item-Total Correlation	Cronbach's Alpha if Item Deleted
EWB1	20.85	10.028	.346	.524
EWB2	20.41	11.235	.458	.504
EWB3	21.53	8.865	.379	.506
EWB4	20.36	11.065	.356	.528
EWB5	21.78	9.062	.281	.582

R: The `alpha` function in the `psych` package

Create new data frame that contains only the variables to be analyzed

Command: `newdataframe <- subset(dataframe,,select = c(variable, variable, variable...))`

Example: `df11 <- subset(df1,,select = c(EWB1,EWB2,EWB3,EWB4,EWB5))`

Remove anyone with NAs on any variable in the new data frame

Command: `newdataframe <- na.omit(newdataframe)`

Example: `df11 <- na.omit(df11)`

Calculate Cronbach's alpha

Command: `alpha(newdataframe)`

Example: `alpha(df11)`

Example script:
```
setwd("e:/R output")
df1 <- read.csv("EWB_NA.csv")
library(psych)
df11 <- subset(df1, ,select = c(EWB1,EWB2,EWB3,EWB4,EWB5))
df11 <- na.omit(df11)
alpha(df11)
```

```
> setwd("e:/R output")
> df1 <- read.csv("EWB_NA.csv")
> library("psych")
> df11 <- subset(df1, , select = c(EWB1, EWB2, EWB3,EWB4,EWB5))
> df11 <- na.omit(df11)
> alpha(df11)
```

Reliability analysis
Call: alpha(x = df11)

raw_alpha	std.alpha	G6(smc)	average_r	S/N	ase	mean	sd	median_r
0.58	0.62	0.6	0.25	1.7	0.064	5.2	0.75	0.25

lower alpha upper	95% confidence boundaries
0.46 0.58 0.71	

Reliability if an item is dropped:

	raw_alpha	std.alpha	G6(smc)	average_r	S/N	alpha se	var.r	med.r
EWB1	0.52	0.58	0.54	0.26	1.4	0.075	0.013	0.26
EWB2	0.50	0.52	0.47	0.21	1.1	0.079	0.011	0.17
EWB3	0.51	0.56	0.51	0.24	1.3	0.078	0.011	0.25
EWB4	0.53	0.57	0.52	0.25	1.3	0.075	0.013	0.25
EWB5	0.58	0.61	0.56	0.28	1.6	0.065	0.012	0.33

Item statistics

	n	raw.r	std.r	r.cor	r.drop	mean	sd
EWB1	102	0.62	0.62	0.46	0.35	5.4	1.23
EWB2	102	0.61	0.70	0.61	0.46	5.8	0.78
EWB3	102	0.68	0.65	0.52	0.38	4.7	1.45
EWB4	102	0.57	0.62	0.48	0.36	5.9	0.95
EWB5	102	0.64	0.57	0.38	0.28	4.5	1.58

Non missing response frequency for each item

	1	2	3	4	5	6	7	miss
EWB1	0.00	0.06	0.06	0.01	0.27	0.51	0.09	0
EWB2	0.00	0.00	0.02	0.02	0.23	0.59	0.15	0
EWB3	0.00	0.06	0.22	0.16	0.17	0.33	0.07	0
EWB4	0.00	0.01	0.01	0.07	0.16	0.52	0.24	0
EWB5	0.02	0.07	0.25	0.18	0.17	0.21	0.11	0

PRINCIPAL COMPONENTS ANALYSIS (VARIMAX ROTATION)

EXAMPLE: Conduct principal components analysis (Varimax) for *ABCD1* to *ABCD11*

SPSS: The FACTOR command

```
FACTOR
    /VARIABLES ABCD1 ABCD2 ABCD3 ABCD4 ABCD5 ABCD6 ABCD7 ABCD8 ABCD9 ABCD10 ABCD11
    /MISSING LISTWISE
    /ANALYSIS ABCD1 ABCD2 ABCD3 ABCD4 ABCD5 ABCD6 ABCD7 ABCD8 ABCD9 ABCD10 ABCD11
    /PRINT INITIAL KMO EXTRACTION ROTATION
    /CRITERIA MINEIGEN(1) ITERATE(25)
    /EXTRACTION PC
    /CRITERIA ITERATE(25)
    /ROTATION VARIMAX
    /METHOD=CORRELATION.
```

Factor Analysis

KMO and Bartlett's Test

Kaiser-Meyer-Olkin Measure of Sampling Adequacy.		.851
Bartlett's Test of Sphericity	Approx. Chi-Square	500.984
	df	55
	Sig.	.000

Communalities

	Initial	Extraction
ABCD1	1.000	.570
ABCD2	1.000	.832
ABCD3	1.000	.678
ABCD4	1.000	.577
ABCD5	1.000	.577
ABCD6	1.000	.691
ABCD7	1.000	.501
ABCD8	1.000	.601
ABCD9	1.000	.534
ABCD10	1.000	.672
ABCD11	1.000	.673

Extraction Method: Principal Component Analysis.

Total Variance Explained

Component	Initial Eigenvalues			Extraction Sums of Squared Loadings			Rotation Sums of Squared Loadings		
	Total	% of Variance	Cumulative %	Total	% of Variance	Cumulative %	Total	% of Variance	Cumulative %
1	4.664	42.401	42.401	4.664	42.401	42.401	2.908	26.439	26.439
2	1.230	11.184	53.585	1.230	11.184	53.585	2.197	19.975	46.414
3	1.011	9.193	62.778	1.011	9.193	62.778	1.800	16.365	62.778
4	.774	7.041	69.819						
5	.714	6.495	76.314						
6	.599	5.444	81.758						
7	.587	5.334	87.092						
8	.447	4.064	91.156						
9	.380	3.455	94.611						
10	.318	2.894	97.505						
11	.274	2.495	100.000						

Extraction Method: Principal Component Analysis.

Component Matrix[a]

	Component		
	1	2	3
ABCD1	-.601	-.042	.455
ABCD2	.427	-.628	.506
ABCD3	.686	.411	.197
ABCD4	-.724	.172	.151
ABCD5	.751	.052	.096
ABCD6	-.466	.398	.561
ABCD7	.522	.449	.164
ABCD8	-.771	.074	.026
ABCD9	-.650	-.245	-.225
ABCD10	.680	-.400	.223
ABCD11	.769	.218	-.185

Extraction Method: Principal Component
Analysis.

a. 3 components extracted.

Rotated Component Matrix[a]

	Component		
	1	2	3
ABCD1	-.319	.684	.024
ABCD2	.036	-.016	.911
ABCD3	.806	-.124	.114
ABCD4	-.354	.574	-.350
ABCD5	.589	-.337	.340
ABCD6	.092	.808	-.171
ABCD7	.706	-.047	-.003
ABCD8	-.487	.477	-.370
ABCD9	-.681	.127	-.232
ABCD10	.281	-.318	.702
ABCD11	.629	-.521	.074

Extraction Method: Principal Component
Analysis.
Rotation Method: Varimax with Kaiser
Normalization.

R: The `principal` function in the `psych` package

Create new data frame that contains only the variables to be analyzed

Command: `newdataframe <- subset(dataframe,,select = c(variable, variable, variable...))`

Example: `df11 <- subset(df1,,select = c (ABCD1, ABCD2,ABCD3,ABCD4, ABCD5, ABCD6,ABCD7,ABCD8,ABCD9,ABCD10,ABCD11))`

Remove anyone with NAs on any variable in the new data frame

Command: `newdataframe <- na.omit(newdataframe)`

Example: `df11 <- na.omit(df11)`

Ask for KMO and Bartlett tests

Command: `KMO(newdataframe)`
`cortest.bartlett(newdataframe)`

Example: `KMO (df11)`
`cortest.bartlett(df11)`

Run initial analysis to determine the # components with eigenvalues > 1

Command: `principal(newdataframe,nfactors = #variables,rotate = "none")`

Note: `#variables` = # variables included in the analysis

Example: `principal(df11, nfactors =11, rotate = "none")`

(Continued)

(Continued)

> Run second analysis stating # components with eigenvalues >
> 1 found in initial analysis
>
> Command: **principal(*newdataframe*,nfactors=**
>   **#*components*,rotate="varimax")**
>   Note: **#*components*** = # components with eigenvalues > 1
>   in initial analysis
>
> Example: principal(df11, nfactors =3, rotate =
>   "varimax")

Example script:
```
setwd("e:/R output")
df1 <- read.csv("ABCD_NA.csv")
library(psych)
df11 <- subset(df1, ,select = c(ABCD1,
ABCD2,ABCD3,ABCD4,ABCD5, ABCD6,
ABCD7,ABCD8,ABCD9,ABCD10,ABCD11))
df11 <- na.omit(df11)
KMO (df11)
cortest.bartlett(df11)
principal(df11, nfactors =11, rotate = "none")
principal(df11, nfactors =3, rotate = "varimax")
```

```
> setwd("e:/R output")
> df1 <- read.csv("ABCD_NA.csv")
> library("psych")
> df11 <- subset(df1, , select = c(ABCD1, ABCD2, ABCD3, ABCD4, ABCD5, ABCD6,
ABCD7,ABCD8,ABCD9,ABCD10,ABCD11))
> df11 <- na.omit(df11)
> KMO (df11)
Kaiser-Meyer-Olkin factor adequacy
Call: KMO(r = df11)
Overall MSA =  0.85
MSA for each item =
 ABCD1   ABCD2   ABCD3   ABCD4   ABCD5   ABCD6   ABCD7   ABCD8   ABCD9 ABCD10 ABCD11
  0.91    0.65    0.84    0.91    0.90    0.84    0.83    0.90    0.86   0.81   0.83
> cortest.bartlett(df11)
R was not square, finding R from data
$chisq
[1] 500.984

$p.value
[1] 3.234399e-73

$df
[1] 55
```

```
> principal(df11, nfactors = 11, rotate = "none")
Principal Components Analysis
Call: principal(r = df11, nfactors = 11, rotate = "none")
Standardized loadings (pattern matrix) based upon correlation matrix
         PC1   PC2   PC3   PC4   PC5   PC6   PC7   PC8   PC9  PC10  PC11 h2       u2 com
ABCD1  -0.60 -0.04  0.46 -0.28 -0.24  0.06  0.51 -0.05 -0.14  0.08  0.06  1  1.1e-16 4.0
ABCD2   0.43 -0.63  0.51 -0.05  0.22  0.13 -0.17  0.06 -0.01 -0.18  0.19  1  2.2e-16 3.8
ABCD3   0.69  0.41  0.20  0.12 -0.25  0.25  0.14 -0.05  0.25 -0.31 -0.06  1  0.0e+00 3.7
ABCD4  -0.72  0.17  0.15  0.26  0.19 -0.15  0.14  0.51  0.13 -0.05  0.02  1 -2.2e-16 2.9
ABCD5   0.75  0.05  0.10  0.11 -0.25  0.37 -0.12  0.31 -0.20  0.23 -0.07  1  0.0e+00 2.8
ABCD6  -0.47  0.40  0.56  0.38 -0.03 -0.14 -0.28 -0.21 -0.14  0.05  0.01  1  5.6e-16 5.0
ABCD7   0.52  0.45  0.16 -0.29  0.61  0.10  0.09 -0.02 -0.11  0.01 -0.13  1  8.9e-16 3.9
ABCD8  -0.77  0.07  0.03 -0.05  0.14  0.43 -0.10 -0.10  0.33  0.22  0.10  1  0.0e+00 2.5
ABCD9  -0.65 -0.24 -0.23  0.19  0.35  0.18 -0.11 -0.22 -0.15 -0.11  1  1.1e-16 4.2
ABCD10  0.68 -0.40  0.22  0.31  0.10 -0.15  0.22 -0.10  0.21  0.21 -0.22  1 -2.2e-16 3.8
ABCD11  0.77  0.22 -0.19  0.30  0.12 -0.04  0.25 -0.07 -0.05  0.10  0.37  1 -4.4e-16 2.6

                     PC1  PC2  PC3  PC4  PC5  PC6  PC7  PC8  PC9 PC10 PC11
SS loadings         4.66 1.23 1.01 0.77 0.71 0.60 0.59 0.45 0.38 0.32 0.27
Proportion Var      0.42 0.11 0.09 0.07 0.06 0.05 0.05 0.04 0.03 0.03 0.02
Cumulative Var      0.42 0.54 0.63 0.70 0.76 0.82 0.87 0.91 0.95 0.98 1.00
Proportion Explained 0.42 0.11 0.09 0.07 0.06 0.05 0.05 0.04 0.03 0.03 0.02
Cumulative Proportion 0.42 0.54 0.63 0.70 0.76 0.82 0.87 0.91 0.95 0.98 1.00

Mean item complexity = 3.6
Test of the hypothesis that 11 components are sufficient.

The root mean square of the residuals (RMSR) is 0
 with the empirical chi square  0  with prob < NA

Fit based upon off diagonal values = 1
```

```
> principal(df11, nfactors = 3, rotate = "varimax")
Principal Components Analysis
Call: principal(r = df11, nfactors = 3, rotate = "varimax")
Standardized loadings (pattern matrix) based upon correlation matrix
         RC1   RC3   RC2   h2   u2 com
ABCD1  -0.32  0.68  0.02 0.57 0.43 1.4
ABCD2   0.04 -0.02  0.91 0.83 0.17 1.0
ABCD3   0.81 -0.12  0.11 0.68 0.32 1.1
ABCD4  -0.35  0.57 -0.35 0.58 0.42 2.4
ABCD5   0.59 -0.34  0.34 0.58 0.42 2.3
ABCD6   0.09  0.81 -0.17 0.69 0.31 1.1
ABCD7   0.71 -0.05  0.00 0.50 0.50 1.0
ABCD8  -0.49  0.48 -0.37 0.60 0.40 2.9
ABCD9  -0.68  0.13 -0.23 0.53 0.47 1.3
ABCD10  0.28 -0.32  0.70 0.67 0.33 1.7
ABCD11  0.63 -0.52  0.07 0.67 0.33 2.0

                     RC1  RC3  RC2
SS loadings         2.91 2.20 1.80
Proportion Var      0.26 0.20 0.16
Cumulative Var      0.26 0.46 0.63
Proportion Explained 0.42 0.32 0.26
Cumulative Proportion 0.42 0.74 1.00

Mean item complexity = 1.7
Test of the hypothesis that 3 components are sufficient.

The root mean square of the residuals (RMSR) is 0.08
 with the empirical chi square  92.61  with prob < 1.1e-09

Fit based upon off diagonal values = 0.95
```

PRINCIPAL COMPONENTS ANALYSIS (OBLIQUE ROTATION)

EXAMPLE: Conduct principal components analysis (oblique) for *ABCD1* to
ABCD11

SPSS: The FACTOR command

```
FACTOR
   /VARIABLES ABCD1 ABCD2 ABCD3 ABCD4 ABCD5 ABCD6 ABCD7 ABCD8 ABCD9 ABCD10 ABCD11
   /MISSING LISTWISE
   /ANALYSIS ABCD1 ABCD2 ABCD3 ABCD4 ABCD5 ABCD6 ABCD7 ABCD8 ABCD9 ABCD10 ABCD11
   /PRINT INITIAL KMO EXTRACTION ROTATION
   /CRITERIA MINEIGEN(1) ITERATE(25)
   /EXTRACTION PC
   /CRITERIA ITERATE(25) DELTA(0)
   /ROTATION OBLIMIN
   /METHOD=CORRELATION.
```

Factor Analysis

KMO and Bartlett's Test

Kaiser-Meyer-Olkin Measure of Sampling Adequacy.		.851
Bartlett's Test of Sphericity	Approx. Chi-Square	500.984
	df	55
	Sig.	.000

Communalities

	Initial	Extraction
ABCD1	1.000	.570
ABCD2	1.000	.832
ABCD3	1.000	.678
ABCD4	1.000	.577
ABCD5	1.000	.577
ABCD6	1.000	.691
ABCD7	1.000	.501
ABCD8	1.000	.601
ABCD9	1.000	.534
ABCD10	1.000	.672
ABCD11	1.000	.673

Extraction Method: Principal
Component Analysis.

Structure Matrix

	Component		
	1	2	3
ABCD1	-.440	.121	.718
ABCD2	.157	-.900	-.150
ABCD3	.823	-.230	-.276
ABCD4	-.501	.475	.669
ABCD5	.683	-.458	-.477
ABCD6	-.089	.280	.796
ABCD7	.695	-.092	-.167
ABCD8	-.614	.496	.600
ABCD9	-.717	.331	.273
ABCD10	.426	-.771	-.456
ABCD11	.722	-.230	-.627

Extraction Method: Principal Component
Analysis.
 Rotation Method: Oblimin with Kaiser
Normalization.

Component Correlation Matrix

Component	1	2	3
1	1.000	-.278	-.374
2	-.278	1.000	.309
3	-.374	.309	1.000

Extraction Method: Principal Component
Analysis.
 Rotation Method: Oblimin with Kaiser
Normalization.

Total Variance Explained

	Initial Eigenvalues			Extraction Sums of Squared Loadings			Rotation Sums of Squared Loadings [a]
Component	Total	% of Variance	Cumulative %	Total	% of Variance	Cumulative %	Total
1	4.664	42.401	42.401	4.664	42.401	42.401	3.698
2	1.230	11.184	53.585	1.230	11.184	53.585	2.404
3	1.011	9.193	62.778	1.011	9.193	62.778	2.988
4	.774	7.041	69.819				
5	.714	6.495	76.314				
6	.599	5.444	81.758				
7	.587	5.334	87.092				
8	.447	4.064	91.156				
9	.380	3.455	94.611				
10	.318	2.894	97.505				
11	.274	2.495	100.000				

Extraction Method: Principal Component Analysis.

a. When components are correlated, sums of squared loadings cannot be added to obtain a total variance.

Component Matrix [a]

	Component		
	1	2	3
ABCD1	-.601	-.042	.455
ABCD2	.427	-.628	.506
ABCD3	.686	.411	.197
ABCD4	-.724	.172	.151
ABCD5	.751	.052	.096
ABCD6	-.466	.398	.561
ABCD7	.522	.449	.164
ABCD8	-.771	.074	.026
ABCD9	-.650	-.245	-.225
ABCD10	.680	-.400	.223
ABCD11	.769	.218	-.185

Extraction Method: Principal Component Analysis.

a. 3 components extracted.

Pattern Matrix [a]

	Component		
	1	2	3
ABCD1	-.227	-.152	.680
ABCD2	-.062	-.955	.122
ABCD3	.835	-.010	.040
ABCD4	-.243	.253	.500
ABCD5	.540	-.247	-.199
ABCD6	.259	.085	.867
ABCD7	.753	.091	.087
ABCD8	-.401	.272	.366
ABCD9	-.687	.149	-.030
ABCD10	.171	-.666	-.187
ABCD11	.579	.063	-.430

Extraction Method: Principal Component Analysis.
Rotation Method: Oblimin with Kaiser Normalization.

R: The `principal` function in the `psych` and `GPARotation` packages

Create new data frame that contains only the variables to be analyzed

Command: `newdataframe <- subset(dataframe,,select = c(variable, variable, variable...))`

Example: `df11 <- subset(df1,,select = c(ABCD1, ABCD2,ABCD3,ABCD4, ABCD5, ABCD6,ABCD7,ABCD8,ABCD9,ABCD10,ABCD11))`

Remove anyone with NAs on any variable in the new data frame

Command: `newdataframe <- na.omit(newdataframe)`

Example: `df11 <- na.omit(df11)`

(Continued)

(Continued)

Ask for KMO and Bartlett tests

    Command: **KMO(*newdataframe*)**
                      cortest.bartlett(*newdataframe*)

    Example: KMO (df11)
                   cortest.bartlett(df11)

Run initial analysis to determine the # components with eigenvalues → 1

    Command: **principal(*newdataframe*,nfactors = #variables,rotate = "none")**
                      Note: **#variables** = # variables included in the analysis

    Example: principal(df11, nfactors =11, rotate = "none")

Run second analysis stating # components with eigenvalues → 1 found in initial analysis

    Command: **principal(*newdataframe*,nfactors= #components,rotate="oblimin")**
                      Note: **#components** = # components with eigenvalues → 1 in initial analysis

    Example: principal(df11, nfactors = 3, rotate = "oblimin")

Example script:
```
setwd("e:/R output")
df1 <- read.csv("ABCD_NA.csv")
library(psych)
library(GPArotation)
df11 <- subset(df1,,select = c(ABCD1, ABCD2,ABCD3,
ABCD4, ABCD5, ABCD6,ABCD7,ABCD8,ABCD9,ABCD10,ABCD11))
df11 <- na.omit(df11)
KMO (df11)
cortest.bartlett(df11)
principal(df11, nfactors =11, rotate = "none")
principal(df11, nfactors = 3, rotate = "oblimin")
```

```
> setwd("e:/R output")
> df1 <- read.csv("ABCD_NA.csv")
> library(psych)
> library(GPArotation)
> subset(df1,,select = c(ABCD1, ABCD2,ABCD3,ABCD4, ABCD5, ABCD6,ABCD7,ABCD8,AB
CD9,ABCD10,ABCD11))
> df11 <- na.omit(df11)
> KMO (df11)
Kaiser-Meyer-Olkin factor adequacy
Call: KMO(r = df11)
Overall MSA = 0.85
MSA for each item =
 ABCD1  ABCD2  ABCD3  ABCD4  ABCD5  ABCD6  ABCD7  ABCD8  ABCD9 ABCD10 ABCD11
  0.91   0.65   0.84   0.91   0.90   0.84   0.83   0.90   0.86   0.81   0.83
> cortest.bartlett(df11)
R was not square, finding R from data
$chisq
[1] 500.984

$p.value
[1] 3.234399e-73

$df
[1] 55


> principal(df11, nfactors = 11, rotate = "none")
Principal Components Analysis
Call: principal(r = df11, nfactors = 11, rotate = "none")
Standardized loadings (pattern matrix) based upon correlation matrix
         PC1   PC2   PC3   PC4   PC5   PC6   PC7   PC8   PC9  PC10  PC11 h2      u2 com
ABCD1  -0.60 -0.04  0.46 -0.28 -0.24  0.06  0.51 -0.05 -0.14  0.08  0.06  1 1.1e-16 4.0
ABCD2   0.43 -0.63  0.51 -0.05  0.22  0.13 -0.17  0.06 -0.01 -0.18  0.19  1 2.2e-16 3.8
ABCD3   0.69  0.41  0.20  0.12 -0.25  0.25  0.14 -0.05  0.25 -0.31 -0.06  1 0.0e+00 3.7
ABCD4  -0.72  0.17  0.15  0.26  0.19 -0.15  0.14  0.51  0.13 -0.05  0.02  1 -2.2e-16 2.9
ABCD5   0.75  0.05  0.10  0.11 -0.25  0.37 -0.12  0.31 -0.20  0.23 -0.07  1 0.0e+00 2.8
ABCD6  -0.47  0.40  0.56  0.38 -0.03 -0.14 -0.28 -0.21 -0.14  0.05  0.01  1 5.6e-16 5.0
ABCD7   0.52  0.45  0.16 -0.29  0.61  0.10  0.09 -0.02 -0.11  0.01 -0.13  1 8.9e-16 3.9
ABCD8  -0.77  0.07  0.03 -0.05  0.14  0.43 -0.10 -0.10  0.33  0.22  0.10  1 0.0e+00 2.5
ABCD9  -0.65 -0.24 -0.23  0.43  0.19  0.35  0.18 -0.11 -0.22 -0.15 -0.11  1 1.1e-16 4.2
ABCD10  0.68 -0.40  0.22  0.31  0.10 -0.15  0.22 -0.10  0.21  0.21 -0.22  1 -2.2e-16 3.8
ABCD11  0.77  0.22 -0.19  0.30  0.12 -0.04  0.25 -0.07 -0.05  0.10  0.37  1 -4.4e-16 2.6

                        PC1  PC2  PC3  PC4  PC5  PC6  PC7  PC8  PC9 PC10 PC11
SS loadings            4.66 1.23 1.01 0.77 0.71 0.60 0.59 0.45 0.38 0.32 0.27
Proportion Var         0.42 0.11 0.09 0.07 0.06 0.05 0.05 0.04 0.03 0.03 0.02
Cumulative Var         0.42 0.54 0.63 0.70 0.76 0.82 0.87 0.91 0.95 0.98 1.00
Proportion Explained   0.42 0.11 0.09 0.07 0.06 0.05 0.05 0.04 0.03 0.03 0.02
Cumulative Proportion  0.42 0.54 0.63 0.70 0.76 0.82 0.87 0.91 0.95 0.98 1.00

Mean item complexity = 3.6
Test of the hypothesis that 11 components are sufficient.

The root mean square of the residuals (RMSR) is 0
 with the empirical chi square 0 with prob < NA

Fit based upon off diagonal values = 1


> principal(df11, nfactors = 3, rotate = "oblimin")
Principal Components Analysis
Call: principal(r = df11, nfactors = 3, rotate = "oblimin")
Standardized loadings (pattern matrix) based upon correlation matrix
          TC1   TC3   TC2   h2   u2 com
ABCD1   -0.28  0.64  0.17 0.57 0.43 1.5
ABCD2   -0.05  0.07  0.94 0.83 0.17 1.0
ABCD3    0.85  0.09  0.00 0.68 0.32 1.0
ABCD4   -0.30  0.48 -0.23 0.58 0.42 2.2
ABCD5    0.57 -0.17  0.23 0.58 0.42 1.5
ABCD6    0.19  0.86 -0.06 0.69 0.31 1.1
ABCD7    0.76  0.13 -0.09 0.50 0.50 1.1
ABCD8   -0.45  0.35 -0.25 0.60 0.40 2.5
ABCD9   -0.70 -0.06 -0.14 0.53 0.47 1.1
ABCD10   0.21 -0.20  0.65 0.67 0.33 1.4
ABCD11   0.63 -0.38 -0.08 0.67 0.33 1.7
```

```
                      TC1  TC3  TC2
SS loadings           3.22 2.00 1.69
Proportion Var        0.29 0.18 0.15
Cumulative Var        0.29 0.47 0.63
Proportion Explained  0.47 0.29 0.24
Cumulative Proportion 0.47 0.76 1.00

 with component correlations of
       TC1   TC3   TC2
TC1  1.00 -0.36  0.26
TC3 -0.36  1.00 -0.27
TC2  0.26 -0.27  1.00

Mean item complexity =  1.5
Test of the hypothesis that 3 components are sufficient.

The root mean square of the residuals (RMSR) is  0.08
 with the empirical chi square  92.61  with prob <  1.1e-09

Fit based upon off diagonal values = 0.95
```

FACTOR ANALYSIS (PRINCIPAL AXIS FACTORING)

EXAMPLE: Conduct factor analysis (principal axis factoring) for *ABCD1* to
ABCD11

SPSS: The FACTOR command

```
FACTOR
    /VARIABLES ABCD1 ABCD2 ABCD3 ABCD4 ABCD5 ABCD6 ABCD7 ABCD8 ABCD9 ABCD10 ABCD11
    /MISSING LISTWISE
    /ANALYSIS ABCD1 ABCD2 ABCD3 ABCD4 ABCD5 ABCD6 ABCD7 ABCD8 ABCD9 ABCD10 ABCD11
    /PRINT INITIAL KMO EXTRACTION ROTATION
    /CRITERIA MINEIGEN(1) ITERATE(25)
    /EXTRACTION PAF
    /CRITERIA ITERATE(25)
    /ROTATION VARIMAX
    /METHOD=CORRELATION.
```

Factor Analysis

KMO and Bartlett's Test

Kaiser-Meyer-Olkin Measure of Sampling Adequacy.		.851
Bartlett's Test of Sphericity	Approx. Chi-Square	500.984
	df	55
	Sig.	.000

Communalities

	Initial	Extraction
ABCD1	.321	.373
ABCD2	.360	.788
ABCD3	.494	.668
ABCD4	.448	.495
ABCD5	.490	.518
ABCD6	.250	.363
ABCD7	.291	.275
ABCD8	.517	.549
ABCD9	.407	.394
ABCD10	.504	.500
ABCD11	.589	.621

Extraction Method: Principal Axis Factoring.

Total Variance Explained

Factor	Initial Eigenvalues			Extraction Sums of Squared Loadings			Rotation Sums of Squared Loadings		
	Total	% of Variance	Cumulative %	Total	% of Variance	Cumulative %	Total	% of Variance	Cumulative %
1	4.664	42.401	42.401	4.180	38.002	38.002	2.521	22.919	22.919
2	1.230	11.184	53.585	.867	7.881	45.883	1.769	16.080	38.999
3	1.011	9.193	62.778	.499	4.532	50.415	1.256	11.417	50.415
4	.774	7.041	69.819						
5	.714	6.495	76.314						
6	.599	5.444	81.758						
7	.587	5.334	87.092						
8	.447	4.064	91.156						
9	.380	3.455	94.611						
10	.318	2.894	97.505						
11	.274	2.495	100.000						

Extraction Method: Principal Axis Factoring.

Factor Matrix[a]

	Factor		
	1	2	3
ABCD1	-.549	.097	.250
ABCD2	.434	.738	.236
ABCD3	.674	-.320	.335
ABCD4	-.681	-.071	.161
ABCD5	.713	-.038	.093
ABCD6	-.424	-.131	.408
ABCD7	.466	-.187	.153
ABCD8	-.736	-.017	.089
ABCD9	-.597	.111	-.159
ABCD10	.644	.292	.003
ABCD11	.745	-.235	-.103

Extraction Method: Principal Axis Factoring.

a. Attempted to extract 3 factors. More than 25 iterations required. (Convergence=.007). Extraction was terminated.

Rotated Factor Matrix[a]

	Factor		
	1	2	3
ABCD1	-.322	.518	-.030
ABCD2	.073	-.110	.878
ABCD3	.807	-.105	.073
ABCD4	-.381	.535	-.254
ABCD5	.581	-.341	.254
ABCD6	-.044	.586	-.132
ABCD7	.503	-.138	.055
ABCD8	-.481	.505	-.251
ABCD9	-.565	.216	-.170
ABCD10	.328	-.394	.488
ABCD11	.604	-.506	.030

Extraction Method: Principal Axis Factoring.
Rotation Method: Varimax with Kaiser Normalization.

a. Rotation converged in 4 iterations.

Component Matrix[a]

	Component		
	1	2	3
ABCD1	-.601	-.042	.455
ABCD2	.427	-.628	.506
ABCD3	.686	.411	.197
ABCD4	-.724	.172	.151
ABCD5	.751	.052	.096
ABCD6	-.466	.398	.561
ABCD7	.522	.449	.164
ABCD8	-.771	.074	.026
ABCD9	-.650	-.245	-.225
ABCD10	.680	-.400	.223
ABCD11	.769	.218	-.185

Extraction Method: Principal Component
Analysis.

a. 3 components extracted.

Pattern Matrix[a]

	Component		
	1	2	3
ABCD1	-.227	-.152	.680
ABCD2	-.062	-.955	.122
ABCD3	.835	-.010	.040
ABCD4	-.243	.253	.500
ABCD5	.540	-.247	-.199
ABCD6	.259	.085	.867
ABCD7	.753	.091	.087
ABCD8	-.401	.272	.366
ABCD9	-.687	.149	-.030
ABCD10	.171	-.666	-.187
ABCD11	.579	.063	-.430

Extraction Method: Principal Component
Analysis.
Rotation Method: Oblimin with Kaiser
Normalization.

R: The `fa` function in the `psych` and `GPARotation` packages

Create new data frame that contains only the variables to be analyzed

Command: `newdataframe <- subset(dataframe, ,select = c(variable, variable, variable...))`

Example: `df11 <- subset(df1,,select = c (ABCD1, ABCD2,ABCD3,ABCD4, ABCD5, ABCD6,ABCD7,ABCD8,ABCD9,ABCD10,ABCD11))`

Remove anyone with NAs on any variable in the new data frame

Command: `newdataframe <- na.omit(newdataframe)`

Example: `df11 <- na.omit(df11)`

Ask for KMO and Bartlett tests

Command: `KMO(newdataframe)`
            `cortest.bartlett(newdataframe)`

Example: `KMO (df11)`
            `cortest.bartlett(df11)`

Run initial analysis to determine the # factors with eigenvalues → 1

Command: `fa(newdataframe, nfactors = #variables, fm ="pa", SMC = FALSE, rotate = "none")`

Note: *#variables* = # variables included in the analysis

`fm = "pa"` = principal axis factoring

Example:
```
fa(df11, nfactors =11, fm ="pa",
SMC = FALSE, rotate = "none")
```

Run second analysis stating # factors with eigenvalues → 1 found in initial analysis

Command:
```
fa(newdataframe, nfactors = #factors,
fm = "pa" , SMC = FALSE, rotate = "method
of rotation")
```

Note: *#factors* = # factors with eigenvalues → 1 in initial analysis

Example:
```
fa(df11,nfactors =3,fm = "pa",
SMC = FALSE, rotate = "varimax")
```

Example script:
```
setwd("e:/R output")
df1 <- read.csv("ABCD_NA.csv")
library(psych)
library(GPArotation)
df11 <- subset(df1,,select = c(ABCD1, ABCD2,ABCD3,
ABCD4, ABCD5, ABCD6,ABCD7,ABCD8,ABCD9,ABCD10,ABCD11))
df11 <- na.omit(df11)
KMO (df11)
cortest.bartlett(df11)
fa(df11, nfactors =11, fm ="pa",SMC = FALSE,
rotate = "none")
fa(df11, nfactors =3, fm = "pa",SMC = FALSE,
rotate = "varimax")
```

```
> setwd("e:/R output")
> df1 <- read.csv("ABCD_NA.csv")
> library(psych)
> library(GPArotation)
> df11 <- subset(df1,,select = c(ABCD1, ABCD2,ABCD3,ABCD4, ABCD5, ABCD6,ABCD7,ABCD8,AB
CD9,ABCD10,ABCD11))
> df11 <- na.omit(df11)
> KMO (df11)
Kaiser-Meyer-Olkin factor adequacy
Call: KMO(r = df11)
Overall MSA =  0.85
MSA for each item =
 ABCD1  ABCD2  ABCD3  ABCD4  ABCD5  ABCD6  ABCD7  ABCD8  ABCD9 ABCD10 ABCD11
 0.91   0.65   0.84   0.91   0.90   0.84   0.83   0.90   0.86   0.81   0.83
> cortest.bartlett(df11)
R was not square, finding R from data
$chisq
[1] 500.984
```

```
$p.value
[1] 3.234399e-73

$df
[1] 55

> fa(df11, nfactors = 11, fm ="pa", SMC = FALSE, rotate = "none")
The estimated weights for the factor scores are probably incorrect. Try a different factor extraction m
ethod.
Factor Analysis using method = pa
Call: fa(r = df11, nfactors = 11, rotate = "none", SMC = FALSE, fm = "pa")
Standardized loadings (pattern matrix) based upon correlation matrix
         PA1   PA2   PA3   PA4   PA5   PA6   PA7   PA8   PA9  PA10  PA11 h2      u2 com
ABCD1  -0.60 -0.04  0.46 -0.28 -0.24  0.06  0.51 -0.05 -0.14  0.08  0.06  1  1.1e-16 4.0
ABCD2   0.43 -0.63  0.51 -0.05  0.22  0.13 -0.17  0.06 -0.01 -0.18  0.19  1  3.3e-16 3.8
ABCD3   0.69  0.41  0.20  0.12 -0.25  0.25  0.14 -0.05  0.25 -0.31 -0.06  1 -2.2e-16 3.7
ABCD4  -0.72  0.17  0.15  0.26  0.19 -0.15  0.14  0.51  0.13 -0.05  0.02  1 -4.4e-16 2.9
ABCD5   0.75  0.05  0.10  0.11 -0.25  0.37 -0.12  0.31 -0.20  0.23 -0.07  1  0.0e+00 2.8
ABCD6  -0.47  0.40  0.56  0.38 -0.03 -0.14 -0.28 -0.21 -0.14  0.05  0.01  1  5.6e-16 5.0
ABCD7   0.52  0.45  0.16 -0.29  0.61  0.10  0.09 -0.02 -0.11  0.01 -0.13  1  1.0e-15 3.9
ABCD8  -0.77  0.07  0.03 -0.05  0.14  0.43 -0.10 -0.10  0.33  0.22  0.10  1  0.0e+00 2.5
ABCD9  -0.65 -0.24 -0.23  0.43  0.19  0.35  0.18 -0.11 -0.22 -0.15 -0.11  1  2.2e-16 4.2
ABCD10  0.68 -0.40  0.22  0.31  0.10 -0.15  0.22 -0.10  0.21  0.21 -0.22  1  0.0e+00 3.8
ABCD11  0.77  0.22 -0.19  0.30  0.12 -0.04  0.25 -0.07 -0.05  0.10  0.37  1 -4.4e-16 2.6

                       PA1  PA2  PA3  PA4  PA5  PA6  PA7  PA8  PA9 PA10 PA11
SS loadings           4.66 1.23 1.01 0.77 0.71 0.60 0.59 0.45 0.38 0.32 0.27
Proportion Var        0.42 0.11 0.09 0.07 0.06 0.05 0.05 0.04 0.03 0.03 0.02
Cumulative Var        0.42 0.54 0.63 0.70 0.76 0.82 0.87 0.91 0.95 0.98 1.00
Proportion Explained  0.42 0.11 0.09 0.07 0.06 0.05 0.05 0.04 0.03 0.03 0.02
Cumulative Proportion 0.42 0.54 0.63 0.70 0.76 0.82 0.87 0.91 0.95 0.98 1.00

Mean item complexity = 3.6
Test of the hypothesis that 11 factors are sufficient.

The degrees of freedom for the null model are  55  and the objective function was  4.09 with Chi Square
of  500.98
The degrees of freedom for the model are -11  and the objective function was  0

The root mean square of the residuals (RMSR) is  0
The df corrected root mean square of the residuals is  NA

The harmonic number of observations is  128 with the empirical chi square  0  with prob <  NA
The total number of observations was  128  with MLE Chi Square =  0  with prob <  NA

Tucker Lewis Index of factoring reliability = 1.132
Fit based upon off diagonal values = 1


> fa(df11, nfactors = 3, fm = "pa", SMC = FALSE, rotate = "varimax")
Factor Analysis using method = pa
Call: fa(r = df11, nfactors = 3, rotate = "varimax", SMC = FALSE, fm = "pa")
Standardized loadings (pattern matrix) based upon correlation matrix
         PA1   PA3   PA2   h2   u2 com
ABCD1  -0.35  0.49 -0.03 0.36 0.64 1.8
ABCD2   0.07 -0.11  0.91 0.84 0.16 1.0
ABCD3   0.79 -0.09  0.07 0.64 0.36 1.0
ABCD4  -0.40  0.53 -0.25 0.50 0.50 2.3
ABCD5   0.59 -0.32  0.25 0.52 0.48 1.9
ABCD6  -0.04  0.63 -0.12 0.41 0.59 1.1
ABCD7   0.51 -0.12  0.06 0.28 0.72 1.1
ABCD8  -0.50  0.48 -0.24 0.55 0.45 2.4
ABCD9  -0.57  0.20 -0.16 0.39 0.61 1.4
ABCD10  0.35 -0.38  0.48 0.49 0.51 2.8
ABCD11  0.63 -0.47  0.03 0.62 0.38 1.9

                       PA1  PA3  PA2
SS loadings           2.62 1.69 1.28
Proportion Var        0.24 0.15 0.12
Cumulative Var        0.24 0.39 0.51
Proportion Explained  0.47 0.30 0.23
Cumulative Proportion 0.47 0.77 1.00

Mean item complexity = 1.7
Test of the hypothesis that 3 factors are sufficient.

The degrees of freedom for the null model are  55  and the objective function was  4.09 with Chi Square
of  500.98
The degrees of freedom for the model are 25  and the objective function was  0.33

The root mean square of the residuals (RMSR) is  0.04
The df corrected root mean square of the residuals is  0.06

The harmonic number of observations is  128 with the empirical chi square  20.75  with prob <  0.71
The total number of observations was  128  with MLE Chi Square =  39.59  with prob <  0.032

Tucker Lewis Index of factoring reliability = 0.927
RMSEA index = 0.073  and the 90 % confidence intervals are  0.02 0.106
BIC =  -81.71
Fit based upon off diagonal values = 0.99
Measures of factor score adequacy
                                                PA1  PA3  PA2
Correlation of scores with factors             0.88 0.79 0.91
Multiple R square of scores with factors       0.77 0.63 0.83
Minimum correlation of possible factor scores  0.54 0.26 0.67
```

LINEAR REGRESSION

EXAMPLE: Conduct linear regression analysis (IV: *satmath*; DV: *cgpa*)

SPSS: The REGRESSION command

```
REGRESSION
  /MISSING LISTWISE
  /STATISTICS COEFF OUTS R ANOVA
  /CRITERIA=PIN(.05) POUT(.10)
  /NOORIGIN
  /DEPENDENT cgpa
  /METHOD=ENTER satmath.
```

Regression

Variables Entered/Removed[a]

Model	Variables Entered	Variables Removed	Method
1	satmath[b]	.	Enter

a. Dependent Variable: cgpa

b. All requested variables entered.

Model Summary

Model	R	R Square	Adjusted R Square	Std. Error of the Estimate
1	.364[a]	.132	.123	.37890

a. Predictors: (Constant), satmath

ANOVA[a]

Model		Sum of Squares	df	Mean Square	F	Sig.
1	Regression	2.033	1	2.033	14.161	.000[b]
	Residual	13.351	93	.144		
	Total	15.384	94			

a. Dependent Variable: cgpa

b. Predictors: (Constant), satmath

Coefficients[a]

Model		Unstandardized Coefficients B	Unstandardized Coefficients Std. Error	Standardized Coefficients Beta	t	Sig.
1	(Constant)	2.080	.253		8.235	.000
	satmath	.002	.000	.364	3.763	.000

a. Dependent Variable: cgpa

R: The `lm` function in the base package

Conduct linear regression analysis

Commands: *result* <- **lm**(*dv* ~ *iv*, **data** = *dataframe*)
             summary(*result*)

Example: linreg <- lm(cgpa ~ satmath, data = df1)
           summary(linreg)

Example script:
```
setwd("e:/R output")
df1 <- read.csv("COLLEGE_NA.csv")
linreg <- lm(cgpa ~ satmath, data = df1)
summary(linreg)
```

```
> setwd("e:/R output")
> df1 = read.csv("COLLEGE_NA.csv")
>
> linreg <- lm(cgpa ~ satmath, data = df1)
> summary(linreg)

Call:
lm(formula = cgpa ~ satmath, data = df1)

Residuals:
    Min      1Q  Median      3Q     Max
-0.86298 -0.22499 -0.03557  0.23036  1.00334

Coefficients:
             Estimate Std. Error t value Pr(>|t|)
(Intercept) 2.0799407  0.2525699   8.235 1.09e-12 ***
satmath     0.0015927  0.0004232   3.763 0.000294 ***
---
Signif. codes:  0 '***' 0.001 '**' 0.01 '*' 0.05 '.' 0.1 ' ' 1

Residual standard error: 0.3789 on 93 degrees of freedom
  (21 observations deleted due to missingness)
Multiple R-squared:  0.1321,    Adjusted R-squared:  0.1228
F-statistic: 14.16 on 1 and 93 DF,  p-value: 0.0002936
```

MULTIPLE REGRESSION (STANDARD)

EXAMPLE: Conduct standard regression analysis (IVs: *satmath* & *satverb*; DV: *cgpa*)

SPSS: The REGRESSION command

```
REGRESSION
    /MISSING LISTWISE
    /STATISTICS COEFF OUTS R ANOVA
    /CRITERIA=PIN(.05) POUT(.10)
    /NOORIGIN
    /DEPENDENT cgpa
    /METHOD=ENTER satmath satverb.
```

Regression

Variables Entered/Removed[a]

Model	Variables Entered	Variables Removed	Method
1	satverb, satmath[b]	.	Enter

a. Dependent Variable: cgpa

b. All requested variables entered.

Model Summary

Model	R	R Square	Adjusted R Square	Std. Error of the Estimate
1	.392[a]	.154	.135	.37622

a. Predictors: (Constant), satverb, satmath

ANOVA[a]

Model		Sum of Squares	df	Mean Square	F	Sig.
1	Regression	2.362	2	1.181	8.345	.000[b]
	Residual	13.022	92	.142		
	Total	15.384	94			

a. Dependent Variable: cgpa

b. Predictors: (Constant), satverb, satmath

Coefficients[a]

Model		Unstandardized Coefficients		Standardized Coefficients	t	Sig.
		B	Std. Error	Beta		
1	(Constant)	1.680	.363		4.634	.000
	satmath	.001	.000	.337	3.451	.001
	satverb	.001	.001	.149	1.525	.131

a. Dependent Variable: cgpa

R: The `lm` function in the base package

Create output of multiple regression analysis

Commands: *result* <- **lm(***dv ~ iv1 + iv2 + iv3...*, **data =** *dataframe***)**

Example: stanmrc <- lm(cgpa ~ satmath + satverb, data = df1)

Modify output of multiple regression analysis to include standardized coefficients (betas)

Commands: *resultb* <- **lm.beta(***result***)**

Example: stanmrcbetas <- lm.beta(stanmrc)

Display output of multiple regression analysis with standardized coefficients (betas)

Commands: **summary(***resultb***)**

Example: summary(stanmrcbetas)

Example script:
```
setwd("e:/R output")
df1 <- read.csv("COLLEGE_NA.csv")
library(lm.beta)
stanmrc <- lm(cgpa ~ satmath + satverb, data = df1)
stanmrcbetas <- lm.beta(stanmrc)
summary(stanmrcbetas)
```

```
> setwd("e:/R output")
> library("lm.beta")
> df1 = read.csv("COLLEGE_NA.csv")
>
> stanmrc <- lm(cgpa ~ satmath + satverb, data = df1)
> stanmrcbetas <- lm.beta(stanmrc)
> summary(stanmrcbetas)

Call:
lm(formula = cgpa ~ satmath + satverb, data = df1)

Residuals:
    Min      1Q  Median      3Q     Max
-0.86365 -0.24999 -0.03883 0.21822 1.02544

Coefficients:
              Estimate Standardized Std. Error t value Pr(>|t|)
(Intercept) 1.6804492    0.0000000  0.3625998   4.634 1.18e-05 ***
satmath     0.0014748    0.3366103  0.0004273   3.451 0.000844 ***
satverb     0.0008609    0.1487722  0.0005644   1.525 0.130580
---
Signif. codes:  0 '***' 0.001 '**' 0.01 '*' 0.05 '.' 0.1 ' ' 1

Residual standard error: 0.3762 on 92 degrees of freedom
  (21 observations deleted due to missingness)
Multiple R-squared: 0.1536,    Adjusted R-squared: 0.1352
F-statistic: 8.345 on 2 and 92 DF,  p-value: 0.0004673
```

MULTIPLE REGRESSION (HIERARCHICAL WITH TWO STEPS)

EXAMPLE: Conduct hierarchical analysis (IVs: Step 1: *satmath*, Step 2: *satverb*; DV = *cgpa*)

SPSS: The REGRESSION command

```
REGRESSION
  /DESCRIPTIVES MEAN STDDEV CORR SIG N
  /MISSING LISTWISE
  /STATISTICS COEFF OUTS R ANOVA CHANGE ZPP
  /CRITERIA=PIN(.05) POUT(.10)
  /NOORIGIN
  /DEPENDENT cgpa
  /METHOD=ENTER satmath
  /METHOD=ENTER satverb.
```

Regression

Variables Entered/Removed[a]

Model	Variables Entered	Variables Removed	Method
1	satmath[b]	.	Enter
2	satverb[b]	.	Enter

a. Dependent Variable: cgpa

b. All requested variables entered.

Model Summary

Model	R	R Square	Adjusted R Square	Std. Error of the Estimate	Change Statistics R Square Change	Change Statistics F Change	Change Statistics df1	Change Statistics df2	Change Statistics Sig. F Change
1	.36	.13	.12	.38	.13	14.16	1	93	.000
2	.39	.15	.14	.38	.02	2.33	1	92	.131

ANOVA

Model		Sum of Squares	df	Mean Square	F	Sig.
1	Regression	2.03	1	2.03	14.16	.000
	Residual	13.35	93	.14		
	Total	15.38	94			
2	Regression	2.36	2	1.18	8.34	.000
	Residual	13.02	92	.14		
	Total	15.38	94			

Coefficients

Model		Unstandardized Coefficients B	Unstandardized Coefficients Std. Error	Standardized Coefficients Beta	t	Sig.	Correlations Zero-order	Correlations Partial	Correlations Part
1	(Constant)	2.080	.253		8.24	.000			
	satmath	.0016	.0004	.364	3.76	.000	.36	.36	.36
2	(Constant)	1.680	.363		4.63	.000			
	satmath	.0015	.000	.337	3.45	.001	.36	.34	.33
	satverb	.0009	.0006	.149	1.53	.131	.21	.16	.15

R: The `lm`, `lm.beta`, and `lm.deltaR2` functions in the base package

Create new data frame that contains only the variables to be analyzed

Command: `newdataframe <- subset(dataframe, ,select = c(variable, variable, variable...))`

Example: `df11 <- subset(df1, ,select = c(cgpa, satmath, satverb))`

Remove anyone with NAs on any variable in the new data frame

Command: `newdataframe <- na.omit(newdataframe)`

Example: `df11 <- na.omit(df11)`

Conduct the first step of the analysis

Command: `result1 <- lm(dv ~ iv1.., data = newdataframe)`
`result1b <- lm.beta(result1)`
`summary(result1b)`
Note: `result1` = output of regression analysis at first step (no betas)
`result1b` = output of regression analysis at first step (with betas)

Example: `step1 <- lm(cgpa ~ satmath, data = df11)`
`step1b <- lm.beta(step1)`
`summary(step1b)`

Conduct the second step of the analysis and ask for ΔR^2 statistics

Command: `result2 <- lm(dv ~ iv1.., data = newdataframe)`
`result2b <- lm.beta(result2)`
`summary(result2b)`
`lm.deltaR2(result1b, result2b)`
Note: `result2` = output of regression analysis at second step (no betas)
`result2b` = output of regression analysis at second step (with betas)
`lm.deltaR2` = calculate change in R^2

Example: `step2 <- lm(cgpa ~ satmath + satverb, data = df11)`
`step2b <- lm.beta(step2)`
`summary(step2b)`
`lm.deltaR2(step1b, step2b)`

Example script:
```
setwd("e:/R output")
df1 <- read.csv("COLLEGE_NA.csv")
library(lm.beta)
library(lmSupport)
df11 <- subset(df1, ,select = c(cgpa,satmath,satverb))
df11 <- na.omit(df11)
step1 <- lm(cgpa ~ satmath, data =df11)
step1b <- lm.beta(step1)
summary(step1b)
step2 <- lm(cgpa ~ satmath + satverb, data =df11)
step2b <- lm.beta(step2)
summary(step2b)
lm.deltaR2(step1b, step2b)
```

```
> setwd("e:/R output")
> # Install and load lm.beta package to get betas
> library("lm.beta")
> # Install and load lmSupport package to get ΔR2 statistics
> library("lmSupport")
Loading required package: car
> df1 = read.csv("COLLEGE_NA.csv")
>
> #  Create data frame containing only the variables to be analyzed
> df11 <- subset(df1, , select = c(cgpa,satmath,satverb))
>
> # Remove anyone with missing data (NAs) on any variable in the new data frame
> df11 <- na.omit(df11)
>
> # Conduct the first step in the analysis
> step1 <- lm(cgpa ~ satmath, data = df11)
> step1b <- lm.beta(step1)
> summary(step1b)

Call:
lm(formula = cgpa ~ satmath, data = df11)

Residuals:
    Min      1Q   Median      3Q     Max
-0.86298 -0.22499 -0.03557  0.23036  1.00334

Coefficients:
             Estimate Standardized Std. Error t value Pr(>|t|)
(Intercept) 2.0799407    0.0000000  0.2525699   8.235 1.09e-12 ***
satmath     0.0015927    0.3635165  0.0004232   3.763 0.000294 ***
---
Signif. codes:  0 '***' 0.001 '**' 0.01 '*' 0.05 '.' 0.1 ' ' 1

Residual standard error: 0.3789 on 93 degrees of freedom
Multiple R-squared:  0.1321,    Adjusted R-squared:  0.1228
F-statistic: 14.16 on 1 and 93 DF,  p-value: 0.0002936
```

```
> # Conduct the second step in the analysis and get ΔR2 statistics
> step2 <- lm(cgpa ~ satmath + satverb, data = df11)
> step2b <- lm.beta(step2)
> summary(step2b)

Call:
lm(formula = cgpa ~ satmath + satverb, data = df11)

Residuals:
     Min      1Q   Median      3Q      Max
-0.86365 -0.24999 -0.03883 0.21822  1.02544

Coefficients:
            Estimate Standardized Std. Error t value Pr(>|t|)
(Intercept) 1.6804492  0.0000000  0.3625998   4.634 1.18e-05 ***
satmath     0.0014748  0.3366103  0.0004273   3.451 0.000844 ***
satverb     0.0008609  0.1487722  0.0005644   1.525 0.130580
---
Signif. codes:  0 '***' 0.001 '**' 0.01 '*' 0.05 '.' 0.1 ' ' 1

Residual standard error: 0.3762 on 92 degrees of freedom
Multiple R-squared: 0.1536,    Adjusted R-squared: 0.1352
F-statistic: 8.345 on 2 and 92 DF,  p-value: 0.0004673

>
> lm.deltaR2(step1b, step2b)
SSE (Compact) =  13.35145
SSE (Augmented) =  13.02208
Delta R-Squared =  0.02140924
Partial Eta-Squared (PRE) =  0.02466912
F(1,92) = 2.326963, p = 0.1305802
```

MULTIPLE REGRESSION (HIERARCHICAL WITH THREE STEPS)

EXAMPLE: Conduct hierarchical analysis (IVs: Step 1: *hsgpa*, Step 2: *satmath* & *satverb*, Step 3: *sshada* & *sshawm*; DV = cgpa)

SPSS: The REGRESSION command

```
REGRESSION
    /MISSING LISTWISE
    /STATISTICS COEFF OUTS R ANOVA CHANGE
    /CRITERIA=PIN(.05) POUT(.10)
    /NOORIGIN
    /DEPENDENT cgpa
    /METHOD=ENTER hsgpa
    /METHOD=ENTER satmath satverb
    /METHOD=ENTER sshada sshawm.
```

Regression

Variables Entered/Removed

Model	Variables Entered	Variables Removed	Method
1	hsgpa	.	Enter
2	satverb, satmath	.	Enter
3	sshada, sshawm	.	Enter

Model Summary

Model	R	R Square	Adjusted R Square	Std. Error of the Estimate	Change Statistics R Square Change	F Change	df1	df2	Sig. F Change
1	.186	.035	.024	.39961	.035	3.341	1	93	.071
2	.393	.155	.127	.37800	.120	6.467	2	91	.002
3	.537	.288	.248	.35071	.134	8.359	2	89	.000

ANOVA

Model		Sum of Squares	df	Mean Square	F	Sig.
1	Regression	.534	1	.534	3.341	.071
	Residual	14.851	93	.160		
	Total	15.384	94			
2	Regression	2.382	3	.794	5.556	.002
	Residual	13.003	91	.143		
	Total	15.384	94			
3	Regression	4.438	5	.888	7.216	.000
	Residual	10.946	89	.123		
	Total	15.384	94			

Coefficients

Model		Unstandardized Coefficients B	Std. Error	Standardized Coefficients Beta	t	Sig.
1	(Constant)	2.274	.410		5.553	.000
	hsgpa	.206	.113	.186	1.828	.071
2	(Constant)	1.576	.462		3.408	.001
	hsgpa	.043	.116	.039	.368	.714
	satmath	.001	.000	.323	3.079	.003
	satverb	.001	.001	.144	1.462	.147
3	(Constant)	1.388	.432		3.217	.002
	hsgpa	.083	.111	.075	.751	.455
	satmath	.001	.000	.288	2.904	.005
	satverb	.000	.001	.078	.838	.404
	sshada	.001	.004	.034	.329	.743
	sshawm	.014	.004	.356	3.370	.001

R: The `lm`, `lm.beta`, and `lm.deltaR2` functions in the base package

Create new data frame that contains only the variables to be analyzed

Command: `newdataframe <- subset(dataframe,,select = c(variable, variable, variable...))`

Example: `df11 <- subset(df1,,select = c(cgpa,hsgpa, satmath, satverb,sshada,sshawm))`

Remove anyone with NAs on any variable in the new data frame

Command: `newdataframe <- na.omit(newdataframe)`

Example: `df11 <- na.omit(df11)`

(Continued)

(Continued)

Conduct the first step of the analysis

Command:
```
result1 <- lm(dv ~ iv1..., data = newdataframe)
result1b <- lm.beta(result1)
summary(result1b)
```

Example:
```
step1 <- lm(cgpa ~ hsgpa, data = df11)
step1b <- lm.beta(step1)
summary(step1b)
```

Conduct the second step of the analysis and ask for ΔR^2 statistics

Command:
```
result2 <- lm(dv ~ iv1..., data = newdataframe)
result2b <- lm.beta(result2)
summary(result2b)
lm.deltaR2(result1b, result2b)
```

Example:
```
step2 <- lm(cgpa ~ hsgpa + satmath + satverb,
data = df11)
step2b <- lm.beta(step2)
summary(step2b)
lm.deltaR2(step1b, step2b)
```

Conduct the third step of the analysis and ask for ΔR^2 statistics

Command:
```
result3 <- lm(dv ~ iv1..., data = newdataframe)
result3b <- lm.beta(result3)
summary(result3b)
lm.deltaR2(result2b, result3b)
```

Example:
```
step3 <- lm(cgpa ~ hsgpa + satmath + satverb
+sshada +sshawm, data = df11)
step3b <- lm.beta(step3)
summary(step3b)
lm.deltaR2(step2b, step3b)
```

Example script:

```
setwd("e:/R output")
df1<- read.csv("COLLEGE_NA.csv")
library(lm.beta)
library(lmSupport)
df11<- subset(df1,,select =
c(cgpa,hsgpa,satmath,satverb,sshada,sshawm))
df11<- na.omit(df11)
step1<- lm(cgpa~ hsgpa, data = df11)
step1b<- lm.beta(step1)
summary(step1b)
step2<- lm(cgpa~ hsgpa+ satmath+ satverb, data = df11)
step2b<- lm.beta(step2)
summary(step2b)
lm.deltaR2(step1b, step2b)
step3<- lm(cgpa~ hsgpa + satmath + satverb +sshada
+sshawm, data = df11)
step3b<- lm.beta(step3)
summary(step3b)
lm.deltaR2(step2b, step3b)
```

```
> setwd("e:/R output")
> # Install and load lm.beta package to get betas
> library("lm.beta")
> # Install and load lmSupport package to get ΔR2 statistics
> library("lmSupport")
> df1 = read.csv("COLLEGE_NA.csv")
>
> # Create data frame containing only the variables to be analyzed
> df11 <- subset(df1, , select = c(cgpa,hsgpa,satmath,satverb,sshada,sshawm))
>
> # Remove anyone with missing data (NAs) on any variable in the new data frame
> df11 <- na.omit(df11)
>
> # Conduct the first step in the analysis
> step1 <- lm(cgpa ~ hsgpa, data = df11)
> step1b <- lm.beta(step1)
> summary(step1b)

Call:
lm(formula = cgpa ~ hsgpa, data = df11)

Residuals:
     Min       1Q   Median       3Q      Max
-1.05623 -0.29079 -0.04623  0.23906  0.82609

Coefficients:
            Estimate Standardized Std. Error t value Pr(>|t|)
(Intercept)   2.2742       0.0000     0.4095   5.553 2.65e-07 ***
hsgpa         0.2058       0.1862     0.1126   1.828   0.0708 .
---
Signif. codes:  0 '***' 0.001 '**' 0.01 '*' 0.05 '.' 0.1 ' ' 1
```

```
Residual standard error: 0.3996 on 93 degrees of freedom
Multiple R-squared:  0.03468,    Adjusted R-squared:  0.0243
F-statistic: 3.341 on 1 and 93 DF,  p-value: 0.07076


> # Conduct the second step in the analysis and get ΔR2 statistics
> step2 <- lm(cgpa ~ hsgpa + satmath + satverb, data = df11)
> step2b <- lm.beta(step2)
> summary(step2b)

Call:
lm(formula = cgpa ~ hsgpa + satmath + satverb, data = df11)

Residuals:
    Min       1Q   Median       3Q      Max
-0.86954 -0.24337 -0.03368  0.23833  1.02097

Coefficients:
             Estimate Standardized Std. Error t value Pr(>|t|)
(Intercept) 1.5757621    0.0000000  0.4623516   3.408 0.000976 ***
hsgpa       0.0426038    0.0385536  0.1158545   0.368 0.713924
satmath     0.0014147    0.3228847  0.0004594   3.079 0.002743 **
satverb     0.0008351    0.1443145  0.0005713   1.462 0.147291
---
Signif. codes:  0 '***' 0.001 '**' 0.01 '*' 0.05 '.' 0.1 ' ' 1

Residual standard error: 0.378 on 91 degrees of freedom
Multiple R-squared:  0.1548,    Adjusted R-squared:  0.1269
F-statistic: 5.556 on 3 and 91 DF,  p-value: 0.001513

> lm.deltaR2(step1b, step2b)
SSE (Compact) =  14.85083
SSE (Augmented) =  13.00276
Delta R-Squared =  0.1201259
Partial Eta-Squared (PRE) =  0.124442
F(2,91) =  6.466857, p = 0.002365728
warning message:
In lm.deltaR2(step1b, step2b) : 'lm.deltaR2' is deprecated.
Use 'modelCompare' instead.




> # Conduct the last step in the analysis and get ΔR2 statistics
> step3 <- lm(cgpa ~ hsgpa + satmath + satverb +sshada +sshawm, data = df11)
> step3b <- lm.beta(step3)
> summary(step3b)

Call:
lm(formula = cgpa ~ hsgpa + satmath + satverb + sshada + sshawm,
    data = df11)

Residuals:
    Min       1Q   Median       3Q      Max
-0.88272 -0.23106 -0.04463  0.22051  0.94779

Coefficients:
             Estimate Standardized Std. Error t value Pr(>|t|)
(Intercept) 1.3883957    0.0000000  0.4316110   3.217  0.00181 **
hsgpa       0.0830508    0.0751554  0.1106405   0.751  0.45485
satmath     0.0012619    0.2880224  0.0004346   2.904  0.00465 **
satverb     0.0004516    0.0780442  0.0005387   0.838  0.40405
sshada      0.0014194    0.0343889  0.0043134   0.329  0.74288
sshawm      0.0143267    0.3560448  0.0042512   3.370  0.00111 **
---
Signif. codes:  0 '***' 0.001 '**' 0.01 '*' 0.05 '.' 0.1 ' ' 1

Residual standard error: 0.3507 on 89 degrees of freedom
Multiple R-squared:  0.2885,    Adjusted R-squared:  0.2485
F-statistic: 7.216 on 5 and 89 DF,  p-value: 1.034e-05
```

```
> lm.deltaR2(step2b, step3b)
SSE (Compact) =  13.00276
SSE (Augmented) =  10.94649
Delta R-Squared =  0.1336592
Partial Eta-Squared (PRE) =  0.1581409
F(2,89) = 8.359203, p = 0.0004711438
warning message:
In lm.deltaR2(step2b, step3b) : 'lm.deltaR2' is deprecated.
Use 'modelCompare' instead.
```

MULTIPLE REGRESSION (TESTING MODERATOR VARIABLES USING HIERARCHICAL REGRESSION)

EXAMPLE: Conduct hierarchical analysis (IV: *satmath*; Moderator: *satverb*; DV = *cgpa*)

SPSS: The COMPUTE and REGRESSION commands

```
*  Create variable representing SATMATH * SATVERB interaction .
COMPUTE  MATHVERB  =  SATMATH * SATVERB .
VARIABLE LABELS  MATHVERB  "SATMATH * SATVERB (crossproduct)" .
EXECUTE  .
REGRESSION
  /MISSING LISTWISE
  /STATISTICS COEFF OUTS R ANOVA CHANGE
  /CRITERIA=PIN(.05) POUT(.10)
  /NOORIGIN
  /DEPENDENT cgpa
  /METHOD=ENTER satmath satverb
  /METHOD=ENTER MATHVERB.
```

Regression

Variables Entered/Removed

Model	Variables Entered	Variables Removed	Method
1	satverb, satmath	.	Enter
2	MATHVERB		.	Enter

Model Summary

Model	R	R Square	Adjusted R Square	Std. Error of the Estimate	Change Statistics				
					R Square Change	F Change	df1	df2	Sig. F Change
1	.392[a]	.154	.135	.37622	.154	8.345	2	92	.000
2	.491[b]	.241	.216	.35820	.088	10.494	1	91	.002

a. Predictors: (Constant), satverb, satmath

b. Predictors: (Constant), satverb, satmath, MATHVERB

ANOVA

Model		Sum of Squares	df	Mean Square	F	Sig.
1	Regression	2.362	2	1.181	8.345	.000[b]
	Residual	13.022	92	.142		
	Total	15.384	94			
2	Regression	3.709	3	1.236	9.635	.000[c]
	Residual	11.676	91	.128		
	Total	15.384	94			

b. Predictors: (Constant), satverb, satmath

c. Predictors: (Constant), satverb, satmath, MATHVERB

Coefficients

Model		Unstandardized Coefficients		Standardized Coefficients	t	Sig.
		B	Std. Error	Beta		
1	(Constant)	1.680	.363		4.634	.000
	satmath	.001	.000	.337	3.451	.001
	satverb	.001	.001	.149	1.525	.131
2	(Constant)	9.467	2.428		3.898	.000
	satmath	-.011	.004	-2.587	-2.851	.005
	satverb	-.013	.004	-2.322	-3.022	.003
	MATHVERB	.000	.000	4.166	3.239	.002

R: The `lm`, `lm.beta`, and `lm.deltaR2` functions in the base package

Create new data frame that contains only the variables to be analyzed

Command: `newdataframe <- subset(dataframe, ,select = c(variable, variable, variable...))`

Example: `df11<- subset(df1,, select =c(cgpa, satmath, satverb))`

Remove anyone with NAs on any variable in the new data frame

Command: `newdataframe <- na.omit(newdataframe)`

Example: `df11<- na.omit(df11)`

Conduct the first step of the analysis (main effects)

Command: `result1<- lm(dv ~ iv1 + iv2, data = newdataframe)`
`result1b<- lm.beta(result1)`
`summary(result1b)`

Example:
```
maineffs <- lm(cgpa ~ satmath + satverb, data
=df11)
maineffsb <- lm.beta(maineffs)
summary(maineffsb)
```

Conduct the second step of the analysis (moderating effect)

Command:
```
result2 <- lm(dv ~ iv1 + iv2 + iv1 * iv2,
data = newdataframe)
result2b <- lm.beta(result2)
summary(result2b)
lm.deltaR2(result1b, result2b)
```

Example:
```
moderator <- lm(cgpa ~ satmath + satverb +
satmath * satverb, data =df11)
moderatorb <- lm.beta(moderator)
summary(moderatorb)
lm.deltaR2(maineffsb, moderatorb)
```

Example script:
```
setwd("e:/R output")
df1 <- read.csv("COLLEGE_NA.csv")
library(lm.beta)
library(lmSupport)
df11 <- subset(df1,,select =c(cgpa, satmath,satverb))
df11 <- na.omit(df11)
maineffs <- lm(cgpa ~ satmath + satverb, data =df11)
maineffsb <- lm.beta(maineffs)
summary(maineffsb)
moderator <- lm(cgpa ~ satmath + satverb + satmath *
satverb, data =df11)
moderatorb <- lm.beta(moderator)
summary(moderatorb)
lm.deltaR2(maineffsb, moderatorb)
```

```
> setwd("e:/R output")
> # Install and load lm.beta package to get betas
> library("lm.beta")
> # Install and load lmSupport package to get ΔR2 statistics
> library("lmSupport")
> df1 = read.csv("COLLEGE_NA.csv")
>
> # Create data frame containing only the variables to be analyzed
> df11 <- subset(df1, , select = c(cgpa,satmath,satverb))
>
> # Remove anyone with missing data (NAs) on any variable in the new data frame
> df11 <- na.omit(df11)
>
> # Conduct the first step of the analysis (main effects)
> maineffs <- lm(cgpa ~ satmath + satverb, data = df11)
> maineffsb <- lm.beta(maineffs)
> summary(maineffsb)

Call:
lm(formula = cgpa ~ satmath + satverb, data = df11)

Residuals:
    Min      1Q  Median      3Q     Max
-0.86365 -0.24999 -0.03883 0.21822 1.02544

Coefficients:
             Estimate Standardized Std. Error t value Pr(>|t|)
(Intercept) 1.6804492    0.0000000  0.3625998   4.634 1.18e-05 ***
satmath     0.0014748    0.3366103  0.0004273   3.451 0.000844 ***
satverb     0.0008609    0.1487722  0.0005644   1.525 0.130580
---
Signif. codes:  0 '***' 0.001 '**' 0.01 '*' 0.05 '.' 0.1 ' ' 1

Residual standard error: 0.3762 on 92 degrees of freedom
Multiple R-squared:  0.1536,    Adjusted R-squared:  0.1352
F-statistic: 8.345 on 2 and 92 DF,  p-value: 0.0004673

> # Conduct the second step of the analysis (moderating effect)
> moderator <- lm(cgpa ~ satmath + satverb + satmath * satverb, data = df11)
> summary(moderator)

Call:
lm(formula = cgpa ~ satmath + satverb + satmath * satverb, data = df11)

Residuals:
    Min      1Q  Median      3Q     Max
-0.85911 -0.19652 0.00064 0.24681 0.87847

Coefficients:
                  Estimate Std. Error t value Pr(>|t|)
(Intercept)      9.467e+00  2.428e+00   3.898 0.000185 ***
satmath         -1.134e-02  3.975e-03  -2.851 0.005385 **
satverb         -1.344e-02  4.446e-03  -3.022 0.003261 **
satmath:satverb  2.343e-05  7.234e-06   3.239 0.001673 **
---
Signif. codes:  0 '***' 0.001 '**' 0.01 '*' 0.05 '.' 0.1 ' ' 1

Residual standard error: 0.3582 on 91 degrees of freedom
Multiple R-squared:  0.2411,    Adjusted R-squared:  0.2161
F-statistic: 9.635 on 3 and 91 DF,  p-value: 1.378e-05

> lm.deltaR2(maineffsb, moderator)
SSE (Compact) = 13.02208
SSE (Augmented) = 11.67569
Delta R-Squared = 0.08751697
Partial Eta-Squared (PRE) = 0.1033934
F(1,91) = 10.49379, p = 0.001672992
```

MULTIPLE REGRESSION (PORTRAYING A SIGNIFICANT MODERATING EFFECT)

EXAMPLE: Investigate moderating effect of *satverb* on the relationship between *satmath* and *cgpa*

Note: This example will portray a significant moderating effect by dichotomizing one continuous predictor variable based on a median split (*satverb*) and calculating two linear regression equations predicting the criterion variable (*cgpa*) from the other predictor variable (*satverb*). In other words, we are investigating how *satverb* moderates the relationship between *satmath* and *cgpa* (the relationship between *satmath* and *cgpa* for those with "low" *satverb* scores versus those with "high" *satverb* scores)

SPSS: The FREQUENCIES and REGRESSION commands

```
FREQUENCIES VARIABLES=satverb
  /ORDER=ANALYSIS.
```

Frequencies

satverb

		Frequency	Percent	Valid Percent	Cumulative Percent
Valid	330	1	.9	1.1	1.1
	350	1	.9	1.1	2.1
	370	1	.9	1.1	3.2
	400	1	.9	1.1	4.2
	420	1	.9	1.1	5.3
	450	3	2.6	3.2	8.4
	470	3	2.6	3.2	11.6
	480	4	3.4	4.2	15.8
	490	1	.9	1.1	16.8
	500	13	11.2	13.7	30.5
	510	3	2.6	3.2	33.7
	520	2	1.7	2.1	35.8
	530	6	5.2	6.3	42.1
	540	4	3.4	4.2	46.3
	550	9	7.8	9.5	55.8
	560	6	5.2	6.3	62.1
	570	5	4.3	5.3	67.4
	580	5	4.3	5.3	72.6
	590	1	.9	1.1	73.7
	600	10	8.6	10.5	84.2
	610	5	4.3	5.3	89.5
	620	2	1.7	2.1	91.6
	630	1	.9	1.1	92.6
	635	1	.9	1.1	93.7
	650	2	1.7	2.1	95.8
	680	2	1.7	2.1	97.9
	700	1	.9	1.1	98.9
	740	1	.9	1.1	100.0
	Total	95	81.9	100.0	
Missing	999	21	18.1		
Total		116	100.0		

```
*  Investigate significant moderating effect by dichotomizing SATVERB .
IF  (SATVERB le 550) NSATVERB  =  1 .
IF  (SATVERB gt 550) NSATVERB  =  2 .
FORMATS   NSATVERB (F2.0) .
VARIABLE LABELS   NSATVERB   "Dichotomized SATVERB" .
VALUE LABELS   NSATVERB   1   "<= 550 (Low) "   2   "> 550 (High)"  .
EXECUTE   .


*  Linear regression:  Low SATVERB .
TEMPORARY .
SELECT IF  (NSATVERB eq 1) .
REGRESSION
  /MISSING LISTWISE
  /STATISTICS COEFF OUTS R ANOVA
  /CRITERIA=PIN(.05) POUT(.10)
  /NOORIGIN
  /DEPENDENT  cgpa
  /METHOD=ENTER  satmath  .
```

Regression

Variables Entered/Removed[a]

Model	Variables Entered	Variables Removed	Method
1	satmath	.	Enter

a. Dependent Variable: cgpa

Model Summary

Model	R	R Square	Adjusted R Square	Std. Error of the Estimate
1	.153[a]	.023	.004	.37703

a. Predictors: (Constant), satmath

ANOVA

Model		Sum of Squares	df	Mean Square	F	Sig.
1	Regression	.173	1	.173	1.220	.275
	Residual	7.250	51	.142		
	Total	7.423	52			

Coefficients

Model		Unstandardized Coefficients		Standardized Coefficients	t	Sig.
		B	Std. Error	Beta		
1	(Constant)	2.57	.352		7.301	.000
	satmath	.0007	.001	.153	1.104	.275

```
*  Linear regression:  High SATVERB  .
TEMPORARY .
SELECT IF (NSATVERB eq 2) .
REGRESSION
  /MISSING LISTWISE
  /STATISTICS COEFF OUTS R ANOVA
  /CRITERIA=PIN(.05) POUT(.10)
  /NOORIGIN
  /DEPENDENT  cgpa
  /METHOD=ENTER  satmath  .
```

Regression

Variables Entered/Removed[a]

Model	Variables Entered	Variables Removed	Method
1	satmath	.	Enter

a. Dependent Variable: cgpa

Model Summary

Model	R	R Square	Adjusted R Square	Std. Error of the Estimate
1	.506[a]	.256	.237	.37165

a. Predictors: (Constant), satmath

ANOVA

Model		Sum of Squares	df	Mean Square	F	Sig.
1	Regression	1.899	1	1.899	13.745	.001
	Residual	5.525	40	.138		
	Total	7.423	41			

Coefficients

Model		Unstandardized Coefficients		Standardized Coefficients	t	Sig.
		B	Std. Error	Beta		
1	(Constant)	1.64	.400		4.097	.000
	satmath	.0024	.001	.506	3.707	.001

R: The `transform`, `lm`, `cut` and `ggplot` functions in the base and `ggplot2` packages

Create new data frame that contains only the variables to be analyzed

Command: `newdataframe <- subset(dataframe,,select = c(variable, variable, variable...))`

Example: `df11 <- subset(df1,,select = c(cgpa, satmath,satverb))`

Remove anyone with NAs on any variable in the new data frame

Command: `newdataframe <- na.omit(newdataframe)`

Example: `df11 <- na.omit(df11)`

Create frequency distribution table for one of the predictor variables

Command: **`transform(table(newdataframe$var), cumFreq = cumsum(Freq), pct = prop.table(Freq)*100)`**
Note: `newdataframe$var` = the moderator variable

Example: `transform(table(df11$satverb), cumFreq = cumsum(Freq), pct = prop.table(Freq)*100)`

Create two data frames based on median split of the moderator variable

Command: `subsample1dataframe <- newdataframe [which(newdataframe$var expression)  ,]`
`subsample2dataframe <- newdataframe [which(newdataframe$var expression)  ,]`
Note: `subsample1dataframe` = data frame, lower half of dichotomized variable
`subsample2dataframe` = data frame, upper half of dichotomized variable
`expression` = mathematical basis of how variable will be dichotomized

Example: `lowsatverb <- df11 [which(df11$satverb <= 550)  ,]`
`highsatverb <- df11 [which(df11$satverb > 550)  ,]`

Conduct linear regression analysis for each half of the moderator variable

Command: `subsample1reg <- lm(dv ~ iv, data = subsample1dataframe)`
`summary(subsample1reg)`
`subsample2reg <- lm(dv ~ iv, data = subsample2dataframe)`
`summary(subsample2reg)`
Note: `subsample1reg` = linear regression, lower half of dichotomized variable
`subsample2reg` = linear regression, upper half of dichotomized variable

Example: ```
lowsatverbreg <- lm(cgpa ~ satmath,
data = lowsatverb)
summary(lowsatverbreg)
highsatverbreg <- lm(cgpa ~ satmath, data =
highsatverb)
summary(highsatverbreg)
```

Create variable representing dichotomy of moderator variable (to create figure)

Command:    **dataframe$groupingvar <- cut
(newdataframe$var, breaks=c(min, cutpoint,
max), labels=c("Label for Group1"," Label
for Group2"))**
Note: *dataframe$groupingvar* = variable representing
dichotomized moderator
*cutpoint* = cutoff for lower half of dichotomized
moderator variable

Example:    ```
df11$satverbg <- cut(df11$satverb,
breaks=c(200, 550, 800), labels=c("Low SAT
Verbal","High SAT Verbal"))
```

Create figure of two regression lines

Command: **ggplot(*newdataframe*, aes(x = *iv1*, y = *dv*,
linetype = *groupingvar*)) + geom_
smooth(method=lm, se=FALSE, color="black",
fullrange=TRUE) + xlim(*minX*, *maxX*) + ylim(*minY*,
maxY) + labs(x = "*iv1*",y = "*dv*") + theme_bw() +
theme(panel.grid.major = element_blank(), panel.
grid.minor = element_blank()) + theme(legend.
title = element_blank()) + theme(legend.key =
element_rect(color = "white"))**
Note: *iv1* = non-dichotomized predictor
groupingvar = dichotomized predictor
minX, *maxX* = minimum and maximum, non-
dichotomized predictor
labs(x="*iv1*",y="*dv*") = labels for predictor and
dependent variables

Example: ```
ggplot(df11, aes(x = satmath, y =
cgpa, linetype = satverbg)) + geom_
smooth(method=lm, se=FALSE, color="black",
fullrange=TRUE) + xlim(200,800) +
ylim(0,4) + labs(x = "SAT Math",y = "College
GPA") + theme_bw() + theme(panel.grid.
major = element_blank(), panel.grid.minor
= element_blank()) + theme(legend.title
= element_blank()) + theme(legend.key =
element_rect(color = "white"))
```
```

Example script:

```
setwd("e:/R output")
df1 <- read.csv("COLLEGE_NA.csv")
library(lm.beta)
library(lmSupport)
library(ggplot2)
df11 <- subset(df1,,select = c(cgpa, satmath, satverb))
df11 <- na.omit(df11)
transform(table(df11$satverb), cumFreq = cumsum(Freq),
pct = prop.table(Freq)*100)
lowsatverb <- df11 [which(df11$satverb <= 550) ,]
highsatverb <- df11 [which(df11$satverb > 550) ,]
lowsatverbreg <- lm(cgpa ~ satmath, data = lowsatverb)
summary(lowsatverbreg)
highsatverbreg <- lm(cgpa ~ satmath, data = highsatverb)
summary(highsatverbreg)
df11$satverbg <- cut(df11$satverb, breaks=c(200, 550,
800), labels=c("Low SAT Verbal"," High SAT Verbal"))
ggplot(df11, aes(x = satmath, y = cgpa,
linetype = satverbg)) + geom_smooth
(method=lm,se=FALSE,color="black", fullrange=TRUE)
+ xlim(200, 800) + ylim(0, 4) + labs(x = "SAT Math", y =
"College GPA") + theme_bw() + theme(panel.grid.major
= element_blank(), panel.grid.minor = element_blank()) +
theme(legend.title = element_blank()) + theme(legend.
key = element_rect(color = "white"))
```

```
> setwd("e:/R output")
> df1 = read.csv("COLLEGE_NA.csv")
>
> # Create data frame containing only the variables to be analyzed
> df11 <- subset(df1, , select = c(cgpa,satmath,satverb))
>
> # Remove anyone with missing data (NAs) on any variable in the new data frame
> df11 <- na.omit(df11)
>
> # Create frequency distribution table for one of the predictor variables
> transform(table(df11$satverb), cumFreq = cumsum(Freq), pct = prop.table(Freq)*100)
```

```
     Var1 Freq cumFreq       pct
1     330    1       1   1.052632
2     350    1       2   1.052632
3     370    1       3   1.052632
4     400    1       4   1.052632
5     420    1       5   1.052632
6     450    3       8   3.157895
7     470    3      11   3.157895
8     480    4      15   4.210526
9     490    1      16   1.052632
10    500   13      29  13.684211
11    510    3      32   3.157895
12    520    2      34   2.105263
13    530    6      40   6.315789
14    540    4      44   4.210526
15    550    9      53   9.473684
16    560    6      59   6.315789
17    570    5      64   5.263158
18    580    5      69   5.263158
19    590    1      70   1.052632
20    600   10      80  10.526316
21    610    5      85   5.263158
22    620    2      87   2.105263
23    630    1      88   1.052632
24    635    1      89   1.052632
25    650    2      91   2.105263
26    680    2      93   2.105263
27    700    1      94   1.052632
28    740    1      95   1.052632
```

```
> # Create two data frames based on dichotomy of one of the predictor variables into two subsamples
> lowsatverb <- df11[which(df11$satverb <= 550) ,]
> highsatverb <- df11[which(df11$satverb > 550) ,]
>
> # Conduct linear regression analysis for each subsample and get results of analysis
> lowsatverbreg <- lm(cgpa ~ satmath, data = lowsatverb)
> summary(lowsatverbreg)

Call:
lm(formula = cgpa ~ satmath, data = lowsatverb)

Residuals:
     Min       1Q   Median       3Q      Max
-0.84092 -0.25966 -0.01158  0.25908  0.92495

Coefficients:
              Estimate Std. Error t value Pr(>|t|)
(Intercept) 2.5678725  0.3517243   7.301 1.82e-09 ***
satmath     0.0006826  0.0006181   1.104    0.275
---
Signif. codes:  0 '***' 0.001 '**' 0.01 '*' 0.05 '.' 0.1 ' ' 1

Residual standard error: 0.377 on 51 degrees of freedom
Multiple R-squared:  0.02336,   Adjusted R-squared:  0.004206
F-statistic:  1.22 on 1 and 51 DF,  p-value: 0.2746
```

```
> highsatverbreg <- lm(cgpa ~ satmath, data = highsatverb)
> summary(highsatverbreg)

Call:
lm(formula = cgpa ~ satmath, data = highsatverb)

Residuals:
     Min       1Q   Median       3Q      Max
-0.88249 -0.17045 -0.03045  0.20733  0.80455

Coefficients:
              Estimate Std. Error t value Pr(>|t|)
(Intercept) 1.6372689  0.3996333   4.097 0.000198 ***
satmath     0.0023519  0.0006344   3.707 0.000634 ***
---
Signif. codes:  0 '***' 0.001 '**' 0.01 '*' 0.05 '.' 0.1 ' ' 1

Residual standard error: 0.3716 on 40 degrees of freedom
Multiple R-squared:  0.2558,    Adjusted R-squared:  0.2371
F-statistic: 13.75 on 1 and 40 DF,  p-value: 0.0006345
```

```
> # Create a variable representing dichotomy of one of the predictor variables in order to create figure
> df11$satverbg <- cut(df11$satverb, breaks=c(200, 550, 800), labels=c("Low SAT Verbal"," High SAT Verba
l"))
>
> # Install and load the ggplot2 library to create figure
> library("ggplot2")
>
> # Create figure of two regression lines
> ggplot(df11, aes(x = satmath, y = cgpa, linetype = satverbg)) + geom_smooth(method=lm,se=FALSE,color="
black", fullrange=TRUE) + xlim(200,800)+ ylim(0,4) + labs(x = "SAT Math", y = "College GPA")  + theme_bw
() + theme(panel.grid.major = element_blank(), panel.grid.minor = element_blank()) + theme(legend.title
= element_blank())+ theme(legend.key = element_rect(color = "white"))
```

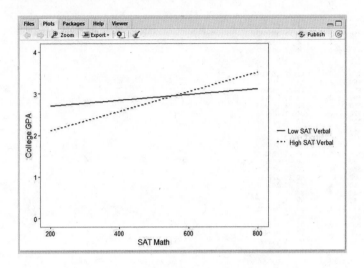

MULTIPLE REGRESSION (STEPWISE)

EXAMPLE: Conduct stepwise regression analysis (IVs: *satmath, satverb, sshada, sshawm, sshata, sshaea*; DV: *cgpa*)

SPSS: The REGRESSION command

```
REGRESSION
  /MISSING LISTWISE
  /STATISTICS COEFF OUTS R ANOVA
  /CRITERIA=PIN(.05) POUT(.10)
  /NOORIGIN
  /DEPENDENT cgpa
  /METHOD=STEPWISE satmath satverb sshada sshawm sshata sshaea.
```

Regression

Variables Entered/Removed[a]

Model	Variables Entered	Variables Removed	Method
1	sshawm		Stepwise (Criteria: Probability-of-F-to-enter <= .050, Probability-of-F-to-remove >= .100).
2	satmath		Stepwise (Criteria: Probability-of-F-to-enter <= .050, Probability-of-F-to-remove >= .100).
3	sshaea		Stepwise (Criteria: Probability-of-F-to-enter <= .050, Probability-of-F-to-remove >= .100).

a. Dependent Variable: cgpa

Model Summary

Model	R	R Square	Adjusted R Square	Std. Error of the Estimate
1	.411[a]	.169	.160	.37082
2	.524[b]	.275	.259	.34828
3	.554[c]	.306	.284	.34242

a. Predictors: (Constant), sshawm

b. Predictors: (Constant), sshawm, satmath

c. Predictors: (Constant), sshawm, satmath, sshaea

ANOVA[a]

Model		Sum of Squares	df	Mean Square	F	Sig.
1	Regression	2.596	1	2.596	18.879	.000[b]
	Residual	12.788	93	.138		
	Total	15.384	94			
2	Regression	4.225	2	2.113	17.416	.000[c]
	Residual	11.159	92	.121		
	Total	15.384	94			
3	Regression	4.715	3	1.572	13.403	.000[d]
	Residual	10.670	91	.117		
	Total	15.384	94			

a. Dependent Variable: cgpa

b. Predictors: (Constant), sshawm

c. Predictors: (Constant), sshawm, satmath

d. Predictors: (Constant), sshawm, satmath, sshaea

Coefficients[a]

Model		Unstandardized Coefficients		Standardized Coefficients	t	Sig.
		B	Std. Error	Beta		
1	(Constant)	2.654	.092		28.804	.000
	sshawm	.017	.004	.411	4.345	.000
2	(Constant)	1.838	.239		7.688	.000
	sshawm	.015	.004	.379	4.251	.000
	satmath	.001	.000	.327	3.665	.000
3	(Constant)	1.736	.240		7.225	.000
	sshawm	.010	.004	.246	2.249	.027
	satmath	.002	.000	.347	3.934	.000
	sshaea	.010	.005	.222	2.043	.044

a. Dependent Variable: cgpa

R: The `lm` and `step` functions in the base package

Create new data frame that contains only the variables to be analyzed

Command:
```
newdataframe <- subset(dataframe,,select =
c(variable, variable, variable...))
```

Example:
```
df11<- subset(df1,,select = c
(cgpa,satmath,satverb, sshada,
sshawm,sshata,sshaea))
```

Create output of stepwise multiple regression analysis

Commands:
```
result1 <- lm(dv ~ iv1 + iv2 + iv3..., data
= newdataframe)
result2 <- step(result1, test="F", direction
= "both")
```
Note: `result1` = full model (all predictor variables)

`result2` = model based on result of stepwise regression analysis

`direction = "both"` = request stepwise method

Example:
```
allvars <- lm(cgpa ~ satmath + satverb + sshada
+ sshawm + sshata + sshaea, data = df11)
stepmrc<-step(allvars,test="F",direction=
"both")
```

Modify output of multiple regression analysis to include standardized coefficients (betas)

Commands:
```
result2b <- lm.beta(result2)
```

Example:
```
stepmrcbetas <- lm.beta(stepmrc)
```

Display output of multiple regression analysis with standardized coefficients (betas)

Commands:
```
summary(result2b)
```

Example:
```
summary(stepmrcbetas)
```

Example script:
```
setwd("e:/R output")
df1 <- read.csv("COLLEGE_NA.csv")
library(lm.beta)
df11 <- subset(df1, ,select =
c(cgpa,satmath,satverb,sshada,
sshawm,sshata,sshaea))
allvars <- lm(cgpa ~ satmath + satverb + sshada + sshawm +
sshata + sshaea, data =df11)
stepmrc<-step(allvars,test="F",direction="both")
stepmrcbetas <- lm.beta(stepmrc)
summary(stepmrcbetas)
```

```
> setwd("e:/R output")
> df1 <- read.csv("COLLEGE_NA.csv")
> library("lm.beta")
> df11 <- subset(df1, , select = c(cgpa,satmath,satverb,sshada,sshawm,sshata,sshaea))
> allvars <- lm(cgpa ~ satmath + satverb + sshada + sshawm + sshata + sshaea, data = df11)
> stepmrc<-step(allvars,test="F",direction="both")
Start:  AIC=-196.11
cgpa ~ satmath + satverb + sshada + sshawm + sshata + sshaea

          Df Sum of Sq     RSS     AIC F value    Pr(>F)
- sshada   1   0.01552  10.420 -197.97  0.1313 0.7179728
- sshata   1   0.10801  10.512 -197.13  0.9135 0.3418047
- satverb  1   0.19472  10.599 -196.34  1.6469 0.2027510
<none>                  10.404 -196.11
- sshawm   1   0.57226  10.977 -193.02  4.8402 0.0304243 *
- sshaea   1   0.60808  11.012 -192.71  5.1431 0.0257873 *
- satmath  1   1.69133  12.096 -183.80 14.3052 0.0002828 ***
---
Signif. codes:  0 '***' 0.001 '**' 0.01 '*' 0.05 '.' 0.1 ' ' 1

Step:  AIC=-197.96
cgpa ~ satmath + satverb + sshawm + sshata + sshaea

          Df Sum of Sq     RSS     AIC F value    Pr(>F)
- sshata   1   0.10270  10.523 -199.03  0.8772 0.3515031
- satverb  1   0.18984  10.610 -198.25  1.6215 0.2062009
<none>                  10.420 -197.97
+ sshada   1   0.01552  10.404 -196.11  0.1313 0.7179728
- sshawm   1   0.55952  10.979 -195.00  4.7790 0.0314328 *
- sshaea   1   0.62444  11.044 -194.44  5.3336 0.0232329 *
- satmath  1   1.71000  12.130 -185.53 14.6057 0.0002451 ***
---
Signif. codes:  0 '***' 0.001 '**' 0.01 '*' 0.05 '.' 0.1 ' ' 1
Step:  AIC=-199.03
cgpa ~ satmath + satverb + sshawm + sshaea

          Df Sum of Sq     RSS     AIC F value  Pr(>F)
- satverb  1   0.14723  10.670 -199.71  1.2593 0.264777
<none>                  10.523 -199.03
+ sshata   1   0.10270  10.420 -197.97  0.8772 0.351503
+ sshada   1   0.01022  10.512 -197.13  0.0865 0.769351
- sshawm   1   0.48034  11.003 -196.79  4.1084 0.045630 *
- sshaea   1   0.52383  11.046 -196.42  4.4803 0.037048 *
- satmath  1   1.60954  12.132 -187.51 13.7664 0.000358 ***
---
Signif. codes:  0 '***' 0.001 '**' 0.01 '*' 0.05 '.' 0.1 ' ' 1

Step:  AIC=-199.71
cgpa ~ satmath + sshawm + sshaea

          Df Sum of Sq     RSS     AIC F value    Pr(>F)
<none>                  10.670 -199.71
+ satverb  1   0.14723  10.523 -199.03  1.2593 0.2647771
+ sshata   1   0.06009  10.610 -198.25  0.5097 0.4770998
+ sshada   1   0.00760  10.662 -197.78  0.0641 0.8006726
- sshaea   1   0.48945  11.159 -197.45  4.1744 0.0439309 *
- sshawm   1   0.59297  11.263 -196.57  5.0573 0.0269357 *
- satmath  1   1.81426  12.484 -186.79 15.4733 0.0001632 ***
---
Signif. codes:  0 '***' 0.001 '**' 0.01 '*' 0.05 '.' 0.1 ' ' 1


> stepmrcbetas <- lm.beta(stepmrc)
> summary(stepmrcbetas)

Call:
lm(formula = cgpa ~ satmath + sshawm + sshaea, data = df11)

Residuals:
     Min      1Q   Median      3Q     Max
-0.91498 -0.20417 -0.06254  0.23335 0.93235

Coefficients:
              Estimate Standardized Std. Error t value Pr(>|t|)
(Intercept) 1.7358477    0.0000000   0.2402595   7.225 1.49e-10 ***
satmath     0.0015213    0.3472195   0.0003867   3.934 0.000163 ***
sshawm      0.0098937    0.2458778   0.0043995   2.249 0.026936 *
sshaea      0.0095174    0.2224688   0.0046582   2.043 0.043931 *
---
Signif. codes:  0 '***' 0.001 '**' 0.01 '*' 0.05 '.' 0.1 ' ' 1

Residual standard error: 0.3424 on 91 degrees of freedom
  (21 observations deleted due to missingness)
Multiple R-squared:  0.3065,    Adjusted R-squared:  0.2836
F-statistic: 13.4 on 3 and 91 DF,  p-value: 2.555e-07
```

MULTIPLE REGRESSION (BACKWARD)

EXAMPLE: Conduct backward regression analysis (IVs: *satmath, satverb, sshada, sshawm, sshata*; DV: *cgpa*)

SPSS: The REGRESSION command

```
REGRESSION
    /MISSING LISTWISE
    /STATISTICS COEFF OUTS R ANOVA
    /CRITERIA=PIN(.05) POUT(.10)
    /NOORIGIN
    /DEPENDENT cgpa
    /METHOD=BACKWARD satmath satverb sshada sshawm sshata.
```

Regression

Variables Entered/Removed

Model	Variables Entered	Variables Removed	Method
1	sshata, satmath, satverb, sshada, sshawm[b]	.	Enter
2		sshata	Backward (criterion: Probability of F-to-remove >= .100).
3		sshada	Backward (criterion: Probability of F-to-remove >= .100).
4		satverb	Backward (criterion: Probability of F-to-remove >= .100).

b. All requested variables entered.

Model Summary

Model	R	R Square	Adjusted R Square	Std. Error of the Estimate
1	.533[a]	.284	.244	.35176
2	.533[b]	.284	.252	.34985
3	.531[c]	.282	.258	.34841
4	.524[d]	.275	.259	.34828

a. Predictors: (Constant), sshata, satmath, satverb, sshada, sshawm

b. Predictors: (Constant), satmath, satverb, sshada, sshawm

c. Predictors: (Constant), satmath, satverb, sshawm

d. Predictors: (Constant), satmath, sshawm

ANOVA

Model		Sum of Squares	df	Mean Square	F	Sig.
1	Regression	4.372	5	.874	7.067	.000[b]
	Residual	11.012	89	.124		
	Total	15.384	94			
2	Regression	4.369	4	1.092	8.923	.000[c]
	Residual	11.016	90	.122		
	Total	15.384	94			
3	Regression	4.338	3	1.446	11.912	.000[d]
	Residual	11.046	91	.121		
	Total	15.384	94			
4	Regression	4.225	2	2.113	17.416	.000[e]
	Residual	11.159	92	.121		
	Total	15.384	94			

b. Predictors: (Constant), sshata, satmath, satverb, sshada, sshawm

c. Predictors: (Constant), satmath, satverb, sshada, sshawm

d. Predictors: (Constant), satmath, satverb, sshawm

e. Predictors: (Constant), satmath, sshawm

Coefficients

Model		Unstandardized Coefficients B	Std. Error	Standardized Coefficients Beta	t	Sig.
1	(Constant)	1.579	.346		4.569	.000
	satmath	.001	.000	.319	3.427	.001
	satverb	.001	.001	.090	.964	.337
	sshada	.002	.004	.052	.508	.613
	sshawm	.014	.005	.348	3.064	.003
	sshata	-.001	.004	-.017	-.164	.870
2	(Constant)	1.586	.341		4.653	.000
	satmath	.001	.000	.317	3.469	.001
	satverb	.001	.001	.088	.956	.342
	sshada	.002	.004	.051	.500	.618
	sshawm	.014	.004	.340	3.294	.001
3	(Constant)	1.610	.336		4.788	.000
	satmath	.001	.000	.312	3.451	.001
	satverb	.001	.001	.088	.964	.337
	sshawm	.015	.004	.365	4.034	.000
4	(Constant)	1.838	.239		7.688	.000
	satmath	.001	.000	.327	3.665	.000
	sshawm	.015	.004	.379	4.251	.000

R: The `lm` and `step` functions in the base package

Create new data frame that contains only the variables to be analyzed

Command: ***newdataframe* <- subset(*dataframe*, ,select = c(*variable, variable, variable...*))**

Example: `df11<- subset(df1,,select = c(cgpa,satmath, satverb, sshada,sshawm,sshata))`

Create output of backward multiple regression analysis

Commands: ***result1* <- lm(*dv ~ iv1 + iv2 + iv3...*, data = *newdataframe*)**
***result2* <- step(*result1*, test="F", direction = "backward")**
Note: ***result1*** = full model (all predictor variables)
result2 = model based on result of backward regression analysis
direction = "backward" = request backward method

Example: `allvars <- lm(cgpa ~ satmath + satverb + sshada + sshawm + sshata, data =df11)`
`backmrc<-step(allvars,test="F",direction="backward")`

Modify output of multiple regression analysis to include standardized coefficients (betas)

Commands: ***result2b* <- lm.beta(*result2*)**

Example: `backmrcbetas <- lm.beta(backmrc)`

Display output of multiple regression analysis with standardized coefficients (betas)

Commands: **summary(*result2b*)**

Example: `summary(backmrcbetas)`

Example script:
```
setwd("e:/R output")
df1 <- read.csv("COLLEGE_NA.csv")
library(lm.beta)
df11<- subset(df1,,select =
c(cgpa,satmath,satverb,sshada,sshawm, sshata))
allvars <- lm(cgpa ~ satmath + satverb + sshada + sshawm +
sshata, data =df11)
backmrc<-step(allvars,test="F",direction="backward")
backmrcbetas <- lm.beta(backmrc)
summary(backmrcbetas)
```

```
> setwd("e:/R output")
> df1 <- read.csv("COLLEGE_NA.csv")
> library("lm.beta")
> df11 <- subset(df1, , select = c(cgpa,satmath,satverb,sshada,sshawm,sshata))
> allvars <- lm(cgpa ~ satmath + satverb + sshada + sshawm + sshata, data = df11)
> backmrc<-step(allvars,test="F",direction="backward")
Start:  AIC=-192.71
cgpa ~ satmath + satverb + sshada + sshawm + sshata

          Df Sum of Sq    RSS     AIC F value    Pr(>F)
- sshata   1   0.00332 11.016 -194.68  0.0268 0.8702214
- sshada   1   0.03189 11.044 -194.44  0.2577 0.6129427
- satverb  1   0.11510 11.128 -193.72  0.9302 0.3374246
<none>                  11.012 -192.71
- sshawm   1   1.16167 12.174 -185.18  9.3883 0.0028897 **
- satmath  1   1.45350 12.466 -182.93 11.7468 0.0009247 ***
---
Signif. codes:  0 '***' 0.001 '**' 0.01 '*' 0.05 '.' 0.1 ' ' 1

Step:  AIC=-194.68
cgpa ~ satmath + satverb + sshada + sshawm

          Df Sum of Sq    RSS     AIC F value    Pr(>F)
- sshada   1   0.03065 11.046 -196.42  0.2504 0.6179973
- satverb  1   0.11183 11.128 -195.72  0.9137 0.3417037
<none>                  11.016 -194.68
- sshawm   1   1.32843 12.344 -185.87 10.8534 0.0014113 **
- satmath  1   1.47253 12.488 -184.76 12.0307 0.0008049 ***
---
Signif. codes:  0 '***' 0.001 '**' 0.01 '*' 0.05 '.' 0.1 ' ' 1

Step:  AIC=-196.42
cgpa ~ satmath + satverb + sshawm

          Df Sum of Sq    RSS     AIC F value    Pr(>F)
- satverb  1   0.11286 11.159 -197.45  0.9297 0.3374952
<none>                  11.046 -196.42
- satmath  1   1.44541 12.492 -186.74 11.9072 0.0008497 ***
- sshawm   1   1.97564 13.022 -182.79 16.2752 0.0001138 ***
---
Signif. codes:  0 '***' 0.001 '**' 0.01 '*' 0.05 '.' 0.1 ' ' 1

Step:  AIC=-197.45
cgpa ~ satmath + sshawm

          Df Sum of Sq    RSS     AIC F value    Pr(>F)
<none>                  11.159 -197.45
- satmath  1    1.6291 12.788 -186.51  13.431 0.0004137 ***
- sshawm   1    2.1921 13.351 -182.41  18.073 5.095e-05 ***
---
Signif. codes:  0 '***' 0.001 '**' 0.01 '*' 0.05 '.' 0.1 ' ' 1


> backmrcbetas <- lm.beta(backmrc)
> summary(backmrcbetas)

Call:
lm(formula = cgpa ~ satmath + sshawm, data = df11)

Residuals:
    Min      1Q  Median      3Q     Max
-0.85837 -0.20074 -0.05195  0.24173  0.93614

Coefficients:
            Estimate Standardized Std. Error t value Pr(>|t|)
(Intercept) 1.8377538    0.0000000  0.2390456   7.688 1.6e-11 ***
satmath     0.0014324    0.3269346  0.0003909   3.665 0.000414 ***
sshawm      0.0152604    0.3792491  0.0035897   4.251 5.1e-05 ***
---
Signif. codes:  0 '***' 0.001 '**' 0.01 '*' 0.05 '.' 0.1 ' ' 1

Residual standard error: 0.3483 on 92 degrees of freedom
  (21 observations deleted due to missingness)
Multiple R-squared: 0.2746,    Adjusted R-squared: 0.2589
F-statistic: 17.42 on 2 and 92 DF,  p-value: 3.851e-07
```

MULTIPLE REGRESSION (FORWARD)

EXAMPLE: Conduct forward regression analysis (IVs: *satmath, satverb, sshada, sshata, sshaea*; DV: *cgpa*)

SPSS: The REGRESSION command

```
REGRESSION
  /MISSING LISTWISE
  /STATISTICS COEFF OUTS R ANOVA
  /CRITERIA=PIN(.05) POUT(.10)
  /NOORIGIN
  /DEPENDENT cgpa
  /METHOD=FORWARD satmath satverb sshada sshata sshaea.
```

Regression

Variables Entered/Removed

Model	Variables Entered	Variables Removed	Method
1	satmath	.	Forward (Criterion: Probability-of-F-to-enter <= .050)
2	sshaea	.	Forward (Criterion: Probability-of-F-to-enter <= .050)

Model Summary

Model	R	R Square	Adjusted R Square	Std. Error of the Estimate
1	.364[a]	.132	.123	.37890
2	.518[b]	.268	.252	.34989

a. Predictors: (Constant), satmath

b. Predictors: (Constant), satmath, sshaea

ANOVA

Model		Sum of Squares	df	Mean Square	F	Sig.
1	Regression	2.033	1	2.033	14.161	.000[b]
	Residual	13.351	93	.144		
	Total	15.384	94			
2	Regression	4.122	2	2.061	16.834	.000[c]
	Residual	11.263	92	.122		
	Total	15.384	94			

b. Predictors: (Constant), satmath

c. Predictors: (Constant), satmath, sshaea

Coefficients

Model		Unstandardized Coefficients		Standardized Coefficients	t	Sig.
		B	Std. Error	Beta		
1	(Constant)	2.080	.253		8.235	.000
	satmath	.002	.000	.364	3.763	.000
2	(Constant)	1.770	.245		7.224	.000
	satmath	.002	.000	.376	4.211	.000
	sshaea	.016	.004	.369	4.130	.000

R: The `lm` and `step` functions in the base package

Create new data frame that contains only the variables to be analyzed

Command: `newdataframe <- subset(dataframe, ,select = c(variable, variable, variable...))`

Example: `df11 <- subset(df1, ,select = c(cgpa, satmath,satverb, sshada,sshata,sshaea))`

Remove anyone with NAs on any variable in the new data frame

Command: `newdataframe <- na.omit(newdataframe)`

Example: `df11 <- na.omit(df11)`

Create output of forward multiple regression analysis

Commands: `nullmodel <- lm(dv ~ 1, data = newdataframe)`
`fullmodel <- lm(dv ~ iv1 + iv2..., data = newdataframe)`
`result1 <- step(nullmodel, scope = list (lower=nullmodel, upper=fullmodel), test="F", direction = "forward")`
Note: `nullmodel` = model with no predictors (starting point)
`fullmodel` = model with all predictors (possible ending point)
`result1` = model based on result of forward regression analysis
`direction = "forward"` = request forward method

(Continued)

(Continued)

Example:
```
nullmodel <- lm(cgpa ~ 1, data =df11)
fullmodel <- lm(cgpa ~ satmath + satverb +
sshada + sshata + sshaea, data =df11)
forwmrc <- step(nullmodel, scope =
list(lower =nullmodel,upper =fullmodel),
test="F", direction = "forward")
```

Modify output of multiple regression analysis to include standardized coefficients (betas)

Commands: ***result1b <- lm.beta(result1)***

Example: ```forwmrcbetas <- lm.beta(forwmrc)```

Display output of multiple regression analysis with standardized coefficients (betas)

Commands: **summary(*result1b*)**

Example: ```summary(forwmrcbetas)```

Example script:
```
setwd("e:/R output")
df1 <- read.csv("COLLEGE_NA.csv")
library(lm.beta)
df11 <- subset(df1, ,select =
c(cgpa,satmath,satverb,sshada,sshata, sshaea))
df11 <- na.omit(df11)
nullmodel <- lm(cgpa ~ 1, data =df11)
fullmodel <- lm(cgpa ~ satmath + satverb + sshada + sshata +
sshaea,data=df11)
forwmrc <- step(nullmodel, scope = list(lower =
nullmodel,upper =fullmodel), test="F",
direction = "forward")
forwmrcbetas <- lm.beta(forwmrc)
summary(forwmrcbetas)
```

```
> setwd("e:/R output")
> df1 <- read.csv("COLLEGE_NA.csv")
> library("lm.beta")
> df11 <- subset(df1, , select = c(cgpa,satmath,satverb,sshada,sshata,sshaea))
> df11 <- na.omit(df11)
> nullmodel <- lm(cgpa ~ 1, data = df11)
> fullmodel <- lm(cgpa ~ satmath + satverb + sshada + sshata + sshaea, data = df11)
> forwmrc <- step(nullmodel, scope = list(lower = nullmodel,upper = fullmodel), test="F",
direction = "forward")
Start: AIC=-170.95
cgpa ~ 1

          Df Sum of Sq    RSS     AIC F value    Pr(>F)
+ satmath  1   2.03296 13.351 -182.41 14.1607 0.0002936 ***
+ sshaea   1   1.95119 13.433 -181.83 13.5083 0.0003970 ***
+ sshata   1   1.03014 14.354 -175.53  6.6742 0.0113400 *
+ satverb  1   0.67619 14.708 -173.22  4.2756 0.0414417 *
+ sshada   1   0.66532 14.719 -173.15  4.2037 0.0431498 *
<none>                 15.384 -170.95
---
Signif. codes:  0 '***' 0.001 '**' 0.01 '*' 0.05 '.' 0.1 ' ' 1

Step: AIC=-182.41
cgpa ~ satmath

          Df Sum of Sq    RSS     AIC F value    Pr(>F)
+ sshaea   1   2.08863 11.263 -196.57 17.0609 7.962e-05 ***
+ sshada · 1   0.75666 12.595 -185.96  5.5271 0.02086 *
+ sshata   1   0.53393 12.818 -184.29  3.8324 0.05330 .
+ satverb  1   0.32937 13.022 -182.79  2.3270 0.13058
<none>                 13.351 -182.41
---
Signif. codes:  0 '***' 0.001 '**' 0.01 '*' 0.05 '.' 0.1 ' ' 1

Step: AIC=-196.58
cgpa ~ satmath + sshaea

          Df Sum of Sq    RSS     AIC F value Pr(>F)
+ satverb 1  0.259860 11.003 -196.79  2.1492 0.1461
<none>                11.263 -196.57
+ sshada  1  0.008665 11.254 -194.65  0.0701 0.7918
+ sshata  1  0.001504 11.261 -194.59  0.0122 0.9125

Step: AIC=-196.79
cgpa ~ satmath + sshaea + satverb

          Df Sum of Sq    RSS     AIC F value Pr(>F)
<none>                11.003 -196.79
+ sshata 1 0.0235267 10.979 -195.00  0.1929 0.6616
+ sshada 1 0.0030742 11.000 -194.82  0.0252 0.8743


> forwmrcbetas <- lm.beta(forwmrc)
> summary(forwmrcbetas)

Call:
lm(formula = cgpa ~ satmath + sshaea + satverb, data = df11)

Residuals:
    Min      1Q   Median      3Q     Max
-0.97783 -0.19959 -0.03901  0.23116 0.97827

Coefficients:
            Estimate Standardized Std. Error t value Pr(>|t|)
(Intercept) 1.4196241    0.0000000  0.3411554   4.161 7.17e-05 ***
satmath     0.0015409    0.3516954  0.0003953   3.898 0.000185 ***
sshaea      0.0155227    0.3628419  0.0037986   4.086 9.42e-05 ***
satverb     0.0007654    0.1322775  0.0005221   1.466 0.146094
---
Signif. codes:  0 '***' 0.001 '**' 0.01 '*' 0.05 '.' 0.1 ' ' 1

Residual standard error: 0.3477 on 91 degrees of freedom
Multiple R-squared: 0.2848,    Adjusted R-squared: 0.2612
F-statistic: 12.08 on 3 and 91 DF,  p-value: 1e-06
```

CANONICAL CORRELATION ANALYSIS

EXAMPLE: Set 1: *Instruct, Faculty, Relfac, TGuide, TPSK*

Set 2: *Fplan1, Fplan2, Fplan3, Fplan4, Fplan5, Fplan6*

SPSS: The MANOVA command

```
MANOVA   INSTRUCT  FACULTY  RELFAC  TGUIDE  TPSK  with
                FPLAN1  FPLAN2  FPLAN3  FPLAN4  FPLAN5  FPLAN6
   /PRINT  signif(eigen  dimenr)
   /NOPRINT  signif(univ)
   /DISCRIM  standardized  correlations  alpha (1.0)
   /DESIGN  .
```

Manova

* * * * * * * * * * * * * * * * * * A n a l y s i s   o f   V a r i a n c e -- Design 1 * * * * * * * * *

EFFECT .. WITHIN CELLS Regression
Multivariate Tests of Significance (S = 5, M = 0, N = 49)

Test Name	Value	Approx. F	Hypoth. DF	Error DF	Sig. of F
Pillais	.89058	3.75640	30.00	520.00	.000
Hotellings	1.59607	5.23512	30.00	492.00	.000
Wilks	.31249	4.52235	30.00	402.00	.000
Roys	.53246				

- -

Eigenvalues and Canonical Correlations

Root No.	Eigenvalue	Pct.	Cum. Pct.	Canon Cor.	Sq. Cor
1	1.13883	71.35237	71.35237	.72970	.53246
2	.35492	22.23689	93.58925	.51181	.26195
3	.07819	4.89893	98.48819	.26930	.07252
4	.02197	1.37625	99.86443	.14661	.02149
5	.00216	.13557	100.00000	.04647	.00216

- -

Standardized canonical coefficients for DEPENDENT variables
        Function No.

Variable	1	2	3	4	5
instruct	-.77918	-.08374	.41321	.74059	-.58451
faculty	.29620	-.31638	.62851	-.55718	.83098
relfac	-.50869	-.33919	-.55480	-.81966	-.36173
tguide	.16580	.96958	.45622	-.17633	-.19059
tpsk	-.22770	.36361	-.48527	.36121	.84235

- -

Correlations between DEPENDENT and canonical variables
        Function No.

Variable	1	2	3	4	5
instruct	-.83499	-.06097	.51253	.19021	.01431
faculty	-.36395	-.20737	.65164	-.35911	.52053
relfac	-.71331	.07449	-.17480	-.67359	-.03682
tguide	-.22390	.84035	.30566	-.37818	-.08501
tpsk	-.57735	.38438	-.29310	.11142	.64853

- -
Variance in dependent variables explained by canonical variables

CAN. VAR.	Pct Var DEP	Cum Pct DEP	Pct Var COV	Cum Pct COV
1	34.43906	34.43906	18.33727	18.33727
2	18.12425	52.56331	4.74760	23.08487
3	17.94415	70.50746	1.30131	24.38618
4	15.48597	85.99343	.33285	24.71903
5	14.00657	100.00000	.03024	24.74928

- -
Standardized canonical coefficients for COVARIATES
          CAN. VAR.

COVARIATE	1	2	3	4	5
fplan1	-.04010	-.49568	-.42115	-.39075	-1.24411
fplan2	-.84187	.03993	.37998	.13845	.93274
fplan3	-.06498	.61656	-.88979	-.11292	-.03982
fplan4	.42248	-.38065	-.16798	-.64434	1.30405
fplan5	.00136	.24496	.55739	-.75847	-.88485
fplan6	-.45545	-.23689	-.10538	1.25165	-.15429

- -
Correlations between COVARIATES and canonical variables
          CAN. VAR.

Covariate	1	2	3	4	5
fplan1	-.44948	-.68308	-.40981	-.32114	-.23432
fplan2	-.93444	-.06025	.03231	-.28779	.18112
fplan3	-.47621	.47673	-.68536	-.21763	.02695
fplan4	-.31497	-.66076	-.29399	-.40401	.28459
fplan5	-.68157	-.00949	.24234	-.47496	-.18205
fplan6	-.65508	-.50948	-.19783	.21509	-.05457

- -
Variance in covariates explained by canonical variables

CAN. VAR.	Pct Var DEP	Cum Pct DEP	Pct Var COV	Cum Pct COV
1	20.36525	20.36525	38.24778	38.24778
2	6.08484	26.45009	23.22925	61.47703
3	.99473	27.44482	13.71662	75.19365
4	.23944	27.68426	11.13993	86.33358
5	.00740	27.69165	3.42573	89.75931

R: The cc function in the CCA and candisc packages

Create a new data frame containing selected variables

Command: `newdataframe <- subset(dataframe,,select =c(variable, variable, variable...))`

Example: `df11 <- subset(df1,,select = c(fplan1, fplan2,fplan3, fplan4,fplan5,fplan6, instruct, faculty,relfac,tguide, tpsk))`

Remove anyone with NAs on any variable in the data frame

Command: `newdataframe <- na.omit(newdataframe)`

Example: `df11 <- na.omit(df11)`

(Continued)

(Continued)

Identify and define the two sets of variables

Command: *set1* <- *newdataframe* [, *startcol*:*endcol*]
                    set2 <- *newdataframe* [, *startcol*:*endcol*]
                    Note: *set1* = label for first set of variables
                          startcol:*endcol* = location of variables in data
                          frame (column numbers)
                          set2 = label for second set of variables

Example: major <- df11[, 7:11] # aspects of major (cols 7-11 of
                  data frame)
                  outcome <- df11[, 1:6] # outcomes (cols 1-6 of data
                  frame)

Conduct the canonical correlation analysis

Command:

```
result1 <- cc(set1, set2)  # conduct CCA
ev <- (1 - result1$cor^2)  # conduct dimension reduction
analysis
n <- dim(set1)[1]
p <- length(set1)
q <- length(set2)
k <- min(p, q)
m <- n - 3/2 - (p + q)/2
w <- rev(cumprod(rev(ev)))
d1 <- d2 <- f <- vector("numeric", k)
for (i in 1:k) {
s <- sqrt((p^2 * q^2 - 4)/(p^2 + q^2 - 5))
si <- 1/s
d1[i] <- p * q
d2[i] <- m * s - p * q/2 + 1
r <- (1 - w[i]^si)/w[i]^si
f[i] <- r * d2[i]/d1[i]
p <- p - 1
q <- q - 1}
pv <- pf(f, d1, d2, lower.tail = FALSE)
(dmat <- cbind(WilksL = w, F = f, df1 = d1, df2 =
d2, p = pv))
result1$cor  # calculate canonical correlation for each dimension
(root)
result2 <- cancor(set1, set2)     # calculate redundancy
index
redundancy(result2)
s1 <- diag(sqrt(diag(cov(set1))))  # standardized
coefficients (set1)
s1 %*% result1$xcoef
```

```
result3<- comput(set1, set2, result1)  # structure
coefficients (set1)
result3[3:3]
s2 <- diag(sqrt(diag(cov(set2))))  # standardized
coefficients (set2)
s2 %*% result1$ycoef
result3[6:6]  # structure coefficients (set2)
```

Example:
```
         cc1 <- cc(major, outcome)
ev <- (1 - cc1$cor^2)
n <- dim(major)[1]
p <- length(major)
q <- length(outcome)
k <- min(p, q)
m <- n - 3/2 - (p + q)/2
w <- rev(cumprod(rev(ev)))
d1 <- d2 <- f <- vector("numeric", k)
for (i in 1:k) {
s <- sqrt((p^2 * q^2 - 4)/(p^2 + q^2 - 5))
si <- 1/s
d1[i] <- p * q
d2[i] <- m * s - p * q/2 + 1
r <- (1 - w[i]^si)/w[i]^si
f[i] <- r * d2[i]/d1[i]
p <- p - 1
q <- q - 1}
pv <- pf(f, d1, d2, lower.tail = FALSE)
(dmat <- cbind(WilksL = w, F = f, df1 = d1, df2 =
d2, p = pv))
cc1$cor
cc2<- cancor(major, outcome)
redundancy(cc2)
s1 <- diag(sqrt(diag(cov(major))))
s1 %*% cc1$xcoef
cc3<- comput(major, outcome, cc1)
cc3[3:3]
s2 <- diag(sqrt(diag(cov(outcome))))
s2 %*% cc1$ycoef
cc3[6:6]
```

Example script:
```
setwd("e:/R output")
df1 <- read.csv("PSYCH_NA.csv")
library(CCA)
library(candisc)
df11 <- subset(df1,,select = c(fplan1,fplan2,fplan3,
fplan4,fplan5,fplan6,instruct, faculty,relfac,tguide,
tpsk))
df11 <- na.omit(df11)
major <- df11[, 7:11]
outcome <- df11[, 1:6]
cc1 <- cc(major, outcome)
ev <- (1 - cc1$cor^2) # conduct dimension reduction analysis
  n <- dim(major)[1]
  p <- length(major)
  q <- length(outcome)
  k <- min(p, q)
  m <- n - 3/2 - (p + q)/2
  w <- rev(cumprod(rev(ev)))
  d1 <- d2 <- f <- vector("numeric", k)
  for (i in 1:k) {
  s <- sqrt((p^2 * q^2 - 4)/(p^2 + q^2 - 5))
  si <- 1/s
  d1[i] <- p * q
  d2[i] <- m * s - p * q/2 + 1
  r <- (1 - w[i]^si)/w[i]^si
  f[i] <- r * d2[i]/d1[i]
  p <- p - 1
  q <- q - 1}
  pv <- pf(f, d1, d2, lower.tail = FALSE)
  (dmat <- cbind(WilksL = w, F = f, df1 = d1,
  df2 = d2, p = pv))
cc1$cor # calculate canonical correlation for each dimension (root)
cc2 <- cancor(major, outcome) # calculate redundancy index
redundancy(cc2)
s1 <- diag(sqrt(diag(cov(major)))) # standardized
coefficients (set1)
s1 %*% cc1$xcoef
cc3 <- comput(major, outcome, cc1) # structure coefficients
(set1)
cc3[3:3]
s2 <- diag(sqrt(diag(cov(outcome)))) # standardized
coefficients (set2)
s2 %*% cc1$ycoef
cc3[6:6] # structure coefficients (set2)
```

```
> setwd("e:/R output")
> df1 <- read.csv("PSYCH_NA.csv")
> library(CCA)
> library(candisc)
> df11 <- subset(df1,,select = c(fplan1,fplan2,fplan3, fplan4,fplan5,fplan6,instruct,
  faculty,relfac,tguide, tpsk))
> df11 <- na.omit(df11)
> major <- df11[, 7:11]
> outcome <- df11[, 1:6]
> cc1 <- cc(major, outcome)
> ev <- (1 - cc1$cor^2)    # conduct dimension reduction analysis
> n <- dim(major)[1]
> p <- length(major)
> q <- length(outcome)
> k <- min(p, q)
> m <- n - 3/2 - (p + q)/2
> w <- rev(cumprod(rev(ev)))
> d1 <- d2 <- f <- vector("numeric", k)
> for (i in 1:k) {
+     s <- sqrt((p^2 * q^2 - 4)/(p^2 + q^2 - 5))
+     si <- 1/s
+     d1[i] <- p * q
+     d2[i] <- m * s - p * q/2 + 1
+     r <- (1 - w[i]^si)/w[i]^si
+     f[i] <- r * d2[i]/d1[i]
+     p <- p - 1
+     q <- q - 1}
> pv <- pf(f, d1, d2, lower.tail = FALSE)
> (dmat <- cbind(WilksL = w, F = f, df1 = d1, df2 = d2, p = pv))
           WilksL         F df1      df2            p
[1,]    0.3124925 4.5223481  30 402.0000 7.360892e-13
[2,]    0.6683698 2.1696008  20 335.9290 2.861621e-03
[3,]    0.9055854 0.8599024  12 270.1581 5.885500e-01
[4,]    0.9763936 0.4125620   6 206.0000 8.702087e-01
[5,]    0.9978409       NaN   2      NaN          NaN
> cc1$cor    # calculate canonical correlation for each dimension (root)
[1] 0.7296956 0.5118078 0.2692956 0.1466074 0.0464658

> cc2<- cancor(major, outcome) #  calculate redundancy index
> redundancy(cc2)

Redundancies for the X variables & total X canonical redundancy

    Xcan1     Xcan2     Xcan3     Xcan4     Xcan5 total X|Y
0.1833727 0.0474760 0.0130131 0.0033285 0.0003024 0.2474928

Redundancies for the Y variables & total Y canonical redundancy

    Ycan1     Ycan2     Ycan3     Ycan4     Ycan5 total Y|X
2.037e-01 6.085e-02 9.947e-03 2.394e-03 7.396e-05 2.769e-01
> s1 <- diag(sqrt(diag(cov(major))))   # standardized coefficients (set1)
> s1 %*% cc1$xcoef
            [,1]        [,2]        [,3]        [,4]        [,5]
[1,] -0.7791773 -0.08373569 -0.4132058  0.7405942 -0.5845129
[2,]  0.2961993 -0.31637707 -0.6285099 -0.5571755  0.8309817
[3,] -0.5086903 -0.33919329  0.5548010 -0.8196583 -0.3617347
[4,]  0.1657994  0.96957863 -0.4562205 -0.1763262 -0.1905867
[5,] -0.2276956  0.36360907  0.4852700  0.3612143  0.8423544
> cc3<- comput(major, outcome, cc1)  # structure coefficients (set1)
> cc3[3:3]
$corr.X.xscores
               [,1]        [,2]        [,3]        [,4]        [,5]
instruct -0.8349936 -0.06097199 -0.5125257  0.1902127  0.01430682
faculty  -0.3639501 -0.20737120 -0.6516383 -0.3591070  0.52052594
relfac   -0.7133149  0.07448932  0.1747954 -0.6735904 -0.03682072
tguide   -0.2238983  0.84035217 -0.3056639 -0.3781814 -0.08500729
tpsk     -0.5773478  0.38438466  0.2931019  0.1114208  0.64853271
```

```
> s2 <- diag(sqrt(diag(cov(outcome))))   # standardized coefficients (set2)
> s2 %*% cc1$ycoef
            [,1]         [,2]         [,3]         [,4]         [,5]
[1,]  -0.040095692 -0.49568348  0.4211545 -0.3907477 -1.24411494
[2,]  -0.841865831  0.03992503 -0.3799804  0.1384545  0.93274007
[3,]  -0.064984035  0.61655538  0.8897867 -0.1129202 -0.03981725
[4,]   0.422476184 -0.38065184  0.1679821 -0.6443365  1.30404546
[5,]   0.001364563  0.24495518 -0.5573858 -0.7584674 -0.88484832
[6,]  -0.455448860 -0.23688873  0.1053795  1.2516484 -0.15428990
> cc3[6:6]     # structure coefficients (set2)
$corr.Y.yscores
            [,1]         [,2]         [,3]         [,4]         [,5]
fplan1 -0.4494792 -0.683081109  0.40981260 -0.3211364 -0.2343175
fplan2 -0.9344416 -0.060245060 -0.03230985 -0.2877884  0.1811205
fplan3 -0.4762125  0.476728528  0.68535629 -0.2176302  0.0269512
fplan4 -0.3149700 -0.660757400  0.29398619 -0.4040112  0.2845871
fplan5 -0.6815735 -0.009486752 -0.24233762 -0.4749648 -0.1820462
fplan6 -0.6550779 -0.509475612  0.19783362  0.2150948 -0.0545671
```

DISCRIMINANT ANALYSIS (TWO GROUPS)

EXAMPLE: Conduct discriminant analysis with two groups
(IVs: *instruct, faculty, relfac, tguide*; DV: *doagain* (1=Yes, 2=No))

SPSS: The DISCRIMINANT command

```
DISCRIMINANT
  /GROUPS=doagain(1 2)
  /VARIABLES=instruct faculty relfac tguide
  /ANALYSIS ALL
  /PRIORS EQUAL
  /STATISTICS=MEAN STDDEV UNIVF TABLE
  /CLASSIFY=NONMISSING POOLED.
```

Discriminant

Group Statistics

doagain		Mean	Std. Deviation	Valid N (listwise) Unweighted	Weighted
1 Yes	instruct	4.85	.56	78	78.000
	faculty	4.91	.53	78	78.000
	relfac	3.83	.92	78	78.000
	tguide	2.89	1.13	78	78.000
2 No	instruct	4.39	.61	36	36.000
	faculty	4.73	.46	36	36.000
	relfac	3.27	.72	36	36.000
	tguide	3.17	1.31	36	36.000

Tests of Equality of Group Means

	Wilks' Lambda	F	df1	df2	Sig.
instruct	.88	15.88	1	112	.000
faculty	.97	3.36	1	112	.069
relfac	.91	10.61	1	112	.001
tguide	.99	1.40	1	112	.239

Analysis 1

Summary of Canonical Discriminant Functions

Eigenvalues

Function	Eigenvalue	% of Variance	Cumulative %	Canonical Correlation
1	.311[a]	100.0	100.0	.487

a. First 1 canonical discriminant functions were used in the analysis.

Wilks' Lambda

Test of Function(s)	Wilks' Lambda	Chi-square	df	Sig.
1	.76	29.81	4	.000

Standardized Canonical Discriminant Function Coefficients

	Function
	1
instruct	.77
faculty	-.22
relfac	.74
tguide	-.71

Structure Matrix

	Function
	1
instruct	.67
relfac	.55
faculty	.31
tguide	-.20

Pooled within-groups correlations between discriminating variables and standardized canonical discriminant functions
Variables ordered by absolute size of correlation within function.

Functions at Group Centroids

doagain	Function 1
1 Yes	.38
2 No	-.81

Unstandardized canonical

Classification Statistics

Prior Probabilities for Groups

doagain	Prior	Cases Used in Analysis	
		Unweighted	Weighted
1 Yes	.500	78	78.000
2 No	.500	36	36.000
Total	1.000	114	114.000

Classification Results[a]

			Predicted Group Membership		Total
		doagain	1 Yes	2 No	Total
Original	Count	1 Yes	54	24	78
		2 No	13	23	36
	%	1 Yes	69.2	30.8	100.0
		2 No	36.1	63.9	100.0

a. 67.5% of original grouped cases correctly classified.

R: The `lda` and `predict` functions in the MASS package

Create a new data frame containing selected variables

Command: `newdataframe <- subset(dataframe,,select =c(variable, variable, variable...))`

Example: `df11 <- subset(df1,,select = c(doagain,instruct,faculty, relfac,tguide))`

Remove anyone with NAs on any variable in the data frame

Command: `newdataframe <- na.omit(newdataframe)`

Example: `df11 <- na.omit(df11)`

Conduct the discriminant analysis

Command: *result* <- **lda**(*dv ~ iv1 + iv2 + ..., ***data = *dataframe*, **prior** = **c**(*#,#*)/*sum of #*s)
result

Example: discrim <- lda(doagain ~ instruct + faculty + relfac + tguide, data = df11, prior = c(1,1)/2)
discrim

Determine accuracy of prediction of group membership

Command: *resultpred* <- **predict**(*result*) # predict group membership
table(*newdataframe$dv*, *resultpred$***class**) # classification summary table *classtable* <- **table**(*newdataframe$dv*, *resultpred$***class**)
diag(prop.table(*classtable*, **1))** # % correct predictions for each group
sum(diag(prop.table(*classtable*)))# % correct predictions for total sample

Example: predict <- predict(discrim)
table(df11$doagain, predict$class)
classtable <- table(df11$doagain, predict$class)
diag(prop.table(classtable, 1))
sum(diag(prop.table(classtable)))

Example script:
```
setwd("e:/R output")
df1 <- read.csv("PSYCH_NA.csv")
library(MASS)
df11 <- subset(df1,,select =
c(doagain,instruct,faculty,relfac,tguide))
df11 <- na.omit(df11)
discrim <- lda(doagain ~ instruct + faculty + relfac +
tguide, data = df11, prior = c(1,1)/2)
```

(Continued)

(Continued)

```
discrim
predict <- predict(discrim)          # predict group membership
table(df11$doagain, predict$class) # classification summary
table
classtable <- table(df11$doagain, predict$class)
diag(prop.table(classtable, 1)) # % correct predictions for
each group
sum(diag(prop.table(classtable))) # % correct predictions for
total sample
```

```
> setwd("e:/R output")
> df1 <- read.csv("PSYCH_NA.csv")
> df11 <- subset(df1, , select = c(doagain,instruct,faculty,relfac,tguide))
> df11 <- na.omit(df11)
> library("MASS")
> discrim <- lda(doagain ~ instruct + faculty + relfac + tguide, data = df11, prior
  = c(1, 1)/2)
> discrim
Call:
lda(doagain ~ instruct + faculty + relfac + tguide, data = df11,
    prior = c(1, 1)/2)

Prior probabilities of groups:
  1   2
0.5 0.5

Group means:
   instruct  faculty   relfac   tguide
1 4.849817 4.913462 3.834020 2.885897
2 4.388889 4.725694 3.267361 3.169444

Coefficients of linear discriminants:
               LD1
instruct -1.3445501
faculty   0.4425590
relfac   -0.8530562
tguide    0.5984212
> psychpred <- predict(discrim)     # predict group membership
> table(df11$doagain, psychpred$class)    # classification summary table

     1  2
  1 54 24
  2 13 23
> classtable <- table(df11$doagain, psychpred$class)
> diag(prop.table(classtable, 1))      # % correct predictions for each group
        1         2
0.6923077 0.6388889
> sum(diag(prop.table(classtable)))     # % correct predictions for total sample
[1] 0.6754386
```

DISCRIMINANT ANALYSIS (THREE GROUPS)

EXAMPLE: Conduct discriminant analysis with three groups (IVs: *riskgain, riskloss, moneyr, age*; DV: *ncateg* (1=Disagree, 2=Unsure, 3=Agree))

SPSS: The DISCRIMINANT command

```
DISCRIMINANT
  /GROUPS=ncateg(1 3)
  /VARIABLES=riskgain riskloss moneyr age
  /ANALYSIS ALL
  /PRIORS EQUAL
  /STATISTICS=MEAN STDDEV UNIVF TABLE
  /CLASSIFY=NONMISSING POOLED.
```

Discriminant

Group Statistics

ncateg		Mean	Std. Deviation	Valid N (listwise) Unweighted	Valid N (listwise) Weighted
1 Disagree	riskgain	2.1343	1.65049	67	67.000
	riskloss	5.1194	1.87909	67	67.000
	moneyr	3.3390	.76924	67	67.000
	age	29.0149	8.36749	67	67.000
2 Unsure	riskgain	1.0833	.93732	36	36.000
	riskloss	5.1389	1.95890	36	36.000
	moneyr	2.8452	.72472	36	36.000
	age	35.5278	8.21666	36	36.000
3 Agree	riskgain	1.5152	1.82211	33	33.000
	riskloss	4.1212	2.28798	33	33.000
	moneyr	2.7186	.73842	33	33.000
	age	32.2727	10.63976	33	33.000
Total	riskgain	1.7059	1.59684	136	136.000
	riskloss	4.8824	2.03691	136	136.000
	moneyr	3.0578	.79632	136	136.000
	age	31.5294	9.27916	136	136.000

Tests of Equality of Group Means

	Wilks' Lambda	F	df1	df2	Sig.
riskgain	.920	5.763	2	133	.004
riskloss	.955	3.140	2	133	.047
moneyr	.875	9.521	2	133	.000
age	.912	6.379	2	133	.002

Analysis 1

Summary of Canonical Discriminant Functions

Eigenvalues

Function	Eigenvalue	% of Variance	Cumulative %	Canonical Correlation
1	.380[a]	84.4	84.4	.525
2	.070[a]	15.6	100.0	.257

a. First 2 canonical discriminant functions were used in the analysis.

Wilks' Lambda

Test of Function(s)	Wilks' Lambda	Chi-square	df	Sig.
1 through 2	.677	51.337	8	.000
2	.934	8.956	3	.030

Standardized Canonical Discriminant Function Coefficients

	Function 1	Function 2
riskgain	.558	-.403
riskloss	.172	.803
moneyr	.677	.419
age	-.661	.389

Structure Matrix

	Function	
	1	2
moneyr	.590	.388
age	-.476	.370
riskgain	.464	-.258
riskloss	.156	.734

Functions at Group Centroids

	Function	
ncateg	1	2
1 Disagree	.615	.030
2 Unsure	-.690	.321
3 Agree	-.495	-.412

Unstandardized canonical discriminant functions evaluated at group means

Classification Statistics

Prior Probabilities for Groups

		Cases Used in Analysis	
ncateg	Prior	Unweighted	Weighted
1 Disagree	.333	67	67.000
2 Unsure	.333	36	36.000
3 Agree	.333	33	33.000
Total	1.000	136	136.000

Classification Results[a]

			Predicted Group Membership			
		ncateg	1 Disagree	2 Unsure	3 Agree	Total
Original	Count	1 Disagree	45	12	10	67
		2 Unsure	5	21	10	36
		3 Agree	9	9	15	33
	%	1 Disagree	67.2	17.9	14.9	100.0
		2 Unsure	13.9	58.3	27.8	100.0
		3 Agree	27.3	27.3	45.5	100.0

a. 59.6% of original grouped cases correctly classified.

R: The `lda` and `predict` functions in the `MASS` package

Create a new data frame containing selected variables

Command: ***newdataframe* <- subset(*dataframe*,,select =c(*variable*, *variable*, *variable*...))**

Example: `df11 <- subset(df1,,select = c(ncateg,riskgain,riskloss, moneyr,age))`

Remove anyone with NAs on any variable in the data frame

Command: ***newdataframe* <- na.omit(*newdataframe*)**

Example: `df11 <- na.omit(df11)`

Conduct the discriminant analysis

Command: ***result* <- lda(*dv* ~ *iv1* + *iv2* + ..., data = *dataframe*, prior = c(#,#,#)/*sum of* #s)**
result

Example: `discrim <- lda(ncateg ~ riskgain + riskloss + moneyr + age, data = df11, prior = c(1,1,1)/3)`
`discrim`

Determine accuracy of prediction of group membership

Command: ***resultpred* <- predict(*result*)** # predict group membership
table(*newdataframe*$*dv*, *resultpred*$class) # classification summary table   ***classtable* <- table(*newdataframe*$*dv*, *resultpred*$class)**
diag(prop.table(*classtable*, 1)) # % correct predictions for each group
sum(diag(prop.table(*classtable*))) # % correct predictions for total sample

Example: `predict <- predict(discrim)`
`table(df11$ncateg, predict$class)`
`classtable <- table(df11$ncateg, predict$class)`
`diag(prop.table(classtable, 1))`
`sum(diag(prop.table(classtable)))`

Example script:

```
setwd("e:/R output")
df1 <- read.csv("MISC_NA.csv")
library(MASS)
df11 <- subset(df1,,select =
c(ncateg,riskgain,riskloss,moneyr,age))
df11 <- na.omit(df11)
discrim <- lda(ncateg ~ riskgain + riskloss + moneyr + age,
data = df11, prior = c(1,1,1)/3)
discrim
predict <- predict(discrim)    # predict group membership
table(df11$ncateg, predict$class) # classification summary table
classtable <- table(df11$ncateg, predict$class)
diag(prop.table(classtable, 1)) # % correct predictions for
each group
sum(diag(prop.table(classtable))) # % correct predictions for
total sample
```

```
> setwd("e:/R output")
> df1 <- read.csv("MISC_NA.csv")
> df11 <- subset(df1, , select = c(ncateg,riskgain,riskloss,moneyr,age))
> df11 <- na.omit(df11)
> library("MASS")
> discrim <- lda(ncateg ~ riskgain + riskloss + moneyr + age, data = df11, prior
= c(1,1,1)/3)
> discrim
Call:
lda(ncateg ~ riskgain + riskloss + moneyr + age, data = df11,
    prior = c(1, 1, 1)/3)

Prior probabilities of groups:
        1          2          3
0.3333333 0.3333333 0.3333333

Group means:
  riskgain riskloss   moneyr      age
1 2.134328 5.119403 3.339019 30.34328
2 1.083333 5.138889 2.845238 34.97222
3 1.515152 4.121212 2.718615 32.27273

Coefficients of linear discriminants:
                LD1         LD2
riskgain  0.36322261  0.32659108
riskloss  0.11162165 -0.40291946
moneyr    1.02745350 -0.40050230
age      -0.05040471 -0.03776673

Proportion of trace:
   LD1    LD2
0.7637 0.2363

> predict <- predict(discrim)        # predict group membership
> table(df11$ncateg, predict$class)    # classification summary table

     1  2  3
  1 45 12 10
  2  5 21 10
  3  9  9 15
> classtable <- table(df11$ncateg, predict$class)
> diag(prop.table(classtable, 1))       # % correct predictions for each group
        1         2         3
0.6716418 0.5833333 0.4545455
> sum(diag(prop.table(classtable)))     # % correct predictions for total sample
[1] 0.5955882
```

CROSS-TABULATION AND THE CHI-SQUARE TEST OF INDEPENDENCE

SPSS: The CROSSTABS command

```
CROSSTABS
  /TABLES=nage BY ncateg
  /FORMAT=AVALUE TABLES
  /STATISTICS=CHISQ
  /CELLS=COUNT ROW COLUMN
  /COUNT ROUND CELL.
```

Crosstabs

nage * ncateg Crosstabulation

			ncateg			
			1 Disagree	2 Unsure	3 Agree	Total
nage	1 < 30	Count	42	10	17	69
		% within nage	60.9%	14.5%	24.6%	100.0%
		% within ncateg	62.7%	25.6%	48.6%	48.9%
	2 30+	Count	25	29	18	72
		% within nage	34.7%	40.3%	25.0%	100.0%
		% within ncateg	37.3%	74.4%	51.4%	51.1%
Total		Count	67	39	35	141
		% within nage	47.5%	27.7%	24.8%	100.0%
		% within ncateg	100.0%	100.0%	100.0%	100.0%

Chi-Square Tests

	Value	df	Asymptotic Significance (2-sided)
Pearson Chi-Square	13.541[a]	2	.001
Likelihood Ratio	13.988	2	.001
Linear-by-Linear Association	3.659	1	.056
N of Valid Cases	141		

a. 0 cells (0.0%) have expected count less than 5. The minimum expected count is 17.13.

R: The `CrossTable` function in the `gmodels` package

Convert a numeric variable to a factor (if variable is a numeric variable)

    Command: *dataframe$factor* <- **factor**(*data frame$numvar*, **labels = c(**"*label*", "*label*", "*label*"...))

                Note: *dataframe$factor* = name of factor

                      dataframe$numvar = numeric independent variable

                      label = label to level of factor based on numeric independent variable

    Example:
```
df1$nage.f <- factor(df1$nage, labels =
c("< 30", "30+"))
df1$ncateg.f <- factor(df1$ncateg, labels
= c("Control", "Life events", "No life
events"))
```

Run the CrossTable function to calculate chi-square statistic

    Command: **CrossTable(***dataframe$rowvar*, *dataframe$colvar*, **digits = #, prop.r = TRUE, prop.c = TRUE, prop.t = FALSE, prop. chisq = FALSE, chisq = TRUE)**

                Note: *dataframe$rowvar* = variable represented in rows of table

                      dataframe$colvar = variable represented in columns of table

                      digits = # = number of decimal places reported for percentages

                      prop.r = TRUE = report row percentages

                      prop.c = TRUE = report column percentages

                      prop.t = FALSE = do not report total percentages

                      prop.chisq = FALSE = don't report contribution of each cell to chi-square

                      chisq = TRUE = report chi-square test of independence

    Example:
```
CrossTable(df1$nage.f, df1$ncateg.f, digits
= 3, prop.r=TRUE, prop.c=TRUE, prop.t=FALSE,
prop.chisq=FALSE, chisq=TRUE)
```

Example script:

```
setwd("e:/R output")
df1 <- read.csv("MISC_NA.csv")
library(gmodels]
df1$nage.f <- factor(df1$nage, labels = c("< 30",
"30+"))
df1$ncateg.f <- factor(df1$ncateg, labels =
c("Control", "Life events", "No life events"))
CrossTable(df1$nage.f, df1$ncateg.f, digits =3, prop.
r=TRUE, prop.c=TRUE, prop.t=FALSE, prop.chisq=FALSE,
chisq=TRUE)
```

```
> setwd("e:/R output")
> df1 <- read.csv("MISC_NA.csv")
> library("gmodels")
> df1$nage.f <- factor(df1$nage, labels = c("< 30", "30+"))
> df1$ncateg.f <- factor(df1$ncateg, labels = c("Control", "Life events", "No life events"))
> CrossTable(df1$nage.f, df1$ncateg.f, digits = 3, prop.r=TRUE, prop.c=TRUE, prop.t=FALSE, prop.chisq=
FALSE, chisq=TRUE)


   Cell Contents
|-------------------------|
|                       N |
|             N / Row Total |
|             N / Col Total |
|-------------------------|


Total Observations in Table:  141


             | df1$ncateg.f
  df1$nage.f |      Control |  Life events | No life events |    Row Total |
-------------|--------------|--------------|--------------|--------------|
        < 30 |           42 |           10 |           17 |           69 |
             |        0.609 |        0.145 |        0.246 |        0.489 |
             |        0.627 |        0.256 |        0.486 |              |
-------------|--------------|--------------|--------------|--------------|
         30+ |           25 |           29 |           18 |           72 |
             |        0.347 |        0.403 |        0.250 |        0.511 |
             |        0.373 |        0.744 |        0.514 |              |
-------------|--------------|--------------|--------------|--------------|
Column Total |           67 |           39 |           35 |          141 |
             |        0.475 |        0.277 |        0.248 |              |
-------------|--------------|--------------|--------------|--------------|


Statistics for All Table Factors


Pearson's Chi-squared test
------------------------------------------------------------
Chi^2 =  13.54071      d.f. =  2      p =  0.001147285
```

FURTHER RESOURCES

- Swirl: http://swirlstats.com
- edX: https://www.edx.org/course/data-science-r-basics
- Personality project: http://personality-project.org/r/r.guide.html
- Quick-R: http://www.statmethods.net
- Learning Statistics with R: https://learningstatisticswithr.com/
- R for Psychological Science: http://psyr.djnavarro.net/
- R for Data Science: https://r4ds.had.co.nz/
- Little Book of R for Multivariate Analysis: https://little-book-of-r-for-multivariate-analysis.readthedocs.io/en/latest/index.html
- Seek: https://rseek.org/